The Good Book of
Southern
Baking

The Good Book of
Southern Baking

A Revival of Biscuits, Cakes, and Cornbread

Kelly Fields

with Kate Heddings

Photographs by Oriana Koren

LORENA JONES BOOKS
An imprint of **TEN SPEED PRESS**
California | New York

Contents

For Shari, Audrey, Jean, and all the womxn who have, and continue to, nourish the South

Introduction

I'm going to get right to the point: I wrote this book to bury y'all in cornbread and biscuits. Not just ordinary cornbread and biscuits, but the best dang ones you've ever had. I've spent *twenty years* figuring out how to perfect every dessert in my repertoire, and it's high time I share those honed recipes. My cornbread? It's made with a mix of cornmeal, corn flour, and buttermilk that sits in the fridge overnight, which plumps up that cornmeal and makes a killer moist and supremely corny-tasting loaf. And my biscuits are made with Italian-style 00 flour. I know that's not Southern, but damn, that flour creates some of the flakiest biscuits you will ever taste.

While I've worked in pastry kitchens under amazing chefs, I've also learned a lot from plain old trial and error. And even the absolute disasters were fun. That's 'cause baking is meant to be fun. I took two and a half years to get my chocolate chip cookie just right, and now I sell more than ten thousand cookies a week at my New Orleans restaurant and bakery, Willa Jean. Baking doesn't need to be laborious or scary, y'all. The pastry of the American South was born out of ingenuity, simplicity, and intuition. A handful, a dollop, and just a pinch are how ingredients have been measured for centuries, and I'll be damned if that hasn't worked, and worked deliciously. It's a beautiful thing to get to know your ingredients well enough to just "feel" them, to know instinctively that you need a splash of this or another pinch of that. It's how we do it in the South . . . and I personally rejoice in the beauty of it. Calm down, put your phone away, take a deep breath, get your hands in the flour, and let them do the work.

How did I get here? It was a long and winding road that began when I was a kid growing up on the water in the low country of South Carolina. That was a pretty idyllic place. My mom had a beautiful garden and grew most of her own produce, which we used for baking, canning, and jamming—my mom treated preserving like an Olympic sport. We also regularly went to farmers' markets and pick-your-own fruit farms. My mom baked everything, from fruit pies and cobblers to biscuits, cakes, and cookies. The door to our house was never locked, and neighborhood kids came and went, grabbing cookies along the way. We were kind of the neighborhood cookie factory. My mom was also known for her cakes. She made carrot cake (it took me years to understand why anyone would want to put vegetables in a cake), Mississippi mud cake, and even a better-than-sex cake (a sweet concoction of chocolate, cream, caramel, and coconut). Let me tell you, when my two siblings and I first had that cake as little kids, we were all like, *ooohhhh.*

My mom's mother, Audrey McDowell, was also a great baker. As far back as I can remember, every time we visited, she would make her apple cake, which was super, super moist and had a perfect pure apple taste. My bakery, Willa Jean, is actually named after my father's mother. She was a terrible cook, but she was sassy and stubborn and sarcastic, and she was my biggest cheerleader and life coach. (I get my personality from her.) Whenever I was a pain in the ass, my dad called me Willa Jean Junior, which stuck as my nickname. I always thought it was a compliment, and needless to say, my grandma got a real kick out of it.

After high school, I moved to New Orleans and started working in bakeries and pastry shops. I went to work for Susan Spicer, who back then had a gourmet shop called Spice Inc. It took two years for me to realize that I could actually make baking a career. I really didn't know it was a valid choice until I went to work for Susan, where I saw a successful woman doing something she loved to do, and it was a real *oh shit* moment. Grandma Willa Jean and I started talking, and she told me that if you find something you love to do that much, don't look anywhere else—go do it. Grandma paid my rent while I was working for Susan, supporting my desire to dive right into the industry and work for the best chef, the one I would grow to emulate. Grandma Willa Jean also made me promise never to tell my cousins that she was footing the bill!

At a staff meeting in late 1999, Susan announced that she was closing Spice Inc. to open Herbsaint with chef Donald Link. I took that as an opportunity to go to culinary school. I went to Charleston to attend Johnson & Wales University, again with Grandma's support. In 2002, not long after graduating from school, I went back to NOLA and applied for a job in the pastry kitchen at Restaurant August—as the pastry chef! When I started, I was in way over my head; I should never have been in that position. It was sink or swim . . . and I swam.

To be honest, the chef de cuisine who ran the kitchen at August really pushed me to succeed. He was a classically trained guy, and I came in really rough around the edges. He didn't think I should be there. He told me I wouldn't last a month, so out of spite, I changed the menu. When I started at August, there were five desserts on the menu that were constantly rotating. I threw away the existing menu and created themed tasting plates. I wasn't allowed to take August's signature bread pudding off the menu, and customers always wanted the other signature NOLA desserts: crème brûlée and cheesecake. So, I figured that instead of serving them separately, I'd put them all together on one tasting plate that I called A Taste of New Orleans. I also created a chocolate tasting plate and a farmers' market plate, as well as one rotating dessert plate that usually had a dairy focus. Each had at least three components, but some nights a plate could have as

many as nine components. These new-style desserts took off, and there was no longer any doubt about whether I should be running the pastry kitchen at August.

In the wake of Hurricane Katrina in 2005, I took a few years off and traveled. A lot. Then I lived in San Francisco and worked under the maniacal badass Shuna Lydon at Sens, where the focus was on southern Mediterranean desserts. Shuna had the résumé I wanted: she had worked at the French Laundry, Bouchon, Citizen Cake, and even with Claudia Fleming at Gramercy Tavern! I knew I needed to work under her, but it was intense. Very intense. I learned a lot about mentorship, leadership, and organization from her. It was the first real position where I got to see and learn business management and not just food.

At Sens, I befriended chef Michael Dotson, and he and I traveled to Scotland before he opened a gastropub called Martin's West in Redwood City, California. I was the pastry chef there, but I also helped run the savory kitchen. We were trying to do Scottish food, like haggis and corn dogs, for Americans (which is pretty funny to me now), back before the gastropub trend in America. One of the partners, Moira Beveridge (who is now Moira Beveridge Dotson) is Scottish. We went to learn about the Scottish approach to eating, since their farm-to-table approach to life was beyond anything I had experienced, even in San Francisco. There was a restaurant in Edinburgh named Martins back in the day, run by a fellow named Martin Irons. He was one of the restaurateurs who inspired Alice Waters's passion and mission for championing farm-to-table cooking. I figured out how to make the best sticky toffee pudding there, and we had a lot of fun.

I also traveled throughout Europe and the Middle East. Traveling and living in other places exposed me to so many different flavor combos, developing my palate and food memory in ways that continue to inform my daily baking. Just eating strawberries in those places made the journey worth it. For example, I tried strawberries served simply with elderflower in Scotland and then roasted with quince in Israel, and realized how the same ingredient can have a distinctly different personality across the globe. My travels have allowed me to learn, hands on, about seasonings and spices in a way that would not have been possible otherwise.

In 2010, when I was in New Zealand, I got an email from Michael Gulotta, then the executive chef at August. He shared his goals and aspirations for the restaurant and told me there was no one he wanted to do it with other than me. So, I went back. The time was right.

The thing is, when Hurricane Katrina hit New Orleans back in 2005, I lost every notebook and recipe I had accumulated during my career. As soon as I arrived safely at my mom's house in the days after the storm, I wrote down every single recipe I could recall in a little red notebook. I remember sitting in bookstores and coffee shops with that notebook, closing my eyes and literally moving my body as if I were making the things I wanted to recall. Muscle memory is an incredible thing, and it helped me resolidify the foundational recipes that have ultimately shaped my career. Truth be told, I still use that notebook to this day. It inspires me as I flip through it, seeing where recipes started and the journeys I have taken through making those recipes in different parts of the world. It's stained and falling apart—as well worn as my favorite pastry cookbook. While thinking about getting back to my roots when I returned to New Orleans, and again before I opened Willa Jean, this notebook was the reminder of where I had come from and the measure of the growth I had experienced. That little notebook spent a good eight years in my left back pocket and is the figurative glue that binds this very book together.

Back at August once again, I wiped the pastry slate clean and started over. I created reimagined versions of desserts people had loved at the restaurant, blending in all sorts of things I had learned about while traveling. The waiters hated me for inventing new stuff, 'cause every day they had to learn something new! The cheesecake, which was a classic, got a makeover with raw goat's-milk cheese, white chocolate, and burnt honey ice cream. The flavors were all hyperlocal, but this was a step farther than I had taken the cheesecake before. Now it didn't bore me, and it stood on its own. I was always playing with would-be new dishes.

My years at August were paramount. Doing such high-end food for so long gave me the space and support to really experiment with ingredients and get seriously molecular. I developed a relationship with ingredients that I never would have any other way. I learned to always highlight the personality of the main ingredient and never to put more than three or four flavors on one plate. This principle applies to everything we make at Willa Jean. I never could have come up with my idea of a perfect chocolate chip cookie if I hadn't gotten to know chocolate the way I did at August. Ditto bananas, pineapple, vanilla. . . .

You'll see a little of me in everything we make at Willa Jean and in this book. I'm drawn to the seemingly simple, nostalgic, and nourishing approach to food. I love to celebrate all the beauty of the South, from our rich and somber histories, influences, and traditions to the bounty of our lands. These recipes are merely guidelines and suggestions, not rules, and should be flexible to fit your tastes and preferences. If I've learned one thing over the years, it's that my best self emerged once I stopped being so serious. I used to break everything apart and examine it and make it crazy complex, but you know what? Having fun and keeping things simple has made me happier and more successful than ever.

Recipe for Success

Here's a brief overview of the ingredients, techniques, and equipment I think are most important for successful baking. I am pretty low-key about most things when it comes to baking, but I feel some guidance is always helpful, and who doesn't like a little extra help now and then?

The Ingredients

In most cases, you can use whatever suits you, but I suggest reading this first, so you make the best choices for your baking.

Baking Powder

In my biscuit experimentation process, a huge revelation was that most baking powder is alluminated. I really prefer non-alluminated (aka aluminum-free) baking powder. Because it's made without aluminum, it doesn't have that unpleasant metallic taste that can turn a great biscuit bad. Most domestic brands are alluminated, but you can generally find aluminum-free baking powder at Whole Foods and Trader Joe's.

Butter

There's always a lot of discussion about butter in baked goods, and rightfully so. The first rule of thumb is simple: delicious butter imparts a delicious butter flavor. I recommend baking with butter you actually would want to eat. If you've never tried several different butters side by side for flavor, now's a good time to do that! You'll find no two butters taste exactly alike due to factors such as where each is made, what the cows were eating, whether any fermentation happened, and a host of other manufacturing variables. You'll also find that when it comes to locally made butters, the butter flavor changes throughout the year based on the cows' diet. I recommend using a higher-end butter with a higher fat content, around 82 percent. For comparison, most commercially made American butter contains about 80 percent butterfat. So, if your local market carries European-style butter, I recommend grabbing that to taste test and use for these recipes.

I call for unsalted butter in all these recipes, so the salt level can be decided and controlled by the baker. Salt levels vary so widely among butter brands that it's best to just start with none and add your own.

Beyond flavor, butter plays an important role in the structure of pastry. Where, when, and how it's introduced, the size of the pieces, and its temperature when incorporated (or not) all have a direct impact on final results. Therefore, it is important to follow the instructions in each of these recipes regarding butter. They're all given on purpose. I promise.

Chocolate

Chocolate is as important an ingredient as any in this book. I'll say it over and over again: if you don't work with a high-quality, delicious chocolate, you will never have a high-quality, delicious outcome. Leave the cheaper chocolate for Halloween and make the same investment in chocolate as you would in butter or produce.

Chocolate is usually characterized in the basic categories of dark, milk, and white. However, in more recent years, subcategories have developed, with experiments in chocolate leading to wonderful flavors, which I detail on page 14. You'll also notice there is a percentage associated with each specific chocolate. This number indicates the amount of cacao mass, or pure cacao solids, in the chocolate. The higher the percentage, the more chocolatey-tasting the chocolate. In dark and semisweet chocolates, this means a stronger, often more bitter, flavor. In white chocolate, the higher the percentage, the less sweet the chocolate.

When purchasing and using chocolate, buy in either bar or *fève* (coin) form, as you'll be chopping most of it.

I pretty much bake exclusively with Valrhona chocolate. I find their chocolate to be the most consistent, versatile, and delicious. Valrhona offers a wide variety of products, all delicious, but below are my favorites and the ones I recommend for the best results.

Dark chocolate. Dark chocolate ranges from about 65% to 100% cacao (unsweetened chocolate). For a workhorse dark chocolate, I recommend Valrhona Guanaja 70% cacao. It has long-lasting flavor, and it's beautifully bitter and nuanced with floral notes. You'll see that I suggest dark chocolates with specific cacao percentages in my recipes. That is because, in my experience, they are the ones that I believe produce the best taste and texture in that recipe. Every dark chocolate tastes different and has different qualities. I encourage you to do side-by-side tastings of dark chocolates with different cacao percentages to find the ones you like most.

Milk chocolate. For all-purpose milk chocolate, I love Valrhona Jivara 40% cacao, which is creamy and rich with hints of malt flavor. And for a really special touch, I often use, and call for, Valrhona Caramélia, in which the sugar is caramelized before being mixed with the chocolate, resulting in a really soft, rich, salted butter–caramel flavor.

Gianduja. This is milk chocolate made with about 30% hazelnut paste. It was developed in Turin, Italy, in Napoleon's time, and it's often melted and served as a spread, much like that other popular condiment. Valrhona offers their version of hazelnut milk chocolate, Azélia 35% cacao, which is a warm milky chocolate with the rich nuance of toasted hazelnuts. It works wonderfully in the Chocolate-Hazelnut Flan (page 137), as well as in just about any other recipe that calls for milk chocolate when you want to add some hazelnut flavor.

White chocolate. This is my least favorite "chocolate." I've participated in many an argument that white chocolate is not actually chocolate. Thankfully, Valrhona makes Ivorie 35% cacao, which is a smooth white chocolate with hints of vanilla. It contains less sugar than most white chocolates.

Dulcey Blond. Valrhona's Dulcey Blond 32% cacao is a smooth and creamy chocolate that's made by roasting the sugar and the milk solids during the chocolate-making process. The result is a warm golden color and a toasty, slightly salty chocolate with undertones of baked shortbread. It is a phenomenal chocolate, in my opinion, and there is no real substitute.

Cocoa powder. Cocoa powder is generally available in two forms: natural and Dutch-processed. In this book, I almost always use Dutch-processed cocoa powder, which is alkalized to neutralize its acidity, mellowing the acidic floral flavor and giving the cocoa a dark, rich color. Compared to natural cocoa powder, Dutch-processed cocoa has a deeper, more chocolatey flavor and reacts differently to chemical leaveners, such as baking soda and baking powder. I always recommend sticking to the form of cocoa powder specified in any recipe.

Coconut

The coconut options available seem to be growing by the day. For the purposes of this book, I call for two primary types: shredded and flakes.

Shredded coconut. This is the most common form used in baking. It's shredded small and thin, and typically, it isn't completely dried, thereby retaining some of its natural sweetness and moisture. When I call for shredded coconut in recipes, I'm referring to sweetened shredded coconut. If you only have unsweetened, it's a little drier and will create a chewier texture in whatever you're baking.

Coconut flakes. These are the large, wide shavings of coconut. While flakes aren't best used within a batter or frosting, they are gorgeous on a finished product and add a great burst of flavor and texture. I find it best to toast coconut flakes before using to add some depth to their flavor, and it looks stunning, too. You can spread the flakes on a baking sheet and bake at 350°F for about 7 minutes, until toasty and fragrant, or spread the flakes evenly in a dry skillet and toast over medium heat until golden and fragrant.

Cooking Spray

There is a time and place for the use of nonstick cooking spray in baking. I find a good rule of thumb is that cooking spray is acceptable in any situation when sticking won't make or break your desired outcome (such as for cookies). That being said, pans or baking dishes used for Bundt cakes, upside-down cakes, and other things that need to easily and fully come out of their baking vessels are best liberally buttered (and floured, if the recipe calls for it).

Remember, even neutral-flavor cooking sprays will impart some flavor to your baked goods, so spray lightly and evenly. Any spray bottle or can that doesn't quickly and easily coat the pan might just need to go into the garbage.

You'll see that I often instruct you to lightly spray a pan before lining it with parchment, then I say to spray the top of the paper, too. I like to do this so that the parchment lies flat and is held in place, limiting the likelihood that your batter or crust will seep underneath the paper so it gets baked into your pastry.

Eggs

There are only two real rules on eggs, y'all: get them fresh and get them local. All these recipes use large eggs. Rarely, if ever, will you need to use a cold egg. Grab eggs at your local farmers' market and ask the farmer if they've washed the eggs (which removes the eggs' natural protective layer that prevents bacteria from entering the egg). If they have not been washed, keep them at room temperature, and you'll always be ready to bake.

Extracts

Generally, I am far from being a fan of extracts or any other imitation flavorings. I've come to accept that there is a time and a place for them, and in those moments, it makes a monumental difference to ensure you use an extract with no artificial flavorings or corn syrup. With almond extract specifically, try to find one that is naturally pressed, with a low alcohol content. Stay far away from anything labeled "imitation almond extract," because it tastes like garbage and will make your pastry taste like garbage. I know that sounds harsh, but there's truly no other way to say it, and it sounds less harsh than it'll taste.

Flours

I will preface this section by saying that I purposefully developed most of the recipes in this book to work well with all-purpose flour. Other flours often just don't work as well, taste as great, or yield the best texture when substituted for all-purpose. And I don't want you to go out and buy a bunch of different kinds of flours unless it's truly necessary. When I do call for a flour other than all-purpose, it's intentional—the recipe will not work without using that specific flour. Flours are generally differentiated by their protein percentage, and the higher the protein, the "stronger" the flour. This

The Good Book of Southern Baking

comes into play, for example, when you're using bread flour to make a good hearty, chewy bread, or using pastry flour to make a delicate, tender pastry crust.

All-purpose flour. Welp, it's all in the name. All-purpose flour can almost always be used in any recipe, as it's become incredibly predictable in baking. In the milling process, the wheat berry is separated into parts, and just the center of the berry, the endosperm, is used to make all-purpose flour. It ranges in protein content from 9 to 11 percent, which is considered neutral.

Almond flour. Almond flour is basically ground blanched almonds, with a texture more like cornmeal than flour. I use it in recipes to add both flavor and texture. It is readily available in most stores and also online. If you're interested in making your own, you can purchase raw blanched slivered almonds and process them, 1 cup at a time, in a food processor or high-speed blender into fine powder. I find that an 8-ounce package of nuts yields about 2 cups of almond flour. Because almonds contain oil, make sure to store your almond flour in an airtight container in a cool, dark place to prevent it from going rancid. I recommend keeping it in the freezer.

Cake flour. Cake flour usually has a protein content of 9 percent or less, and US manufacturers almost always bleach it. Bleaching the flour enables the cake to support a higher amount of sugar and fat than unbleached flour in the recipe. Unbleached cake flour is sometimes available in the United States (and the only cake flour available elsewhere), but substituting unbleached flour will directly affect the cake, often creating a much denser texture.

Corn flour, fine cornmeal, and coarse cornmeal. You'll find that in some countries, cornstarch is called corn flour; furthermore, cornmeal is also sometimes called corn flour, so I want to be clear that for my recipes, corn flour is corn flour, cornmeal is cornmeal, and cornstarch is cornstarch. The basic difference among these items is the fineness to which they're ground. I use all three separately, together, and interchangeably throughout this book. I am a huge fan of the different textures they contribute within an item when used together, as well as the differing flavors they lend a product. I generally stick to yellow corn out of habit and buy mine from Anson Mills, but Bob's Red Mill is reliable and available everywhere. Corn flour and cornstarch can be used as thickeners in soups and such but are not interchangeable in the recipes included here. Corn flour is earthy and sweet and can be used in place of, or in addition to, the wheat flour called for in recipes such as pancakes, muffins, biscuits, and most baked goods you want to have a really tender crumb. Corn flour does not contain gluten, so it's not well suited for baked goods that need structure (such as Danish dough, monkey bread, or king cake).

Pastry flour. Pastry flour has an even lower protein percentage than cake flour, often coming in at 8 percent or less, making it perfect for recipes that beg to be flaky, tender, and crumbly. Even though it seems like pastry flour would produce all the qualities you want in a pie dough, I actually call for using all-purpose flour in my pie dough, because dough made with pastry flour can be tricky to work with when making pie; it's challenging to roll out without cracking and difficult to move around. The truth is, the increase in the flakiness of the pie dough when made with pastry flour instead of all-purpose flour is so minute that the peace of mind and ease of using all-purpose flour is worth more. I swear by using pastry flour in my chocolate chip cookies, though, 'cause it keeps the cookie tender.

00 flour. This finely milled, soft, Italian-style wheat flour is categorized not just by protein content but also by the fineness to which the grain is ground. The finest mill of flour available in stores is 00, yet it still maintains about the same percentage of protein as all-purpose flour. I call for it in biscuits because in the US, the type of wheat that it's made from (durum) is strong, but not elastic, giving biscuits a really nice bite without making them chewy or elastic. If you have challenges sourcing 00 flour, substitute all-purpose flour; it will have the least impact on the texture of your baked goods.

Nuts and Nut Butters

Nuts are a secret weapon in delicious baking. They are so incredibly versatile, allowing for experimentation and substitutions to your favorite recipes. I generally have about eight different nuts or nut butters on hand at any given time to mix in, sprinkle, smear, or match whatever my mood might be while I'm baking.

Whole nuts. A fresh nut is a revelation if you've never had one. Growing up, we almost always had fresh walnuts and pecans in a bowl with a nutcracker in the kitchen for a drive-by snack on the way in or out the door. I never fully appreciated this until I was well into my professional career. We are incredibly lucky to have so many nuts growing here in Louisiana and almost year-round access to fresh pecans. If you live in an area with a fresh nut harvest, I highly suggest you give that nut (or legume—hello, peanut!) a try in these recipes. I highly doubt you'll be disappointed. However, if your access is limited, I recommend buying nuts that are vacuum-sealed in packaging rather than buying nuts from bulk bins. Nuts are naturally rich in oils and fats, and air exposure is the biggest catalyst in their spoilage. Let's be honest: no one knows exactly how long those nuts have been in that bulk bin. That being said, because of exposure to air and, in my case, humidity, nuts should be stored in the fridge or the freezer to help preserve their shelf life. If you're feeling a little unsure if your nuts are still usable or not, give them the ol' sniff test first; if they smell sour and slightly ammonia scented, they've likely turned. If you're still on the fence, you can certainly try one—if it's not great, you'll know. . . .

To toast nuts, I spread them on a rimmed baking sheet and set them in a 300°F oven for about 15 minutes, stirring several times, until the nuts are rich and toasty smelling. I like using a low oven temperature 'cause it's a little like confitting the nuts in their own oils.

Nut butters. As delicious as they are, most nut butters are not easily substituted in place of peanut butter in equal amounts. Peanut butter plays a specific role in the structure of cookies that other nut butters will adversely affect. For example, using almond butter in my peanut butter cookie would result in a flatter, more spread-out, crumbly, and crispy cookie. As such, I recommend seeking out cookie recipes that have been developed for specific nut butters. However, in recipes like the banana pudding (page 126), in which I add peanut butter for flavor and not structure, feel free to substitute whichever nut you would like in the recipe. Just be sure to taste your batter before finishing, as you may need to adjust the salt. As for types of peanut butter, use the peanut butter you love. Period.

Salt

Baked goods and desserts deserve to be treated the same way as savory dishes. They require a balance, and salt creates the perfect balance.

Kosher salt. This type of salt can vary much more than you might know. The kind I specifically call for in this book is Diamond Crystal kosher salt. Diamond Crystal is manufactured using a different method than the other widely available kosher salts, making it lighter and less salty tasting than the others. Due to its shape, it also does not require processing with anticaking agents; this helps it keep its nice clean flavor. If you can't find Diamond Crystal, I recommend reducing the salt in the recipe by half and then tasting whatever you're making before you finish mixing to make sure you're on the right track; otherwise, you'll end up with an oversalted disappointment.

Finishing salt. This is what I use to top my chocolate chip cookies. Use Maldon sea salt or any other large-flake sea salt. If you're the adventurous type, experiment with some of the fun flavors on the market, such as vanilla bean salt or even smoked sea salt.

Sweeteners

Sweeteners do so much more for baking and pastry than just sweeten. They build structure (or prevent structure from building, in some cases); affect moisture, pH, and shelf life, and even play the role of starch in items. In cookies, sweeteners impact texture, spread, flavor, moisture, and overall aesthetics. Of the most commonly used sugars (white, light brown, and dark brown), it used to be that the most basic difference was how much of the naturally occurring molasses was removed during processing. However, now almost all brown sugar (both light and dark) that is available in the market is made with white sugar that has molasses added back in.

You can swap sugars in your baking if you wish, but it's important to consider the ideal outcome you want to produce. If you think about how moist and heavy brown sugar is straight out of the bag, for example, you'd want to sub it in recipes where that effect is what you'd want in the final product. It's not as well suited for things like light cake batters or for delicately flavored items, in which granulated sugar will create the perfect lightness and allow nuanced flavors to shine.

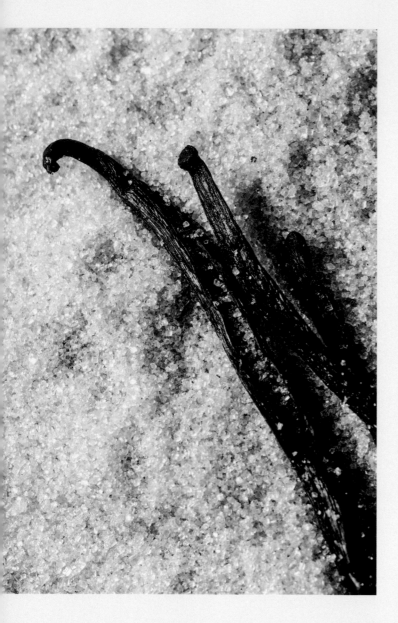

Brown sugar. Both light brown and dark brown sugars are used frequently in my recipes. If your pantry is stocked with light brown sugar but you need to use dark brown, add about 3 percent molasses to the light brown sugar and stir to combine to achieve a workable dark brown sugar. Or, if you're not so good at math, for 1 cup of light brown sugar, stir in roughly 1½ teaspoons of molasses.

Cane syrup and maple syrup. These are interchangeable in the book (as are molasses and sorghum syrup), based on what you may have on hand or what might be specific to your region. I use cane syrup, and not that stuff you find in a can that feels way too incredibly intense, but something far more special: Poirier's Cane Syrup. Charles Poirier grows sugarcane in his backyard, and using the equipment and lessons of his granddaddy, he harvests it, juices it directly into two custom-built 60-gallon New York pattern cast-iron syrup kettles, and cooks it low and slow, skimming it for 24 hours straight. The result is the most beautifully nuanced cane syrup I've ever had the pleasure of tasting, matching the complex notes usually left to sorghum syrup. I highly recommend ordering a bottle or two online, even if just for your future adventures in cornbread.

Granulated sugar. This is colorless, odorless, and relatively neutral in flavor (aside from sweetness, of course) and it's about 99 percent pure sucrose. These recipes are written using standard granulated sugar, which is not to be confused with superfine sugar or coarse sugar.

Powdered sugar. This is also called confectioners' sugar and sometimes 10X (which refers to the number of times the sugar is processed to make it into a powder). It's superfine ground sugar with cornstarch added as an anticaking agent. When any recipe calls for powdered sugar, do yourself a favor and remember to always sift, and sometimes to double sift it, just to prevent little lumps from ending up in your finished baked goods.

Raw sugar. Sometimes marketed under the brand name Sugar In The Raw, raw sugar (aka turbinado sugar) is sugar that has been processed as little as possible in comparison to granulated and still retains some of its natural molasses. The sugar comes in a much larger grain, making it so much fun to use for coating pans to achieve an insanely appealing texture on the crust of baked goods. Its pH and flavor are the same as for brown sugar, but its larger grain prevents it from being an equivalent substitute for brown sugar in this book. If substituted, the size of the grain will directly, usually adversely, affect the structure of your pastry.

Sorghum syrup and molasses. These are staples of the American South, specifically in baking. The biggest difference between sorghum syrup and molasses today is the method of production. Sorghum syrup is made by juicing the sorghum plant and boiling off the water content, leaving the syrup behind. Molasses is a by-product of the sugar-making process, made out of the juice from sugar cane as it is boiled to produce crystallized sugar. Molasses can have several different labels based on how many times the syrup was boiled: first molasses, second molasses, and blackstrap molasses (which can be a little bittersweet). Each boil mellows out the sweetness of the syrup; however, all types of molasses are interchangeable, based on your own taste preference.

Vanilla

Vanilla is one of the most miraculous gifts of nature, and I feel grateful for it every day. The bean is produced by just one species of orchid (of which there are tens of thousands) and only develops if the flower is pollinated, often by hand, within the first 12 hours of opening. After pollination, the bean takes another 9 months to grow before it is harvested, cured, and dried in another 4- to 5-month process. Because of the involved process of growing vanilla, along with the instabilities in trade and climate, vanilla prices have climbed, often more expensive per pound than silver, making it one of the most valuable ingredients in the kitchen.

If substituting vanilla extract for vanilla bean, use 1 tablespoon of extract per bean. If substituting extract for vanilla paste, use an equal amount. One tablespoon of paste is equivalent to one vanilla bean. Again, if substituting for vanilla extract, use an equal amount.

Vanilla extract. Vanilla's flavor cannot be synthetically reproduced, so using pure vanilla extract is the only good option. Pure vanilla extract is sometimes labeled with where the beans were grown, such as Indonesia, Madagascar, or Tahiti. I personally use

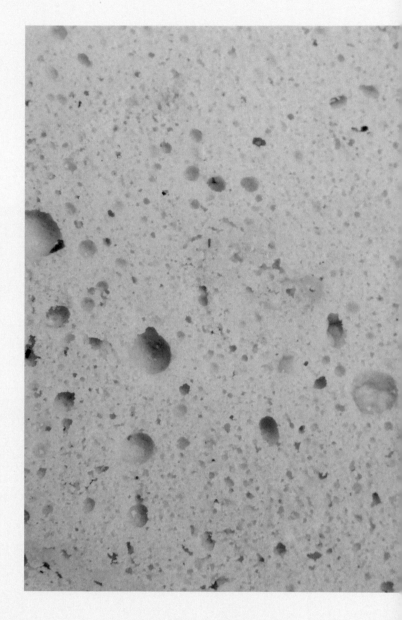

Bourbon vanilla, which is produced from beans grown and harvested in Madagascar, the world's largest supplier of quality vanilla beans.

The extract is made by soaking vanilla pods in a mixture of alcohol and water. Imitation extract is often made with a by-product of the wood pulp industry and lacks the nuanced depth of flavor you get from pure vanilla.

Vanilla bean paste. Vanilla bean paste is a thicker version of vanilla extract, with the addition of bean flecks (the seeds from the pods), which are visible in your final product. Using paste allows for the addition of vanilla flavor without thinning your batter or base with additional liquid. I tend to use vanilla bean paste when preparing something that will show off the flecks, or when I just want that extra pop of vanilla flavor.

Vanilla beans. Also called vanilla pods, vanilla beans are the fruit of the orchid. Once grown, they are dried and cured for months, turning the green pod the deep brown we know and creating that distinct vanilla flavor. When using vanilla beans, we're generally most interested in the tiny seeds inside the pod, but we can also extract flavor from the pod itself. To collect as many of the tiny seeds as possible, I like to lightly heat my vanilla pod (10 seconds in a 325°F oven), then carefully slice open the entire length of the bean with a sharp paring knife. I then use the back of the knife to scrape the insides of the bean to collect the seeds. Because the seeds are bonded in oil, the heat helps them release from the pod more easily. I like to add the seeds directly into the sugar called for in the recipe and rub the seeds and sugar between my fingers to more evenly distribute the seeds, as they like to clump together. (This is a great trick I learned from the wildly talented pastry chef Shuna Lydon.) Once you've collected the seeds, use the scraped pod to flavor sugar or steep in liquids. You can rinse your vanilla bean pod, dry it, and continue to reuse it until you've fully used its power to flavor.

Yeast

This book calls for both instant yeast and active dry yeast. Instant yeast is a smaller particle that can be mixed directly into ingredients and starts working immediately. Active dry yeast needs to be dissolved in lukewarm water until it starts to get foamy before it can be added to ingredients. To be fair, both of these yeasts can be used interchangeably in the same amounts. If you only have active dry yeast, just be sure to activate it before proceeding with the recipe and add about 15 or so minutes to your predicted rising time, since it's a little slower to rise. To activate dry yeast, warm a portion of the liquid called for in the recipe to about 100°F, sprinkle the yeast into the liquid, add a pinch of sugar, and stir. It will take 5 to 15 minutes, depending on the age of your yeast, the temperature of your liquid, and the ambient temperature. Be patient and let the yeast get bubbly and foamy. If you've been patient and the yeast hasn't become bubbly, which sometimes happens, the yeast may be dead and it would be best to throw out the mixture and start over with some fresh yeast. It's better to redo that one step at the beginning than proceed through the entire recipe only to have it fail. On the flip side, if you only have instant yeast, things will activate more quickly, and you'll need to keep an eye on your dough, as it will likely finish rising about 15 minutes earlier than called for.

Techniques and Equipment

This is by no means a comprehensive list of the techniques and equipment I use to make the recipes in this book, but the ones I describe here are the most important ones.

Baking Sheets

In the process of writing this book, I have learned that baking sheets are a heated subject, and opinions vary on what's best. I grew up using whatever we had, and therefore, my opinion on baking sheets has been pretty much nonexistent until recently. If you want the fancy ones that are specifically textured for cookie baking, by all means, get them. However, the condition of the sheet is what's most important: it should be flat and light in color. If your baking sheet is dark and well-worn, it will most likely cause your baked goods to become a little too dark on their bottoms. My go-to baking sheet at home is Nordic Ware baker's half-sheet aluminum pan, which has, surprisingly, been the pan I use most consistently—even more often than the few fancy pans I have with fancy price tags.

I have no horse in the race when it comes to baking sheets with or without a lip. All of mine have lips, because I use them for everything. You can fit more cookies on a lipless pan, but, other than that, there's not enough of an argument for me to own one.

Really, the important thing is to get to know the personality of any equipment you're using, from your oven to your baking sheets. Like every single oven, every sheet will behave differently. Just get to know each one and adjust accordingly, if needed.

Crossover Baking

Crossover baking is the baking that happens AFTER you pull a tray of cookies from the oven and let them sit on the still-hot baking sheet, where your perfectly baked cookies become dark and overbaked. You need to literally stop the baking process as soon as you're able to by transferring the cookies to a wire rack.

I take the approach of slightly underbaking my cookies, pulling them from the oven when the outside edge of the cookie is starting to turn golden and looks just as I'd like the middle of the cookie to look. The centers still appear underdone at this point, but I'll remove the cookies from the oven and let them cool for 5 to 10 minutes on the pan to finish baking perfectly. Then I transfer the cookies to a wire rack, stopping the baking at the perfect moment.

Foil Collars

I like to make foil collars for my pies to help keep the height on the crust and prevent burning. You can buy them ready-made, but I've never used those. I take a large rectangular piece of foil (it should be double the diameter of your pie pan in length, approximately 20 inches long) and fold it in half lengthwise over and over again, until the foil strip is about 2 inches wide. Then I wrap the collar around the lip of the piecrust, folding the ends together where they meet to hold the collar in place.

Ice Cream Scoops

If you make a lot of cookies (and I hope you do), I suggest buying some ice cream scoops to make portioning easy. We use all sizes of ice cream scoops at Willa Jean to portion cookies, and we refer to them by their color. For home use, I most often use a yellow scoop (#20), which is a little over 2 inches in diameter and holds about 1½ ounces, or roughly 3 tablespoons, of dough. I really like to get my nephews involved with scooping dough when I visit—they have a blast helping and racing to scoop the most.

Ingredient Temperatures

The temperature of your ingredients is one of the most critical factors in baking. When a recipe calls for ingredients to be at room temperature, believe it to be true. Not following this simple instruction will prevent you from experiencing a recipe's fullest potential. Making batters is an act of creating and controlling the amount of air trapped within the batter and ensuring the ingredients are fully emulsified, so that when that air expands in the oven, you're left with the lightest, fluffiest baked goods or pastry possible. There is a ton of science I could happily dive into here, but the point of this book is to make baking less intimidating. So, here is a fundamental: when "room temperature" is called for, follow that instruction.

Room-temperature butter means that the butter has been out of the fridge for at least 1 hour. It will divot under the pressure of a fingertip, but should not be melty or greasy. Cheeses and cream also need to be fully room temperature when called for, which means resting at room temperature for about an hour before using. Eggs, too: leave them out at room temperature for an hour or warm them gently in a bowl of warm water before using. Using cold eggs and room-temperature creamed butter will literally destroy a recipe. Don't do it.

Microplane

Since my earliest days in the kitchen, chefs and pastry chefs have loved to utilize home improvement and hardware stores as resources for creative kitchen techniques and efficiencies. The Microplane is the perfect example. It was originally designed and sold as a woodworking tool, but now you'd be hard-pressed to find a knife roll or bar setup without one. They come in all sorts of sizes and shapes these days and are used for all kinds of things. I stick with the original model, though, and use just the Microplane with the shaving blades. It is an efficient tool for shaving chocolate, cheese, citrus rind, and spices.

Rotating during Baking

Rotating baking sheets and pans during baking is a necessity in almost every home oven. Despite technological advances and how well home ovens are made these days, there's almost always an uneven airflow or hot spot. Rotate your baking sheets 180 degrees halfway through each bake (even for savory foods) to ensure the most even results possible.

Scalding

Scalding is heating dairy to the point just before it reaches a full boil, when it starts to bubble at the edges. There are several reasons we bring things to a scald and not to a boil. First, and most important, is temperature. Generally, when we are bringing something up to scald, we'll be combining it with something else, such as eggs or chocolate, both of which have very low cooking temperatures or burn points (cocoa butter is toast at about 127°F), so you want to bring your liquid to JUST the lowest possible temperature at which you can combine the two to make a true emulsion without burning or overcooking either ingredient. The second reason is moisture content. Naturally, when you heat a liquid, evaporation happens. If you heat something long enough to come to a full boil, you're losing liquid that won't be made up by other ingredients in the recipe, and this loss will impact your final product.

Sifting

This is something I will admit I am not a fan of. In most cases, I think it adds preciousness, or just an unnecessary step. In most recipes, simply whisking the ingredients will do the job. So, when I say to sift, I really, really mean it. Sifting is never an option with cocoa powder or powdered sugar, which you must always sift to avoid lumps. (Hell, I even double-sift those.) Also, some recipes call for sifting the dry ingredients into another part of the recipe, such as whipped egg whites. This is also intentional. When you've taken the time and energy to whip egg whites to full volume, don't just dump flour on top and deflate all that love. Instead, gently sift the dry ingredients over the top and carefully fold with a rubber spatula to incorporate.

A Baking Year at a Glance

If you need more excuses to bake beyond holidays like Thanksgiving and Christmas and all of that (not that you do, but should you), well, there is a day to celebrate everything.

First Friday in February—Work Naked Day

First Saturday in February—Eat Ice Cream in Bed Day

First week in May—Teacher Appreciation Week

First Friday in May—No Pants Day

JANUARY	FEBRUARY	MARCH	APRIL	MAY	JUNE
1/17—Ditch New Year's Resolutions Day (most people only last 3 weeks)	Shrove Tuesday (the day before Ash Wednesday)—Eat Pancakes Day 2/20—National Muffin Day 2/21—National Banana Bread Day	3/1—National Peanut Butter Lover's Day 3/8—Women's Day 3/14—Pi Day	4/7—My birthday 4/20—Celebrate Cannabis—if that's your thing	5/11—Eat What You Want Day Second Saturday in May—National Bake Sale Day 5/14—National Buttermilk Biscuit Day 5/18—No Dirty Dishes Day (make cobbler or another one-pan recipe)	June—National Candy Month 6/21—National Peaches-and-Cream Day

Third Friday in December—Ugly Sweater Party (throw a party!)

JULY	AUGUST	SEPTEMBER	OCTOBER	NOVEMBER	DECEMBER
7/7—World Chocolate Day	8/8—Beyoncé and Jay-Z Day in Minnesota	9/5—National Be Late for Something Day	10/1—International Coffee Day	Fourth Thursday in November—Thanksgiving (make ALL the pies)	12/4—National Cookie Day
7/21—National Ice Cream Day	8/13—National Prosecco Day	9/12—National Day of Encouragement	10/31—All Hallow's Eve	11/30—Stay at Home Because You're Well Day (this happens in the UK, but I like it)	12/14—National Monkey Day (pay your furry friends a visit at the zoo and make monkey bread)
7/30—National Cheesecake Day		9/13—Kids Take Over the Kitchen Day			12/17—National Maple Syrup Day
		9/19—National Butterscotch Pudding Day			

A Baking Year at a Glance

Quick Breads, Muffins, Biscuits, and More

Willa Jean Cornbread

Makes one 10-inch round
or one 9 by 5-inch loaf

¾ cup corn flour
(I like using Bob's Red Mill)

¾ cup coarse cornmeal

2⅓ cups buttermilk,
at room temperature

3 tablespoons plus 1½ teaspoons
unsalted butter, melted

2⅓ cups all-purpose flour

4 teaspoons baking powder

¼ teaspoon baking soda

2 tablespoons plus 2 teaspoons
granulated sugar

2 tablespoons plus 2 teaspoons
dark brown sugar

4 eggs, at room temperature

2½ tablespoons honey

1 tablespoon plus 1 teaspoon
kosher salt

Butter for serving

Cane syrup for serving (optional)

This cornbread recipe is a testament to what happens when multiple folks put their heads together and collaborate on a seemingly simple project. The fantastic team at Willa Jean and I dissected cornbread— what we love about it and what we don't—and became absolutely maniacal about creating a version that spoke to all the different things we imagined the perfect cornbread to be. First and foremost, it's about achieving great corn flavor. But almost equally important is texture— we hate dry cornbread. This version—the best version ever—blurs the lines between the texture of traditional cornbread and that of a tender quick bread. Then there's the issue of sweetness, about which there is an ongoing decades-long debate. Some folks believe that cornbread is just cake if you add sugar to it. Folks in the South are *real serious* about their position on this. I can tell you that I've debated it a hundred times over (and often with the same folks over and over again), and I will stand behind and defend my stance: I like a little sugar in my cornbread. But in truth, I believe there is room in this world for all the cornbreads!

At the end of the day, I think the real jewel is the cornbread that you can and will eat all by itself for breakfast, lunch, or dinner, and that you are equally happy crumbling on top of things like red beans and chili. The trick to this perfect cornbread is letting the cornmeal, corn flour, and buttermilk sit overnight; this allows the corn flour to fully hydrate, while the acid from the buttermilk tenderizes the cornmeal, helping to create a tender, almost cakey bread that still retains that slightly gritty texture you expect. The beauty of this cornbread is that you can leave the fully prepared batter in the refrigerator for 2 days before baking it.

1. In a medium bowl, using a wooden spoon, stir the corn flour and cornmeal with the buttermilk until there are no dry pockets remaining. Cover and refrigerate overnight (or for as little as 1 hour if you want to make the cornbread right now).

2. Preheat the oven to 375°F. Coat a 10-inch cast-iron skillet or 9 by 5-inch loaf pan with the 1½ teaspoons butter. In another medium bowl, whisk the all-purpose flour with the baking powder and baking soda. In a large bowl, whisk the granulated sugar and brown sugar with the eggs, honey, and salt. Whisk in the cornmeal mixture until well combined. Add the flour mixture, stirring just until combined, and then stir in 3 tablespoons of the butter.

continued

Willa Jean Cornbread

3. Pour the batter into the prepared skillet or pan. Bake for about 35 minutes, if using a skillet, or 50 to 55 minutes if using a loaf pan, rotating the skillet or pan after 25 minutes, until the cornbread is golden and irresistible and a knife inserted in the middle comes out clean.

4. Slather with butter and cane syrup, if using, cut, and enjoy immediately. Store leftovers loosely wrapped in foil at room temperature for up to 3 days.

Cornbread Pancakes

To make cornbread pancakes, whip 3 egg whites until medium stiff peaks form and fold them into the batter. Voilà! Pancake batter. To cook, lightly oil a skillet and heat over medium heat until hot. Spoon approximately ½ cup of batter into the skillet. Cook for about 1½ minutes, until you see bubbles popping on the surface, and then flip and cook the other side until golden brown. This batter makes about 16 large pancakes.

Cornbread Waffles

Drag out that waffle iron and turn the batter into waffles. Whip 5 egg whites with 2 tablespoons granulated sugar until soft peaks form, then fold them into the cornbread batter. To cook, follow your waffle iron's directions. A standard waffle iron uses about ¾ cup batter per waffle and takes about 3½ minutes to cook each one. This batter makes 8 waffles.

Cornbread Fritters

To make fritters, just add some fresh corn kernels to the batter and deep-fry for delicious little fritters. To make savory corn fritters, stir 2 cups fresh corn kernels, 1 cup sliced scallions, ¼ cup minced jalapeño, 1 tablespoon plus 1 teaspoon kosher salt, and 2 teaspoons freshly ground black pepper into the cornbread batter. In a separate bowl, whip 4 egg whites to soft peaks, then fold them into the batter. Set a brown paper bag on a baking sheet. Fry dollops of the batter in 350°F vegetable or peanut oil for about 2 minutes, until golden. Transfer the fritters to the brown bag to drain, then serve hot. This batter makes about 32 fritters.

Cornbread Croutons

If you have any leftover cornbread after a couple of days, turn it into cornbread croutons for chili or salads. Cut the cornbread into cubes, store in a resealable bag at room temperature for up to 3 days or in the freezer for up to 1 month, and then toast on a baking sheet in a 325°F oven for 7 to 10 minutes, stirring after 4 minutes for even toasting, until light brown on all sides. If frozen, toast straight from the freezer; no need to thaw.

The Jiffy Fix

If you're short on time or gumption and want delicious cornbread immediately, here are some of my favorite ideas for making it special when you aren't making it from scratch. Start with one (8½-ounce) box of Jiffy corn muffin mix. Just follow the package instructions, using egg and milk, unless I've instructed otherwise.

Savory Ideas

Add ⅓ cup sour cream to the batter to make the cornbread more moist and a little tangy.

Replace ⅔ cup milk with buttermilk to make the cornbread more tender (this also makes it a little tangier).

For some pops of texture, stir 1 cup fresh corn kernels into the batter.

To make it extra corny, strain 1 (8-ounce) can creamed corn and stir into the batter, along with 1 additional egg.

Stir 1 cup chopped roasted red bell peppers or roasted pimentos into the batter.

For heat, there are a lot of ways to go at it. Stir 1 cup roasted chopped jalapeños or 1 teaspoon crushed red pepper or cayenne pepper into the batter. Or mix in 3 tablespoons chile paste.

Who doesn't love cheesy cornbread? Fold ¾ cup shredded sharp cheddar into the batter.

Give it some NOLA flair by adding a rounded ¼ teaspoon Cajun spice blend.

Cook and crumble 4 to 6 slices bacon. Fold into the batter.

Cook, drain, and crumble about 1 cup breakfast sausage. Fold into the batter.

Sweet Ideas

Stir 2 tablespoons honey into the batter.

Stir the zest and juice of 1 orange or 2 lemons or limes into the batter.

Sprinkle berries over the bottom of the baking pan or skillet and pour the batter on top.

Toss 2 peeled peaches (cut into thin wedges) with 2 tablespoons light brown sugar and fold into the batter. I recommend sprinkling the top with a little raw sugar for crunchy fun.

Stir 1 teaspoon ground cinnamon into the dry mix.

Stir 1 (15-ounce) can pure pumpkin puree along with ½ teaspoon each ground cinnamon and nutmeg and ¼ teaspoon each ground cloves and cardamom into the batter. Add 1 additional egg, too.

Banana Bread

Makes two 9 by 5-inch loaves

½ cup unsalted butter,
at room temperature, plus
more for greasing the pans

2 tablespoons raw sugar
for coating the pans

3 cups all-purpose flour

2½ teaspoons baking soda

2 teaspoons kosher salt

⅓ cup sour cream,
at room temperature

⅓ cup Creole Cream Cheese
(page 305), mascarpone,
sour cream, fresh ricotta,
or pureed cottage cheese,
at room temperature

1¾ cups firmly packed
dark brown sugar

4 eggs, at room temperature

1 teaspoon vanilla extract

3¼ cups mashed ripe bananas
(about 5)

This is an absolute staple from my childhood. My mom baked banana bread almost every weekend—I can't remember many weekends when we weren't eating it. We didn't just eat it at home, either. One of my best childhood memories is eating griddled banana bread with whipped butter (something I serve at Willa Jean) at Hominy Grill in Charleston.

This recipe, like all my recipes, is about magnifying the personality of the main ingredient, and here it's all about banana. Sometimes I mix in nuts, chocolate chunks, or dried fruit—you can do whatever you want. Truly, I think this is one of my most favorite recipes of all time. Even if the bread gets dried out and old, you can make it into great bread pudding. Try it. You won't be mad about it.

1. Preheat the oven to 350°F. Butter two 9 by 5-inch loaf pans and add 1 tablespoon raw sugar to each. Tilt the pans to coat with the sugar, tapping out the excess.

2. In a medium bowl, whisk the flour with the baking soda and salt. In the bowl of a stand mixer fitted with the paddle attachment or in a large bowl using a handheld mixer, beat the butter, sour cream, cream cheese, and brown sugar on high speed, until light and fluffy, about 1 minute. Beat in the eggs, one at a time, beating well after each addition. Beat in the vanilla. With the mixer on low speed, mix in the dry ingredients. Add the bananas and beat on medium speed for about 15 seconds, just until combined; don't mix longer—you still want some viscosity. Using a large rubber spatula, stir the batter a few times to fully incorporate the banana.

3. Scrape the batter into the prepared loaf pans and bake for 50 to 60 minutes, rotating the pans after 25 minutes, until the loaves are golden brown and springy to the touch.

4. Transfer the pans to a wire rack to cool slightly, then turn the loaves out of the pans and let cool completely before cutting. The loaves can be kept at room temperature, loosely wrapped in foil, for up to 4 days.

Banana Muffins

Butter 24 standard muffin cups and sprinkle with the raw sugar; tap out the excess sugar. Divide the batter among the muffin cups and bake at 350°F for 18 to 20 minutes, rotating the muffin pans after 10 minutes, until the tops are golden brown. Let cool and then store in an airtight container or very loosely wrapped in foil (too tightly wrapped and they get gummy and weird) at room temperature for up to 3 days.

What's Mine Is Yours

For this batter, it's really important to make sure your wet ingredients are at room temperature to prevent the batter from breaking. We puree the bananas at Willa Jean, but it's okay to mash them. A little chunk isn't bad. Coating the pans with some raw sugar adds a really nice texture to the outside of the loaves and also makes them a little caramelized at the edges.

Mom's Zucchini Bread

Makes two 9 by 5-inch loaves

Butter for greasing the pans

3 cups all-purpose flour,
plus more for dusting the pans

1½ teaspoons ground cinnamon

2 teaspoons baking soda

1 teaspoon kosher salt

½ teaspoon baking powder

¾ cup chopped pecans

3 eggs, at room temperature

2 cups granulated sugar

1 cup vegetable oil

2 teaspoons vanilla extract

2 cups coarsely shredded zucchini

1 (8-ounce) can crushed
pineapple, drained

After my complete meltdown over carrots in cake (see my carrot cake recipe on page 259, y'all), my mom kept the real name of this bread a secret from me until I was mature enough to deal with vegetables in delicious baked goods.

1. Preheat the oven to 325°F. Grease and flour two 9 by 5-inch loaf pans. In a medium bowl, combine the flour, cinnamon, baking soda, salt, baking powder, and pecans.

2. In a large bowl, whisk the eggs lightly. Add the sugar, oil, and vanilla and mix until creamy. Stir in the zucchini and pineapple. Add the dry ingredients, stirring only until the dry ingredients are moistened. Scrape the batter into the prepared loaf pans and bake for 60 to 75 minutes, rotating the pans after 30 minutes, until the loaves are golden brown and springy to the touch.

3. Transfer the pans to a wire rack to cool for 10 minutes. Turn the loaves out of the pans and let cool completely before cutting. The loaves can be wrapped in plastic wrap or foil or stored in an airtight container at room temperature for up to 3 days.

Zucchini Bread Improv

My zucchini bread recipe is a basis for inspiration, not a mandate. Feel free to add any of these things to the batter along with the zucchini and pineapple:

Finely grated zest of 2 lemons

Finely grated zest of 1 orange

1½ cups berries (I will put blueberries in anything)

1½ cups fresh or dried cranberries

¼ teaspoon warming spices, such as ground cardamom, ginger, fennel, freshly ground black pepper, curry powder, or freshly grated nutmeg

Or substitute:

½ cup coarse cornmeal for ½ cup all-purpose flour

½ cup shredded carrots for ½ cup shredded zucchini

Pumpkin Bread with Pumpkin Seed Streusel

Makes one 9 by 5-inch loaf

Pumpkin Seed Streusel

¾ cup hulled pumpkin seeds

1¼ cups all-purpose flour

½ cup firmly packed light brown sugar

1 teaspoon kosher salt

¾ cup unsalted butter, at room temperature

Bread

Butter for greasing the pan and spreading on the bread

⅓ cup raw sugar for coating the pan

3 cups all-purpose flour

2 teaspoons baking soda

1 teaspoon kosher salt

1 teaspoon ground cinnamon

¾ teaspoon ground nutmeg

¼ teaspoon ground cloves

¼ teaspoon ground ginger

¼ teaspoon ground cardamom

1 (15-ounce) can pure pumpkin puree, 1⅓ cups measured out and the remainder (about ⅓ cup) reserved for another use

3 eggs, at room temperature

1 cup vegetable oil

½ cup cane syrup

¼ cup brewed coffee, at room temperature

2½ cups granulated sugar

1 recipe Whipped Cranberry Cream Cheese (page 306) for serving

Growing up in and around Charleston, I had the good fortune to have many, many weekend morning treats at Hominy Grill, which helped shaped my style of hospitality and vision for my own restaurant. Every single breakfast visit started with whichever quick bread they were offering on the menu, often served warm with delicious butter and jam.

By the time fall rolls around in New Orleans and the summer heat finally breaks, the abundance of pumpkins and squashes shifts our menus and our eating. In honor of Hominy Grill, I always add this pumpkin bread with pumpkin seed streusel to the griddled bread snacks we offer at Willa Jean and serve it with a delicious cranberry spread for optimal enjoyment.

1. Make the streusel. Preheat the oven to 350°F. Spread the pumpkin seeds on a rimmed baking sheet and toast in the oven for 15 minutes, or until aromatic and toasty, stirring every 5 minutes. Let cool. In a medium bowl, combine the pumpkin seeds with the flour, brown sugar, and salt.

2. In a medium saucepot set over medium heat, cook the butter until golden brown, fragrant, and nutty smelling. Pour the butter through a fine-mesh strainer into a heat-resistant bowl, leaving the browned sediment at the bottom of the saucepan. Let the browned butter cool until solidified, about 30 minutes.

3. Add the cooled browned butter to the pumpkin seed mixture and rub it between your palms until everything is thoroughly combined. At this point, you can store the streusel in an airtight container in the fridge for up to 5 days.

4. Make the bread. Lightly coat a 9 by 5-inch loaf pan with butter. Place the raw sugar in the pan and tilt to coat evenly. Tap out any excess.

5. In a medium bowl, sift together the flour, baking soda, salt, cinnamon, nutmeg, cloves, ginger, and cardamom. In the bowl of a stand mixer fitted with the paddle attachment or in a large bowl using a handheld mixer, combine the pumpkin, eggs, oil, cane syrup, and coffee and beat until well incorporated. Alternately beat in the granulated sugar and the sifted dry ingredients in stages, beating well after each addition.

6. Pour the batter into the prepared pan. Top with the streusel. Bake for 70 to 75 minutes, rotating the pan after 35 minutes, until the top is golden brown and a knife comes out clean when inserted into the center. Transfer the pan to a wire rack and let cool for 20 minutes, then turn the loaf out of the pan onto the rack and cool completely.

7. Slice the loaf into ¾-inch-thick slices. Butter both sides of the bread with soft butter and griddle in a pan over medium heat until each side is nice and toasty. Serve with the cream cheese. The loaf can be wrapped in plastic wrap or foil and stored at room temperature for 4 to 5 days.

What's Mine Is Yours

Whip a couple tablespoons of the leftover pumpkin puree into the Cranberry Cream Cheese.

Bran muffins are one of the most overlooked breakfast muffins. When done well, they're flavorful and moist. The muffins here take on an almost oatmeal-like texture, which I love. That amazing texture (and flavor) comes from toasting the bran. Toasting also helps alleviate any stale bran flavor that might come from the bran sitting in the back of your pantry for who knows how long. It's the same as toasting your spices to turn up the volume on their flavor.

1. Preheat the oven to 350°F. Spread the bran on a rimmed baking sheet and toast in the oven for about 10 minutes, stirring occasionally to prevent burning, until golden and aromatic. Transfer to a plate to cool.

2. Increase the oven temperature to 400°F. Lightly coat the muffin cups of a standard muffin pan with cooking spray or line with paper muffin cups.

3. In a medium bowl, soak the bran in the water until soft, 3 to 5 minutes. In a large bowl, combine the brown sugar, honey, oil, and egg, and stir until well mixed. Add the bran mixture and stir until combined.

4. In a medium bowl, whisk the flour, baking soda, and salt. Add the orange zest. Add the dry ingredients to the wet ingredients, stirring until combined. Stir in the raisins and cranberries. Spoon the batter into the prepared muffin cups, filling each about three-quarters full. Bake for 15 to 20 minutes, rotating the pan after 8 minutes, until the muffins are golden brown and a cake tester comes out clean when inserted into the center of a muffin.

5. Let the muffins cool in the pans on a wire rack for 5 minutes and then transfer them to the wire rack to cool; don't wait any longer or the steam released will cause them to start to collapse. These muffins keep well at room temperature if they're wrapped well in plastic wrap or foil or stored in an airtight container, for up to 3 days.

Badass Toasted-Bran Muffins

Makes 12 muffins

2¼ cups wheat bran

1 cup water

¾ cup firmly packed light brown sugar

4½ tablespoons honey

4½ tablespoons grapeseed or rice bran oil

1 egg, at room temperature

¾ cup all-purpose flour

1 teaspoon baking soda

Rounded ¼ teaspoon kosher salt

½ teaspoon finely grated orange zest

¼ cup golden raisins

¼ cup dried cranberries

Classic Blueberry Muffins with Streusel

Makes 12 muffins

Streusel

1 cup all-purpose flour

⅓ cup firmly packed
light brown sugar

⅓ cup granulated sugar

½ teaspoon ground cinnamon

½ teaspoon kosher salt

½ cup unsalted butter, melted

1 teaspoon finely grated lemon
or orange zest

Muffins

2 cups all-purpose flour, plus
more for tossing the berries

2 teaspoons baking powder

½ teaspoon kosher salt

½ cup unsalted butter,
at room temperature

1 cup granulated sugar

2 eggs, at room temperature

⅓ cup whole milk,
at room temperature

1 teaspoon vanilla extract

2 cups fresh blueberries
(or frozen, if that's all you have)

Finely grated zest of 1 lemon
or orange

Here's a pretty straightforward and crowd-pleasing streusel-topped muffin. I know y'all do love a basic blueberry muffin. Feel free to make the muffin batter and streusel the night before if you want quick and easy muffins in the morning; just store them separately in airtight containers in the fridge overnight. You'll also just want to break the streusel up with a fork before sprinkling it on the muffins.

1. Make the streusel. In a medium bowl, whisk together the flour, brown sugar, granulated sugar, cinnamon, and salt. Stir in the melted butter and zest, mixing with a fork until the mixture is crumbly and resembles coarse meal.

2. Make the muffins. Preheat the oven to 375°F. Lightly coat the cups of a standard muffin pan with cooking spray. In a large bowl, whisk together the flour, baking powder, and salt. In the bowl of a stand mixer fitted with the paddle attachment or in a large bowl using a handheld mixer, cream the butter and sugar on low speed. Add the eggs, one at a time, beating well after each addition, and mix until well combined and creamy, about 3 minutes. Add the milk and vanilla and beat until well incorporated. Add the dry ingredients in portions, beating until each addition is incorporated before adding more, and then beat until the batter is uniform. Add a pinch of flour to the blueberries and toss to coat well and prevent sticking. Fold the blueberries and zest into the batter.

3. Spoon the batter into the prepared muffin cups, filling them about three-quarters full. Sprinkle on the streusel and bake for about 30 minutes, rotating the pan after 15 minutes, until the muffins are golden brown and a cake tester comes out clean when inserted into the center of a muffin. Let the muffins cool in the pan for about 20 minutes and then transfer them to a wire rack to fully cool; don't wait longer or the steam released will cause the muffins to start to collapse. You can serve these immediately or keep them in an airtight container at room temperature for up to 3 days.

I love lemon–poppy seed muffins, and since it seems that they are obligatory for any baking book, here are mine, y'all. I like to glaze my lemon–poppy seed muffins to give another little pop of lemon flavor, but feel free to skip the step if you're not interested in the extra tartness or added sweetness.

1. Make the muffins. Preheat the oven to 350°F. Coat the cups of a standard muffin pan with cooking spray. In a medium bowl, whisk together the flour, baking powder, baking soda, and salt. In the bowl of a stand mixer fitted with the paddle attachment or in a large bowl using a handheld mixer, cream the butter and sugar until combined. Add the eggs, one at a time, beating well after each addition. Beat in the milk, sour cream, vanilla, lemon zest, and lemon juice until well incorporated and smooth. Fold in the dry ingredients just until incorporated, making sure not to mix more, since doing so will result in dry, tough muffins. Stir in the poppy seeds.

2. Spoon the batter into the prepared muffin cups, filling them about two-thirds full. Bake for 20 to 25 minutes, rotating the pan after 10 minutes, until the muffins are golden brown and a cake tester comes out clean when inserted into the center of a muffin. Let the muffins cool in the pan for 5 to 10 minutes and then transfer them to a wire rack to cool; don't wait any longer or the steam released will cause the muffins to start to collapse.

3. Make the glaze. In a medium bowl, whisk the powdered sugar with the cream and lemon juice until smooth. Drizzle the glaze over the cooled muffins. (If they're not cool, the glaze will slide right off the muffins and wreck their texture.) The muffins can be wrapped in plastic wrap or foil or stored in an airtight container at room temperature for up to 3 days.

Lemon–Poppy Seed Muffins

Makes 12 muffins

Muffins

2½ cups all-purpose flour

2 teaspoons baking powder

¼ teaspoon baking soda

½ teaspoon kosher salt

½ cup unsalted butter, at room temperature

½ cup plus 2 tablespoons granulated sugar

2 eggs, at room temperature

⅔ cup whole milk, at room temperature

¼ cup sour cream, at room temperature

1 teaspoon vanilla extract

2½ tablespoons finely grated lemon zest

2½ tablespoons fresh lemon juice

⅓ cup poppy seeds

Glaze

1 cup powdered sugar, sifted

1 tablespoon heavy cream or whole milk

2 tablespoons fresh lemon juice

Blueberry-Ginger Muffins

Makes 24 muffins

1⅔ cups plus 1 tablespoon
cake flour

1⅔ cups bread flour

¾ teaspoon ground ginger

2 teaspoons baking powder

½ teaspoon baking soda

1½ teaspoons kosher salt

½ cup unsalted butter,
at room temperature

1 cup plus 2 teaspoons firmly
packed light brown sugar

⅓ cup plus 1 teaspoon cane syrup
or molasses

⅓ cup plus 1 teaspoon honey

3 eggs, at room temperature

⅔ teaspoon vanilla extract

½ cup buttermilk,
at room temperature

2⅔ cups fresh blueberries
(or frozen, if that's all you have)

It's really too easy to find mediocre blueberry muffins. So easy, that I had almost given up on ever ordering one again. Then, as luck would have it, I wandered into a café in San Francisco and had all hope restored by a singular muffin. This is a tribute to that experience; a moment I relive every time I bite into one of these. It's beyond any basic model and offers a dark, nuanced depth of flavor that I just adore. If you don't have cane syrup, substitute molasses.

1. Preheat the oven to 350°F. Coat the muffin cups of two standard muffin pans with cooking spray. In a medium bowl, mix the cake flour and bread flour with the ginger, baking powder, baking soda, and salt. In the bowl of a stand mixer fitted with the paddle attachment or in a large bowl using a handheld mixer, cream the butter and brown sugar until light and fluffy. Beat in the cane syrup and honey, then beat in the dry ingredients just until combined. Add the eggs, one at a time, beating well after each addition, then mix in the vanilla and buttermilk. Gently fold in the blueberries.

2. Spoon the batter into the prepared cups, filling them about three-quarters full. Bake for 15 to 20 minutes, rotating the pans after 8 minutes, until the muffins are golden brown and a cake tester comes out clean when inserted into the center of a muffin.

3. Let the muffins cool in the pans for 5 minutes and then transfer them to a wire rack to cool; don't wait any longer or the steam released will cause them to start to collapse. Let cool completely if you're able to wait . . . if not, no big deal—warm muffins are delicious. The muffins can be wrapped well in plastic wrap or stored in an airtight container, bread box, or cake carrier (or even your microwave) at room temperature for about 3 days.

Tall Blueberry Muffins

At Willa Jean, I love to bake these muffins (and just about any other muffin or quick bread) in tall cylinders (about 3½ inches high and 3 inches in diameter) because they look so great. I also love the ratio of surface crunch to inside fluff. To take it to the next level, I brush the muffin cups with soft butter and then sprinkle with raw sugar to create a caramelly crunch. Increase the baking time to 30 to 35 minutes. Makes 18 tall muffins.

What's Mine Is Yours

If you're feeling it, I recommend making a quick fresh ginger puree to substitute for the ground ginger. Roughly chop a big nob of peeled fresh ginger. Put the ginger in a mini food processor or high-speed blender and add just enough water to puree to a paste. Use 1 tablespoon of the ginger puree in place of the ground ginger, adding it to the batter along with the cane syrup and honey.

If you like to use cupcake liners for your muffins, I suggest lightly spraying the pan first to help keep the liners in place while you're filling the muffin cups and then also lightly spraying the insides of the liners just to make the eating tidier.

Glazed Lemon-Cornmeal Muffins

Makes 12 muffins

¾ cup plus 4 teaspoons all-purpose flour

½ cup coarse cornmeal

1 tablespoon baking powder

⅔ teaspoon baking soda

1 teaspoon kosher salt

2 tablespoons plus 2 teaspoons vegetable oil

1 tablespoon plus 1 teaspoon fresh lemon juice

1 tablespoon plus 1 teaspoon maple syrup

2 teaspoons vanilla extract

¼ cup plus 1 teaspoon unsalted butter, at room temperature

⅓ cup plus 1 tablespoon granulated sugar

Very finely grated zest of 2½ lemons

1 egg, at room temperature

¾ cup plus 1 tablespoon ricotta cheese, at room temperature

⅓ cup mascarpone cheese, at room temperature

Glaze

1 cup powdered sugar, sifted

2 tablespoons fresh lemon juice

1 tablespoon buttermilk, milk, or water

My great-uncle Henry in Knoxville, Tennessee, has always judged the quality of the restaurant where I work by asking if he can get a glass of good buttermilk and some cornbread. He combines the two—much like what we call "cush cush" in New Orleans. These muffins never fail to make me think of my sweet, ornery uncle Henry.

1. Make the muffins. Preheat the oven to 350°F. Coat the cups of one standard muffin pan with cooking spray. In a large bowl, whisk together the flour, cornmeal, baking powder, baking soda, and salt. In a medium bowl, stir together the oil, lemon juice, maple syrup, and vanilla.

2. In the bowl of a stand mixer fitted with the paddle attachment or in a large bowl using a handheld mixer, cream the butter, sugar, and lemon zest on medium-high speed for about 2 minutes, until fluffy and combined. Beat in the egg, incorporating well. Stop the mixer and scrape down the sides of the bowl using a rubber spatula. With the mixer on low, add the wet ingredients in several batches, followed by the dry ingredients, ricotta, and mascarpone cheese. Mix until just incorporated.

3. Spoon the batter into the prepared muffin cups, filling them about three-quarters full. Bake for 20 to 25 minutes, rotating the pan after 10 minutes, until the muffins are golden brown and a cake tester comes out clean when inserted into the center of a muffin.

4. Let the muffins cool in the pans for 5 to 10 minutes and then transfer them to a wire rack to cool completely before glazing; don't wait longer or the steam released will cause them to collapse.

5. Make the glaze. In a medium bowl, whisk together the powdered sugar, lemon juice, and buttermilk until smooth. You can adjust the consistency by adding more liquid to thin the glaze or more sugar to thicken it. Drizzle the glaze over the muffins and serve. The muffins can be wrapped in plastic wrap or foil or stored in an airtight container at room temperature for up to 3 days.

I have messed up a lot of biscuits in my time. I've overthought, overworked, underbaked, and overbaked more biscuits than anyone could reasonably justify. I've used the wrong flours and added too little fat—or too much (sure, there's an argument to be made that there's no such thing as too much fat in a biscuit, but nevertheless). I've made biscuits that come out like cake and biscuits that would make better ornamental rocks than food. After seventeen years of professional baking and being surrounded by crazy-talented folks like former Willa Jean baker Mike Carmody (one of the most talented bakers I've ever worked with, whose influence and passion have made me a better cook and person), I learned that Italian-style 00 flour gives biscuits the strength they need without the chew. So-named for how millers grade the texture of flour, 00 flour is most often used for making pizza and pasta, but it works great in biscuits because it absorbs the butter and buttermilk just right, creating the perfect flaky layers you want in a biscuit without the chewy, toothsome texture. My other secret? I *always* freeze these biscuits before baking and take them straight from the freezer to the hot oven: The colder they are, the higher they rise. You know what they say: the higher the hair, the closer to God.

The Baker's Biscuits

Makes 12 large biscuits

6 cups 00 flour, preferably Italian Antimo Caputo flour (cake flour works well, too)

¼ cup plus 2 tablespoons baking powder

2 tablespoons granulated sugar

1 tablespoon kosher salt

¾ cup plus 3 tablespoons cold unsalted butter, grated on the large holes of a box grater and placed in the freezer

3 cups cold buttermilk, plus ¼ cup for brushing on top

All-purpose flour for dusting

1. In a large bowl, mix the 00 flour, baking powder, sugar, and salt. Add the butter and use your hands to cut it into the flour, smearing the mixture between your fingertips to create flakes; there should be a combination of large and small flecks of butter, and the flour will start to take on the color of the butter. Make a well in the center of the dry ingredients and add 1½ cups of the buttermilk. Using a rubber spatula, stir the dry ingredients from the edges into the buttermilk until incorporated. Add the remaining 1½ cups buttermilk and stir just until a shaggy dough forms.

2. Line a baking sheet with parchment paper. Dust your work surface liberally with all-purpose flour. Turn the dough out of the bowl and pat it into a rectangle; it's okay if the dough barely holds together. Fold one-third of the dough to the center, then fold the other third on top, like folding a letter. Using a lightly floured rolling pin, roll the dough into a 6 by 13-inch rectangle and repeat the folding process. Roll again to a 6 by 13-inch rectangle, until about 1 inch thick. Cut the dough into 12 biscuits; each one should be a little less than 3 inches square (there might be some leftover dough). Transfer the biscuits to the prepared baking sheet. Place the baking sheet in the freezer for at least 12 hours and up to overnight, covering the biscuits with plastic wrap once they're frozen.

3. Preheat the oven to 400°F. Bake the frozen biscuits for 40 minutes, rotating the baking sheet after 20 minutes, until the biscuits have risen, are golden, and sound hollow when you flick the bottoms. Serve hot. Store wrapped loosely in foil or plastic wrap at room temperature up to overnight.

What's Mine Is Yours

I dust the sticks of butter in flour before I grate them so they're easier to handle.

What's Mine Is Yours

Don't try to make these biscuits any larger than about 2½ inches or they won't achieve their maximum rise. Larger biscuits would require more dough structure than this recipe provides, as it's a recipe that aims to create as little structure as possible. These should rise 2 to 2½ times their uncooked height. Remember, the more you work the dough, the more you develop and tighten the protein threads in the flour (aka gluten), which will result in a tight, dense, chewy biscuit.

These are the biscuits—straightforward, classic, and simple—that I remember both my mom and her mother, my grandma Mac, whipping up with sausage gravy on Sunday mornings. These are the ones you make on a whim and serve for breakfast, lunch, supper, or dessert (with some fresh fruit). They're called rolled biscuits because they're traditionally rolled and cut. There's no poetry in their name, but they make up for it with their crisp, buttery crust and light, fluffy insides.

Rolled Biscuits

Makes 12 biscuits

3 cups all-purpose flour, plus more for dusting

1 tablespoon plus 1 teaspoon granulated sugar

1 tablespoon baking powder

1½ teaspoons kosher salt

¼ cup plus 2 tablespoons cold unsalted butter, grated on the large holes of a box grater and placed in the freezer

1 cup cold whole milk

Heavy cream for brushing

1. Line a baking sheet with parchment paper or a silicone liner. In a medium bowl, whisk together the flour, sugar, baking powder, and salt. Using your hands, a fork, a pastry blender, or even a stand mixer fitted with the paddle attachment on low speed, cut in the butter until the mixture resembles small peas. Add the milk and mix gently until a dough forms. If the dough seems a touch dry, add a dash of milk and stop mixing as soon as the dough comes together.

2. Lightly dust your work surface with flour. Turn the dough out of the bowl onto the work surface and pat down (or roll, if you're really literal), until the dough is ¾ to 1 inch thick. Using a floured 2-inch biscuit cutter, cut out biscuits as close to one another as is humanly possible to reduce scraps. Transfer the biscuits to the prepared baking sheet. Place the baking sheet in the freezer for at least 30 minutes and up to overnight, covering the biscuits with plastic wrap once they're frozen.

3. Preheat the oven to 425°F. Lightly brush the tops of the frozen biscuits with the cream, being careful not to let it drip down the sides of the biscuits, which can reduce their rise in the oven. Bake for 15 to 20 minutes, rotating the baking sheet after 8 minutes, until the biscuits have risen, are light golden, and sound hollow when you flick the bottoms.

4. Serve immediately. Store wrapped loosely in foil or plastic wrap at room temperature up to overnight.

Angel Biscuits

Makes 6 biscuits

2 (¼-ounce) envelopes active
dry yeast (2½ teaspoons each)

¼ cup warm water

5 cups all-purpose flour,
plus more for dusting

¼ cup granulated sugar

2 teaspoons baking powder

1 teaspoon baking soda

1½ teaspoons kosher salt

½ cup cold unsalted butter,
grated on the large holes of
a box grater and placed in
the freezer, plus 2 tablespoons
unsalted butter, melted

½ cup lard (you can use
vegetable shortening, but
it won't be as delicious)

2 cups cold buttermilk

These quick biscuits do not need to rise, but with three leaveners, they are supremely light and fluffy. That's why they call them angel biscuits, y'all. However, they have also been called bride's biscuits because they're so easy to make that "even a new bride could make them." Seriously? Seriously.

This dough holds well, so you can shape the biscuits and refrigerate them for up to 4 days or freeze them, well wrapped in plastic, for up to 3 months and put them right into the oven from the freezer.

1. Preheat the oven to 400°F. In a small bowl, dissolve the yeast in the warm water. In a medium bowl, whisk together the flour, sugar, baking powder, baking soda, and salt. Using a pastry blender or two table knives, cut the chilled butter and lard into the dry ingredients until the mixture resembles coarse meal. Stir in the buttermilk, then stir in the yeast mixture.

2. Lightly dust your work surface with flour. Using a lightly floured rolling pin, roll the dough into a 6 by 9-inch rectangle. Cut the dough into six 3-inch squares. Transfer the biscuits to a baking sheet. Brush the tops of the biscuits with the melted butter. Bake for 15 to 20 minutes, rotating the baking sheet after 8 minutes, until the biscuits are golden brown on top.

3. Serve warm. Store wrapped loosely in foil or plastic wrap at room temperature up to overnight.

Drop biscuits are defined by how much liquid they have in them—they are too wet to be rolled, so they have to be dropped from a scoop or spoon onto the pan. They're fluffy but not airy—more like moist-fluffy—and the crust isn't as crisp as a rolled biscuit.

1. Preheat the oven to 350°F. In a medium bowl, whisk together the cake flour, all-purpose flour, baking powder, and baking soda. Whisk in the sugar and salt. Using a pastry blender or two table knives, cut the butter into the dry ingredients until the mixture resembles small peas. Stir in the buttermilk and cream until the dough is uniformly mixed.

2. Using two spoons or a 3¼-ounce ice cream scoop (about 6 tablespoons), drop the biscuit dough directly onto a baking sheet. Brush the tops with buttermilk and bake for about 30 minutes, rotating the baking sheet after 15 minutes, until the tops are golden brown.

3. Serve hot. Store overnight in an airtight container or tightly wrapped at room temperature up to overnight.

Drop Biscuits

Makes about 12 biscuits

2 cups cake flour

1 cup all-purpose flour

1 tablespoon plus 1 teaspoon baking powder

¼ teaspoon baking soda

¼ cup granulated sugar

2¼ teaspoons kosher salt

¼ cup plus 2 tablespoons cold unsalted butter, diced

1⅓ cups cold buttermilk, plus more for brushing on top

¼ cup cold heavy cream

What's Mine Is Yours

With all biscuits, I find it best to make the dough before I preheat the oven. Set up the biscuits on the baking sheet, place the sheet in the fridge (or even in the freezer, if you have room), and then preheat your oven. Getting the dough as cold as possible not only helps the biscuits keep their shape while baking, but I also find it produces more rise in the biscuits with the evaporation of moisture.

You don't have to line your baking sheet, but if you do, I prefer to use parchment paper or a silicone liner. Lining your pans not only ensures you'll be able to get your baked goods off the pans, but also really helps reduce the cleanup.

Beaten Biscuits

Makes about 12 biscuits

2 cups all-purpose flour, plus more for dusting

1 teaspoon granulated sugar (optional)

1¼ teaspoons kosher salt

¼ teaspoon baking powder

3 tablespoons lard (you can use vegetable shortening, but it won't be as delicious)

3 tablespoons cold unsalted butter, grated on the large holes of a box grater and placed in a freezer

½ cup cold whole milk

What's Mine Is Yours

There is no household mixer strong enough to survive this dough, but a food processor will get the job done.

The beaten biscuit had fallen into relative obscurity until it was revived by Karl Worley of Biscuit Love in Nashville. I didn't know how good a beaten biscuit could be, because I had never had a good one until I met him. The name is apt—to make it, you beat the hell out of the dough. This is a great alternative to a cracker. Beaten biscuits are dense, thin, crispy, and traditionally served with ham. You can also smear them with pimento cheese, and they won't crumble.

Side confession: I was fascinated by flour when I was a kid. I used to put a spoonful between my cheek and gum and keep it in my mouth until it got chewy. Gross, maybe, but it all makes sense now that I make my living by experimenting with flour. Also, I was born, raised, and schooled with Crisco. To be honest, I liked to eat that, too.

1. Preheat the oven to 375°F. In a large bowl, whisk together the flour, sugar (if using), salt, and baking powder. Using a pastry blender or two table knives, cut the lard and butter into the dry ingredients until the mixture resembles small peas. Make a well in the center of the mixture with your hands and add the milk. Stir until the milk is fully incorporated and a soft dough forms.

2. Lightly dust your work surface with flour. Turn the dough out and knead it about 15 to 20 times by hand. Divide the dough into two equal pieces. Place half of the dough in a food processor and process the hell out of it—8 to 10 minutes nonstop, until it starts to get stretchy and has a "tight" structure. Set aside and repeat with the second piece of dough. Let the dough rest in a cool place for about 15 minutes. (You can also wrap it in plastic wrap and refrigerate overnight.)

3. Line a baking sheet with parchment paper. Roll out the dough to about ¼ inch thick. Using a floured 2-inch biscuit cutter, cut out as many biscuits as you can. You can reroll the scraps and cut more biscuits until all the dough has been used. Transfer the biscuits to the prepared baking sheet. Bake for 15 to 20 minutes, rotating the baking sheet after 8 minutes, until the biscuits are very light brown on top and the bottoms are a deep brown.

4. Serve warm or at room temperature—it doesn't matter, unless you're trying to smear with some pimento cheese because it might just melt if you don't smear and eat it quickly. I recommend making and eating these biscuits the same day, as with most biscuits, but you can make the biscuits a day ahead if you absolutely have to. Store them well wrapped at room temperature. To reheat, pop them into a 325°F oven for 5 to 7 minutes to heat through, if desired.

I am a big fan of a little bite of something sweet with my savory breakfast. This sweet potato biscuit is just sweet enough to satisfy without being overly so. I find these biscuits are best eaten straight from the oven, but they can be reheated later in the day and used for a ham sandwich snack.

Sweet Potato Biscuits

Makes 12 square biscuits

1¼ cups pureed roasted sweet potatoes (from 2 sweet potatoes), chilled

½ cup cold buttermilk

1⅔ cups all-purpose flour, plus more for dusting

1 tablespoon firmly packed light brown sugar

2½ teaspoons baking powder

¼ teaspoon baking soda

1 teaspoon kosher salt

½ cup cold unsalted butter, grated on the large holes of a box grater and placed in the freezer

1. In a small bowl, combine the sweet potatoes and buttermilk. In a large bowl, combine the flour, brown sugar, baking powder, baking soda, and salt. Add the butter to the dry ingredients. Using a pastry blender or two table knives, cut the butter into the dry ingredients until the mixture resembles small peas. Add the sweet potato mixture and stir gently just until incorporated and a soft dough begins to form; don't continue mixing or you will overmix the dough. The dough will be wet and sticky.

2. Coat a baking sheet with cooking spray and line it with parchment paper. Dust your work surface liberally with flour. Turn the dough and pat it into a rough rectangle. Using a lightly floured rolling pin, roll out the dough into a 4 by 12-inch rectangle, about 1 inch thick. Using a floured sharp knife, cut out twelve 2-inch square biscuits. Place the biscuits on the prepared baking sheet. Place the baking sheet in the freezer for at least 30 minutes and up to 2 hours.

3. Preheat the oven to 425°F. Bake for about 15 minutes, rotating the baking sheet after 8 minutes, until the biscuits are golden brown.

4. Serve warm. Store wrapped loosely in foil or plastic wrap at room temperature up to overnight.

What's Mine Is Yours

If you're in the mood for these and don't want to take the time to roast sweet potatoes, feel free to substitute canned sweet potato puree. Or drain the water out of canned "cut" sweet potatoes and puree them in a high-speed blender to make the 1¼ cups puree.

This dough also freezes beautifully. I recommend keeping some of these biscuits in your freezer, unbaked and tightly wrapped, to bake any time the mood strikes. (And that goes for all the biscuits, not just these.)

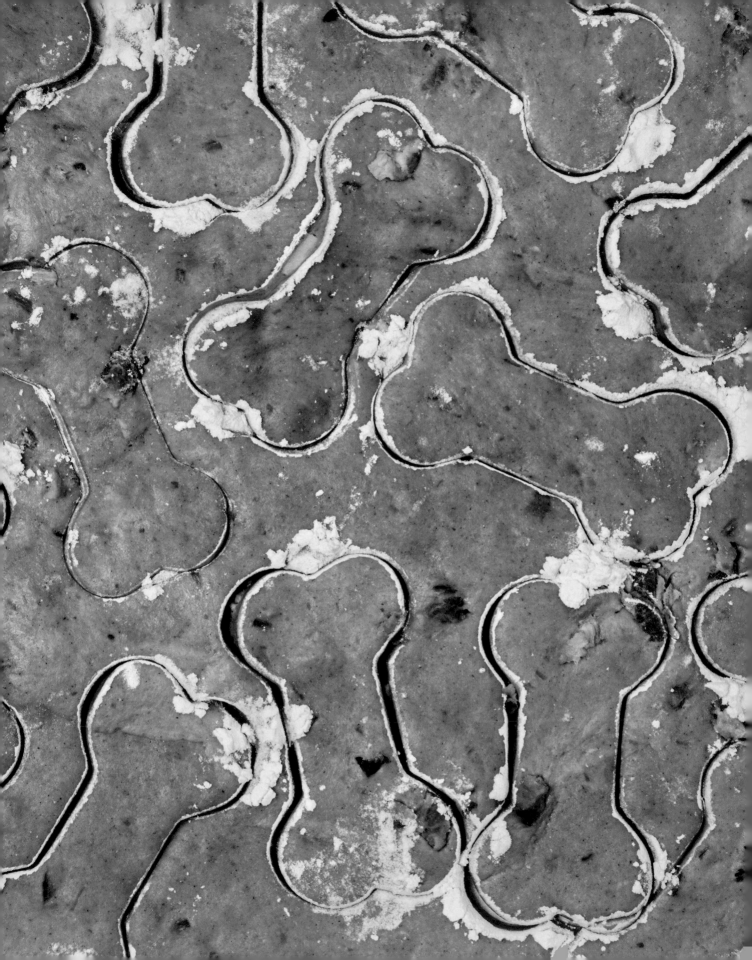

A few years ago, I stood outside a kennel at the local Louisiana ASPCA and was warned that the dog inside was mouthy and not very social, despite his good looks. I liked him immediately and it must have been mutual because he instantly rolled over and gave me his belly to love on. To say it was love at first sight would be an understatement. I hadn't really known I was a dog person until I met this guy, and maybe I hadn't been . . . until then. He was adopted by someone else that same day but was then returned because the person was allergic to dogs (he hadn't known it beforehand). Then he was adopted by someone else and, yes, returned again. For two weeks, I was heartbroken about missing the moment to adopt him (twice), but then his face popped up on the ASPCA website again. I ran out of work immediately to adopt him. Ever since that afternoon, if you know me, you know the great R. S. Kinney (his adopted name was Rocky, which I lengthened to include my favorite band, of course). Kinney is the world's best boy and is highly motivated to do as many stellar acts as possible to get treats. Of the dog biscuits I make, these are his favorites. I thought it only fair to include them in this collection of all the important biscuits in life. In fact, this may be the most important kind.

1. Preheat the oven to 350°F. In a large bowl, mix together the flour, eggs, sweet potato, peanut butter, cinnamon, and bacon (if using). The dough should be dry and pretty stiff, but if you need to add water to work with it more easily, add a few tablespoons at a time and continue mixing.

2. Lightly dust your work surface with flour. Using a lightly floured rolling pin, roll out the dough to about ⅓ inch thick. Using a cookie cutter lightly dipped in flour (the size and shape of the biscuit is really up to you or your dog), cut out as many biscuits as you can. You can reroll the scraps and cut more biscuits until you're left with too little dough to form a full one. Transfer the biscuits, evenly spaced, to a baking sheet and bake for 35 to 40 minutes, rotating the pan after 18 minutes, until the biscuits are golden brown and crispy. Cool completely before serving. Store in an airtight container or resealable bag at room temperature for up to 5 days.

R. S. Kinney's Most Favorite Dog Biscuits

Makes about 24 biscuits

2½ cups all-purpose flour, plus more for dusting

2 eggs, at room temperature

¾ cup pureed roasted sweet potato or pumpkin

¼ cup peanut butter (smooth or chunky–whatever you prefer or have on hand as long as it's xylitol-free)

½ teaspoon ground cinnamon

4 strips bacon, cooked and minced (optional . . . I spoil my dog)

Quick Breads, Muffins, Biscuits, and More

I Really Love Pancakes

Makes 24 delicious pancakes

2½ cups all-purpose flour

2½ cups cake flour

¼ cup granulated sugar

3 tablespoons baking powder

½ teaspoon baking soda

2 teaspoons kosher salt

1 quart cold buttermilk

½ cup cold whole milk

1½ teaspoons vanilla extract

8 eggs, separated, at room temperature

½ cup unsalted butter, melted

⅓ cup cold sour cream

Pancakes are my favorite food, y'all. I like to cook them on a nonstick griddle, but I'm a firm believer that you should be empowered to use your favorite cast-iron pan . . . or whatever you prefer. Always preheat your griddle (or pan) and coat with nonstick cooking spray or coconut oil or another oil with a high smoke point (safflower, vegetable, or canola oil, for example). I set my heat on the cooler side of medium and exercise the most patience, so I can get a beautiful golden brown flapjack that is perfectly cooked through. I love adding chocolate and banana or any seasonal fruit, too.

1. In a large bowl, whisk together the all-purpose flour, cake flour, sugar, baking powder, baking soda, and salt. In a medium bowl, whisk together the buttermilk, whole milk, vanilla, and egg yolks. In two stages, add the wet ingredients to the dry ingredients, stirring just until incorporated.

2. In the bowl of a stand mixer fitted with the whisk attachment or in a large bowl using a handheld mixer, whisk the egg whites on medium-high speed until medium-stiff peaks form, about 2 minutes. Remove the bowl from the mixer and, using a large spatula, gently fold the whipped egg whites into the batter in three portions; be careful not to compress the mixture or it will lose too much volume.

3. Put the melted butter in a medium bowl, add a touch of the batter, and stir together. Add this mixture to the batter and gently fold to incorporate. Fold in the sour cream just until it is fully incorporated and the batter isn't streaky. At this point, you can store the batter in an airtight container in the refrigerator for up to 4 hours before cooking. (After 4 hours, it deflates completely.)

4. Heat a nonstick griddle or cast-iron pan over medium-low heat and coat with cooking spray. Pour or scoop the batter (approximately ½ cup for each pancake) onto the hot griddle and cook for about 3 minutes per side; your cue to flip the pancakes is when air bubbles form in the pancakes and the edges begin to set.

5. The pancakes should be golden brown and perfectly cooked through. Serve hot.

Pancakes with Mix-ins

This recipe is fantastic as is, but feel free to improvise as your mood dictates. Mix in chocolate or butterscotch chips or top the pancakes with fresh berries, banana slices—whatever strikes your fancy. Go nuts!

Coffee cake was a staple in the house throughout my youth. My siblings and I were (very) competitive swimmers and incredibly active all the time. My poor parents had the remarkable task of trying to fill the house with enough food for three growing, active kids who spent about 6 hours a day in the pool practicing and, therefore, working up our already massive appetites. Despite the strength of my mom's baking skills, there were some cases when convenience won, and we'd have store-bought baked goods in the house. Even now, any time I see coffee cake, I remember the feeling of cutting a slice, grabbing a banana, and running off to be in the water by 4:00 A.M. I love to serve this cake topped with additional fresh fruit and a dusting of powdered sugar.

1. Make the fruit topping. In a medium saucepot, whisk together the sugar and cornstarch, then toss in the fruit and lemon juice. Cook the fruit over moderately high heat just until it begins to break down and release its juices. Continue cooking until the juices thicken slightly and begin to bubble slowly, about 4 minutes. Remove from the heat, stir in the vanilla paste, and let cool. The topping can be made up to 3 days ahead of time and stored in an airtight container in the fridge.

2. Make the crumb topping. In a medium bowl, whisk together the flour, brown sugar, granulated sugar, cinnamon, lemon zest, almonds, and salt. Gradually stream in the melted butter, stirring until the ingredients resemble coarse meal. Set aside until ready to use. This topping can be made up to 3 days ahead of time and stored in an airtight container in the fridge. Bring the streusel to room temperature and break up (it will compact a bit during refrigeration) with a fork or your hands.

3. Make the cake. Preheat the oven to 325°F. Liberally butter a 10-inch cake pan with 4-inch-high sides. (If you don't have a 4-inch-deep pan, two 2-inch-deep ones will work.) Place the raw sugar in the pan and tilt to coat evenly. Tap out any excess sugar.

4. In a small bowl, toss the fruit with 3 tablespoons of the flour, coating evenly. In another bowl, whisk the remaining 2 cups plus 2 tablespoons flour with the baking powder and salt. In the bowl of a stand mixer fitted with the paddle attachment or in a large bowl using a handheld mixer, cream the butter and sugar on medium-high speed until light and fluffy, 4 to 5 minutes, stopping to scrape down the sides of the bowl with a rubber spatula. Reduce the speed to low and beat in the eggs, one at a time, beating well after each addition, followed by the vanilla paste and orange zest. With the mixer still running, add the dry ingredients. Mix in the sour cream until incorporated, and then fold in the fruit. Remove the bowl from the mixer and, using a rubber spatula, scrape the batter into the prepared cake pan, spreading it evenly.

continued

Crumby, Fruity Coffee Cake

Makes one 10-inch cake

Fruit Topping

¾ cup granulated sugar

1 teaspoon cornstarch

2¼ cups prepared seasonal fruit (diced, sliced, or halved)

2 teaspoons fresh lemon juice

1 teaspoon vanilla bean paste

Crumb Topping

2½ cups all-purpose flour

1¾ cups firmly packed light brown sugar

1 cup granulated sugar

2 teaspoons ground cinnamon

Finely grated zest of 1 lemon

½ cup sliced or chopped whole raw almonds

1½ teaspoons kosher salt

1 cup plus 2 tablespoons unsalted butter, melted and cooled

Cake

¾ cup unsalted butter, at room temperature, plus more for greasing the pan

Raw sugar for coating

½ cup prepared seasonal fruit (diced, sliced, or halved)

2⅓ cups all-purpose flour

1¼ teaspoons baking powder

1 teaspoon kosher salt

1 cup plus 2 tablespoons granulated sugar

3 eggs, at room temperature

1½ teaspoons vanilla bean paste

Finely grated zest of 1 orange

1 cup sour cream, at room temperature

Quick Breads, Muffins, Biscuits, and More

Crumby, Fruity Coffee Cake

5. Spoon the fruit topping evenly over the top of the cake (don't just pile it all up in the middle; that will prevent the cake from baking evenly and will cause the middle to collapse), being careful to leave a 1-inch border around the edges of the cake to prevent leaking and burning. Depending on the fruit and the time of year, your fruit may be extra juicy. You don't need to add all the juice in the bowl if you feel it might be too much and drip down the sides of the cake and burn in the baking process. Top the cake with the crumb topping, pressing it lightly onto the fruit topping. Place the cake in the oven on the center rack and bake for 55 to 65 minutes, rotating the pan after 30 minutes, until the cake is golden brown and a cake tester comes out clean when inserted into the center.

6. Transfer the pan to a wire rack to cool for 15 minutes. Place a plate on top of the cake pan, invert the cake onto the plate, and remove the pan. Place a serving plate on top of the cake, then invert the cake onto the serving plate so it's right side up. Let cool for 30 minutes, then cut and serve. Store in an airtight container at room temperature for about 3 days.

What's Mine Is Yours

This cake is a real treat during any season. For the fruit, you can use anything from summer berries and stone fruit to apples and pears.

For the fruit topping, if you're using apples and/or pears, be sure to peel the fruit and core it and make tidy slices that are about ¼ inch thick. Once the slices are cooked, let them cool, then fan them around the top of the cake like a pinwheel, slightly overlapping them. It'll take a little bit longer to do but will be worth the even distribution of fruit. If you feel like taking a less fussy approach, you could also just cut the fruit into even squares and spread it over the top of the cake. (Random pro tip: Dot a thin layer of apple butter or other jam on the cake surface before placing the fruit on top for a little added depth of flavor.) If you're using stone fruit, make sure to peel (if you find that kind of thing necessary) and pit them. I recommend halving or quartering cherries and apricots before cooking. Peaches, plums, and nectarines work best when cut into slices about ¼ inch thick. If you're using berries, go with your favorite or a mix of favorites. (Blueberries are my personal favorite.)

Cut all the fruit you're preparing for the cake batter into small pieces— approximately the size of chocolate chips or blueberries. Tossing the fruit in flour helps it evenly distribute in the batter and not sink to the bottom or float to the top.

What's Mine Is Yours

There's an old saying that salt and sugar kill yeast, and this is what I was taught early in my career. While this is true with large amounts of salt, what is actually happening is that the contact between the yeast and salt (and sugar) actually retards the yeast's ability to ferment. So, in addition to adding flavor, salt brings a crucial chemical balance to dough, keeping the yeast in check and ensuring it doesn't get too carried away!

I use SAF instant yeast for "real" bread recipes because it doesn't have to be reconstituted and activated by liquid and is faster acting, so it cuts down your prep and wait-around times tremendously.

Monkey bread isn't really a Southern tradition, but I love it! I make it with praline sauce, so it doesn't seem out of place in a Southern bakery. At Willa Jean, we serve it only at brunch on weekends because we sell so much that we can't keep it up all week long. A bite of this is like that perfect middle bite in a piece of French toast—crusty, soft, and buttery.

1. Make the brioche dough. In the bowl of a stand mixer fitted with the dough hook or in a large bowl with a large wooden spoon, add the bread flour with the yeast, sugar, and salt, making sure the salt and yeast don't touch (see What's Mine Is Yours). Turn the mixer on low and add the eggs and milk; the dough will form into a smooth ball. Once the ball forms, start adding the butter, a little at a time. Increase the speed to medium and beat the dough until it's smooth and silky, about 10 minutes.

2. Loosely cover the bowl with plastic wrap and let it sit in a warm place until the dough has doubled in size, about 1½ hours.

3. Meanwhile, make the praline sauce. In a saucepot, combine 1⅓ cups of the cream with the brown sugar, corn syrup, butter, and salt. Add the vanilla seeds and pod to the pan. Bring the mixture to a boil over high heat, stirring until the sugar has dissolved, then decrease the heat and simmer for about 5 minutes, until thickened. Remove from the heat and stir in the lemon juice and the remaining 1 cup cream. Remove the vanilla pod (rinse, dry, and save it for another use). Pour the praline sauce into a bowl; you can refrigerate this, covered, for up to 3 days. The sauce will need to be gently rewarmed over low heat before using.

4. Preheat the oven to 350°F. Butter a 9-cup Bundt pan. Punch down the dough with your fist to let out any large air bubbles. Divide the dough into approximately 24 golf ball–sized pieces, rolling the balls between your palms so they are smooth.

5. Pour the praline sauce into the prepared baking pan. Put the melted butter in a small bowl. In another small bowl, stir the cinnamon with the sugar. Dip each ball in the melted butter and then roll in the cinnamon sugar. Arrange the balls in the praline sauce around the center of the pan to evenly fill it. Place the pan on a baking sheet to catch any bubbling-over sauce and bake for 55 to 60 minutes, rotating the baking sheet after 30 minutes, until the monkey bread is golden brown. Place a serving platter over the baking pan and very carefully invert the cake onto the platter, then remove the pan.

6. Serve hot or at room temperature. Even though this bread is best eaten the day it is made, you can make it ahead of time and reheat in a 325°F oven until warmed through, 7 to 10 minutes. It is best reheated in the dish in which it was baked and then inverted onto a serving platter when warm.

Praline Monkey Bread

Makes one 9-cup Bundt

Brioche Dough
4¼ cups bread flour

1 tablespoon instant yeast (I use SAF brand)

¼ cup granulated sugar

2 teaspoons kosher salt

4 eggs, at room temperature

½ cup whole milk, at room temperature

1½ cups unsalted butter, at room temperature

Praline Sauce
2⅓ cups heavy cream

2 cups firmly packed dark brown sugar

¼ cup light corn syrup

¾ cup unsalted butter

1 teaspoon kosher salt

1 vanilla bean, split lengthwise and seeds scraped out

1 tablespoon fresh lemon juice

¼ cup unsalted butter, melted, plus more for greasing the pan

2 teaspoons ground cinnamon

¾ cup granulated sugar

Morning Buns

_____

Makes 24 buns

¼ cup unsalted butter,
melted and cooled

¾ cup granulated sugar, plus
more for sprinkling and coating

½ cup firmly packed
light brown sugar

1½ tablespoons ground cinnamon

2 teaspoons finely grated
orange zest

1 "book" Danish Dough (page 314),
rolled out to ⅓ inch thick

1½ cups Pastry Cream (page 303)

Morning buns are generally cinnamon roll–type pastries made with croissant dough. Because we laminate the dough by rolling it out several times and folding in butter to create thin alternating layers to get that buttery, flaky texture for the cinnamon rolls (page 75), I adapted my morning bun to be the love child of a cinnamon roll and kouign-amann (a Breton pastry made with laminated dough, salted butter, and sugar).

1. Using a pastry brush, liberally coat the cups and tops of two standard muffin pans with the butter; sprinkle with an even layer of granulated sugar.

2. In a medium bowl, mix the granulated sugar, brown sugar, cinnamon, and orange zest. Lay the dough on a work surface with one long side closest to you. Using an offset spatula, spread a thin layer of pastry cream across the dough, leaving a 1-inch border along the length of dough closest to you. Sprinkle the cinnamon sugar evenly over the pastry cream. To create the tightest possible roll, starting at the corners farthest from you, pull and roll the dough toward yourself to create a spiral log. Continue rolling up to the 1-inch border of dough at the bottom. Using a pastry brush, brush a bit of water on the border, finish rolling up the log, and press it down just slightly to create a seal. Cut the log crosswise into twenty-four 1-inch-thick rolls and toss each individual roll lightly in granulated sugar to coat.

3. Place one roll in each prepared muffin cup and cover the muffin pans loosely with plastic wrap. Let rise at room temperature for about 2 hours, or until the rolls are approximately 1½ times their original size.

4. Preheat the oven to 350°F. Remove the plastic wrap from the muffin pans. Bake the buns for 40 to 45 minutes, rotating the pans after 20 minutes, until the buns are golden brown.

5. Let the buns cool in the pans for 5 minutes then use a metal spatula to transfer them to a wire rack or serving platter.

6. Serve immediately or cool completely on the wire rack. The buns can be kept in an airtight container at room temperature for up to 2 days.

I've always enjoyed eating a cinnamon roll layer by layer. When I started making them professionally, I was on a quest to make as many layers as possible to increase the joy of pulling them apart. Layering butter into the dough before rolling it all up creates those layers upon layers of joy.

1. Make the rolls. In a medium bowl, mix the granulated sugar and brown sugar with the cinnamon. Lay the dough on a work surface with one long side closest to you. Using an offset spatula, spread a thin layer of pastry cream across the dough, leaving a 1-inch border along the length of dough closest to you. Sprinkle the cinnamon sugar evenly over the pastry cream. To create the tightest possible roll, starting at the corners farthest from you, pull and roll the dough toward you to create a spiral log. Continue rolling up to the 1-inch border of dough at the bottom. Using a pastry brush, brush a bit of water on the border, finish rolling up the log, and press it down just slightly to create a seal.

2. Coat a 9 by 13-inch and a 9 by 9-inch pan with cooking spray. Using a sharp knife (not serrated), cut the log crosswise into twenty-four 1¼-inch-thick rolls and place 15 rolls in the larger pan and 9 in the smaller, evenly spaced. Cover the pans loosely with plastic wrap and let rise at room temperature for about 2 hours, or until the rolls are approximately 1½ times their original size.

3. Make the icing. In a medium bowl, whisk together the powdered sugar, milk, and vanilla until smooth. (You can use more or less milk, based on your personal preference for icing thickness.) Set aside until the rolls are warm from the oven.

4. Preheat the oven to 350°F. Remove the plastic wrap from the pans. Bake the rolls for 40 to 45 minutes, rotating the pans after 20 minutes, until the rolls are golden brown. Let cool in the pans for 5 minutes. Spoon icing over the rolls and serve.

5. Store in an airtight container at room temperature for up to 2 days.

Cinnamon Rolls

Makes 24 rolls

Rolls
1 cup granulated sugar
¼ cup firmly packed light brown sugar
1½ tablespoons ground cinnamon
1 "book" Danish Dough (page 314), rolled out to ⅓ inch thick
1½ cups Pastry Cream (page 303)

Icing
2 cups powdered sugar, sifted
About 3 tablespoons whole milk
1 teaspoon vanilla extract

Sticky Buns

Buns

1 cup granulated sugar

¼ cup firmly packed
light brown sugar

1½ tablespoons ground cinnamon

1 "book" Danish Dough (page 314),
rolled out ⅓ inch thick

½ cups Pastry Cream (page 303)

Sticky Topping

2¼ cups unsalted butter

4 cups firmly packed
light brown sugar

1 tablespoon kosher salt

¾ cup light corn syrup

¾ cup cane syrup

1 tablespoon vanilla extract

2 tablespoons bourbon

4½ cups pecan pieces,
toasted (see page 18)

One of my favorite things about pastry making, and eating in general, is the opportunity to play with texture. Adding this Bourbon-y, caramelly, and nutty glaze to a cinnamon roll enhances the textural contrast. I love to heat these buns and watch the changes in texture as the topping cools.

1. Make the buns. In a medium bowl, mix the granulated sugar and brown sugar with the cinnamon. Lay the dough on a work surface with one long side closest to you. Using an offset spatula, spread a thin layer of pastry cream across the dough, leaving a 1-inch border along the length of dough closest to you. Sprinkle the cinnamon sugar evenly over the pastry cream. To create the tightest possible roll, starting at the corners farthest from you, pull and roll the dough toward you to create a spiral log. Continue rolling up to the 1-inch border of dough at the bottom. Using a pastry brush, brush a bit of water on the dough, finish rolling up the log, and press it down just slightly to create a seal.

2. Lightly coat a baking sheet with cooking spray. Using a sharp knife (not serrated), cut the log crosswise into twenty-four 1¼-inch-thick buns, and place the buns, evenly spaced, on the prepared baking sheet. Cover the baking sheet loosely with plastic wrap and let rise at room temperature for about 2 hours, or until the buns are approximately 1½ times their original size.

3. Preheat the oven to 350°F. Remove the plastic wrap from the baking sheet. Bake the buns for 40 to 45 minutes, rotating halfway through baking, until golden brown.

4. Make the topping. While the buns are in the oven, in a large nonreactive pot, heat the butter, brown sugar, salt, corn syrup, cane syrup, vanilla, and bourbon. Cook, whisking gently as the butter melts to combine the ingredients. Bring to a boil, then remove from the heat and stir in the pecans. Let cool for a few minutes before glazing the sticky buns.

5. Let the buns cool on the baking sheet for 5 minutes. Transfer the buns to a wire rack placed over a baking sheet to catch the sticky glaze runoff as you spoon it over. Spoon the glaze over the buns and then let cool for at least 10 minutes before serving. The buns keep in an airtight container at room temperature for up to 2 days. They are best refreshed in a 325°F oven for 5 minutes.

Fruit Danish

Makes 16 Danish

1 "book" Danish Dough (page 314), rolled out to ¾ inch thick

1½ cups Pastry Cream (page 303) or Cream Cheese Filling (page 304)

About 2½ cups diced or sliced seasonal fruit of your choice

1 egg, at room temperature

1 teaspoon water

2 tablespoons raw sugar

Fruit Danish are one of my favorite breakfast treats. You can literally use whatever fruit is in season or, if you're so inclined, your favorite pie filling, and have a terrific treat so easily. Despite the name, don't be afraid to substitute burrata cheese or ricotta for the pastry cream and pile your savory Danish high with tomatoes, asparagus, or any other ingredient you'd like!

1. Preheat the oven to 350°F. Line a baking sheet with parchment paper or a silicone liner.

2. Very lightly flour your work surface. Lay the dough on the surface and cut it into sixteen 4-inch squares. The key to success here is to work quickly and keep the dough cold. If you find that it's getting soft, just place the squares in the refrigerator for 10 minutes before proceeding.

3. At each corner of each square of dough, make a 1-inch cut toward the center of the square with a sharp knife. Using a fork, poke a few holes in the center of the squares, then scoop about 1 heaping tablespoon of the pastry cream into the center of each square. Top with your fruit and then form a pinwheel: fold the opposite points of the square toward the center and press to seal, forming a pinwheel. Transfer the Danish to the prepared baking sheet and repeat for the other squares.

4. In a small bowl, whisk together the egg and water. Brush the tops of the pinwheels with the egg wash and sprinkle with the sugar. Bake for 20 to 25 minutes, rotating the baking sheet after 10 minutes, until the pastry is golden brown.

5. Serve immediately or let cool on the baking sheet for about 15 minutes. They're best eaten the day they are made. Store in an airtight container at room temperature for up to 1 day. Rewarm them in a 300°F oven for about 7 minutes.

King Cake

Makes one 10-inch cake

Dough

2½ cups bread flour

⅔ cup all-purpose flour

2 teaspoons instant yeast
(I use SAF brand)

2 eggs, at room temperature

1 cup whole milk

2 tablespoons lard (you can
use vegetable shortening,
but it won't be as delicious)

⅓ cup granulated sugar

1 teaspoon kosher salt

¼ cup plus 1 tablespoon
unsalted butter, cut into
pieces and slightly softened

Cinnamon Filling

⅓ cup granulated sugar

¼ cup firmly packed
light brown sugar

1 tablespoon ground cinnamon

¼ cup unsalted butter,
at room temperature

½ teaspoon kosher salt

1 teaspoon vanilla extract

Caramel Crunch

½ cup granulated sugar

½ teaspoon light corn syrup

¼ cup water

Every year in New Orleans, the game of king caking starts to feel more and more like a full-contact sport. Local shops create and serve these cakes each year from Twelfth Night through Mardi Gras day (and yes, it is absolute blasphemy to consume king cake outside of season here). A traditional part of Mardi Gras for the last three hundred years in New Orleans (and beyond), these cakes are more like brioche than "cake" as we know it. The yeast-raised dough is braided, sometimes around various fillings, formed into a ring, and baked. Once it's baked, it's topped with green, purple, and gold sugar to represent faith, justice, and power, respectively, a nod to the "three kings." A token of some sort, be it a bean or plastic baby, is stuffed randomly inside, and tradition states that whoever gets the slice of king cake with the token has to host the next party!

There are as many thoughts, feelings, opinions, and preferences about king cakes in New Orleans as there are king cakes themselves. I take a pretty traditional approach with the dough, but my team and I dreamed up the idea of adding a layer of caramelized sugar to give our cake a fun, shattering crunch. With cream cheese icing for a less-sweet approach, I find myself craving this cake year-round.

1. Make the dough. In a large bowl, whisk together the bread flour and all-purpose flour with the yeast. In the bowl of a stand mixer or in a large bowl using a handheld mixer, whisk the eggs until smooth. Switch to the dough hook or a large wooden spoon, and add the milk, lard, and flour mixture. Mix on low speed for 4 minutes, until a dough starts to form. Stop the mixer and scrape down the sides of the bowl with a rubber spatula. With the mixer on low speed, add the sugar and salt, then increase the speed to medium, and mix for 3 minutes. Decrease the speed to low and add the butter, a little at a time, until fully incorporated. Increase the speed to medium-high and beat the dough for 5 to 7 minutes, until the butter is fully incorporated and the dough becomes silky and shiny.

2. Coat a large baking sheet with cooking spray. Transfer the dough to the baking sheet and press it with the heel of your hand to about ¾ inch thick and as close to a 6 by 10-inch rectangle as possible (it's fine if it's a little wider or longer; you will trim it later). Cover the baking sheet in plastic wrap and refrigerate overnight (the dough can also be frozen if you don't plan to use it the next day, but it will need to thaw overnight in the refrigerator when you're ready for it).

3. Make the cinnamon filling. In the bowl of a stand mixer fitted with the paddle attachment or in a large bowl using a handheld mixer, mix the granulated sugar, brown sugar, cinnamon, butter, salt, and vanilla until a uniform paste forms. The filling can be used right away or stored in an airtight container in the refrigerator for up to 3 days and brought to room temperature before using.

4. Lightly coat a 10-inch-round cake pan with 2-inch-high sides with cooking spray. Cut the dough into two 3 by 5-inch strips. Using a lightly floured rolling pin, roll each piece evenly, maintaining a rectangular shape, until each piece is approximately 6 by 12 inches. Using an offset spatula, spread half of the cinnamon filling on one of the strips of dough, making sure to leave a 1-inch border on all but the long bottom edge. Using a pastry brush, brush the border with water along the upper lip of the dough until slightly wet; this will act as a sealant later. Starting at the bottom edge, roll up the dough like a cinnamon roll. Once rolled, lightly press down to evenly seal the dough; the water will help to fully seal. Using your hands, continue to roll the log to double the length, about 22 inches. Make sure to keep the width of the log consistent. Follow the same process for the second strip of dough.

5. Twist together the two dough logs, one over the other, in a spiral. Once fully twisted, connect the ends together to form a ring shape; pinch to seal if needed. Place the dough in the prepared pan and cover loosely with plastic wrap. Let the dough proof at room temperature (ideally about 75°F) for about 2 hours, until it has risen to about 1½ times its original size and slightly springs back after you press it. (If it does not spring back at all, it has overproofed and should be discarded.)

6. Preheat the oven to 350°F. Line a baking sheet with parchment paper and set a wire rack on the pan. Before baking, spritz the dough with water (or lightly sprinkle water over the dough with your hands) to help keep the crust from hardening. Bake for 30 to 35 minutes, rotating the pan after 15 minutes, until golden brown. Let cool in the pan for 5 minutes, then carefully remove the king cake from the pan and transfer it to the wire rack on the baking sheet. Let cool completely, about 1 hour.

7. Make the caramel crunch. In a small nonreactive saucepot, combine the sugar, corn syrup, and water and bring to a boil over high heat, making sure the sugar fully dissolves. Continue cooking just until the mixture becomes a medium amber color, 6 to 7 minutes. Remove from the heat and ladle the caramel over the cake, creating a thin, even coating over the entire cake. Allow the crunch to set for 15 to 20 minutes.

8. While the cake is setting, make the icing. In the bowl of a stand mixer fitted with the paddle attachment or in a large bowl using a handheld mixer, mix the cream cheese on medium speed until very smooth. Decrease the speed to low and add the powdered sugar in three portions, mixing well after each addition, until a smooth paste forms. Stop the mixer and scrape down the sides of the bowl. With the mixer on low speed, slowly stream in the milk and mix until the icing is well

Cream Cheese Icing

4 ounces cream cheese, at room temperature

4½ cups powdered sugar, sifted

¼ cup whole milk

¼ teaspoon vanilla bean paste

Sanding sugar in Mardi Gras colors (green, purple, and gold) for finishing (optional)

continued

King Cake

combined and smooth. Mix in the vanilla paste. This icing can be stored in an airtight container in the refrigerator for up to 4 days. Bring to room temperature before using.

9. While the cake is still on the wire rack, drizzle the icing over the cake. I like to use a 1-ounce ice cream scoop (about 2 tablespoons) to drop a bit of icing over the higher ridges on the top of the cake, and then I pour the icing as I move away from the cake, so it kind of waterfalls down the sides. (I think it looks pretty awesome this way.) If you're sticking true to Mardi Gras tradition, sprinkle the sanding sugar over the top and allow the cake to sit for at least 30 minutes before transferring it to a serving plate. You can keep the king cake in an airtight container at room temperature for up to 3 days, but it truly is best on the day it is made.

What's Mine Is Yours

The process of letting dough ferment and rise is called proofing in most professional kitchens, and it is the final step before baking in bread making. This process develops flavor and the final structure of the bread, allowing the yeast to feed on the starches in the dough and release carbon dioxide gas to form bubbles within the dough, creating that beautiful tender crumb. Bear in mind that every loaf of bread is going to require a different amount of time to fully proof. An incredible number of variables can affect the results, such as your room temperature, the humidity, the type of dough, the type of wheat, the amount of moisture in the dough, the type of yeast, how long you mix the dough, the temperature of the ingredients going into the mixer, and on and on and on. The only thing you really have to know is what to look for: the moment when you can lightly touch the side of the loaf with your finger and the indent stays—the dough does not "spring back" into place. The timing of this is what you will have to learn for each yeast-raised dough you make. One of the most amazing parts of this process is the control you have over it. Need to slow it down? Put the dough in the refrigerator. Not only will you be working on your own timeline, but this also develops better flavor! Need to speed it up a bit? Place the dough in a warmer spot. To be clear, "warm" is 85° to 90°F. Any temperature above that will speed up the fermentation process too quickly for the structure of the dough to keep up, resulting in a less-than-perfect outcome.

Perfectly proofing dough is an easy thing to master with just a little bit of practice and gives you a really big payoff when your home smells amazing and you're eating freshly baked yeasted breads.

Cookies and Bars

Snickerdoodles

Makes about 24 cookies

Sugar Mix

¼ cup granulated sugar

2 tablespoons ground cinnamon

1½ teaspoons ground cardamom

¼ teaspoon kosher salt

Cookie Dough

2¾ cups all-purpose flour

2 teaspoons cream of tartar

1 teaspoon baking soda

¾ teaspoon kosher salt

1 cup unsalted butter,
at room temperature

1½ cups granulated sugar

2 eggs, at room temperature

1 teaspoon vanilla bean paste

½ teaspoon orange blossom water

The texture of a snickerdoodle is what makes them one of my favorite cookies. The cream of tartar acts as a tenderizer and creates their signature chewy texture, and also adds the slightest tang to the flavor of the dough.

1. Make the sugar mix. In a small bowl, whisk together the sugar, cinnamon, cardamom, and salt. Preheat the oven to 350°F. Line a baking sheet with parchment paper and lightly coat with cooking spray.

2. Make the cookie dough. In a medium bowl, whisk together the flour, cream of tartar, baking soda, and salt. In the bowl of a stand mixer fitted with the paddle attachment or in a large bowl using a handheld mixer, combine the butter and sugar and mix on medium-high speed until light and fluffy, about 4 minutes. Stop the mixer and scrape down the sides of the bowl with a rubber spatula. Return the mixer to medium speed and beat in the eggs, one at a time, mixing well after each addition, followed by the vanilla paste and orange blossom water. Reduce the speed to low and add the dry ingredients in two portions, mixing until fully incorporated after each addition.

3. Using a 1½-ounce ice cream scoop (about 3 tablespoons), portion the dough. Roll the portions into balls, then roll in the sugar mix. Place the cookies on the prepared baking sheet at least 2 to 3 inches apart. Bake for 12 to 14 minutes, rotating the baking sheet after 6 minutes, until the outer edges and the bottoms are golden.

4. Let the cookies cool on the baking sheet for 10 minutes before transferring them to a wire rack to cool completely. The cookies can be stored in an airtight container at room temperature for up to 5 days.

Pecan Sandies

Makes about 24 cookies

4¼ cups all-purpose flour

1 teaspoon ground cinnamon

1¼ teaspoons baking soda

1 teaspoon cream of tartar

1½ teaspoons kosher salt

1 cup unsalted butter,
at room temperature

½ cup granulated sugar,
plus more for rolling

½ cup firmly packed
light brown sugar

1 cup powdered sugar, sifted

1 cup vegetable oil

2 eggs, at room temperature

2 teaspoons vanilla bean paste

2½ cups pecan pieces

Even though my mom baked all the time, especially cookies, pecan sandies were one of the few store-bought sweets that were almost always in the house, and were reserved for her specifically. It wasn't until I was in culinary school that I took an interest in pecan sandies (I was always after chocolate cookies, let's be honest). I was in a class in which we were given a store-bought cookie and its ingredient label and told to replicate the recipe, based on our knowledge of techniques and ingredients and how they interact during mixing and baking. I became obsessed with figuring out how to make pecan sandies. The most interesting part of this cookie for me has always been the texture. Much like my Snickerdoodles (page 86), you'll see cream of tartar in the dough; this helps achieve the unmistakably crispy texture of a great pecan sandie.

1. Preheat the oven to 375°F. In a medium bowl, whisk together the flour, cinnamon, baking soda, cream of tartar, and salt. In the bowl of a stand mixer fitted with the paddle attachment or in a large bowl using a handheld mixer, combine the butter, granulated sugar, brown sugar, and powdered sugar and mix on medium speed until smooth. Stop the mixer and scrape down the sides of the bowl with a rubber spatula. Return the mixer to medium speed and stream in the oil. Once combined, beat in the eggs, one at a time, mixing well after each addition, followed by the vanilla paste.

2. Decrease the speed to low and beat in the dry ingredients in three portions, mixing well after each addition. Stir in the pecans. Cover the bowl with plastic wrap and refrigerate for at least 45 minutes and up to overnight.

3. Line two baking sheets with parchment paper or silicone liners. Using a 1½-ounce ice cream scoop (about 3 tablespoons), portion the dough. Roll the portions into balls, then roll in granulated sugar. Place the cookies on the prepared baking sheets. With the palm of your hand or the flat bottom of a glass, flatten the tops of the dough balls with gentle pressure, not to squish them but to encourage spreading.

4. Bake for 9 to 14 minutes, rotating the baking sheets after 6 minutes, until the outer edges of the cookies are golden.

5. Transfer the cookies to a wire rack to cool. The cookies can be stored in an airtight container at room temperature for up to 3 days.

Pecan-Plus Sandies

I really like to substitute raw sugar for the granulated sugar on the outside of the dough. It's just more fun, in my opinion. You can also substitute other nuts for the pecans, so, yeah, go nuts. Or even consider removing ¾ cup of the nuts and replacing them with ¾ cup chopped dark chocolate.

Iced cookies didn't really register in my life until I first moved to New Orleans and a friend introduced me to them. These cookies are beautifully tender without being crumbly, and they have that full lemon flavor without being oversweet. I love the zing of lemon in the glaze. Play with adding ground spices and minced fresh herbs to the cookie dough for a more unique approach.

1. Make the dough. Preheat the oven to 350°F. Line two baking sheets with parchment paper or silicone liners. In the bowl of a stand mixer fitted with the paddle attachment or using a handheld mixer, combine the butter and powdered sugar and mix on medium-high speed until light and smooth, about 3 minutes. Add the lemon zest, lemon juice, and vanilla and mix to combine. Decrease the speed to low and beat in the flour and salt in two portions; mix just until combined.

2. Using a 1½-ounce ice cream scoop (about 3 tablespoons), scoop mounds of the dough onto the prepared baking sheets, spacing them evenly. Flatten each cookie with the flat bottom of a glass (you can dip it in a tiny bit of water if you find the dough sticks to it). Bake for 12 to 15 minutes, rotating the baking sheets after 6 minutes, until the outer edge of each cookie is golden and the middle is set and dry. Let cool on the baking sheets for 3 to 5 minutes before transferring the cookies to a wire rack to cool completely.

3. Make the glaze. In a medium bowl, whisk together the powdered sugar, lemon zest, lemon juice, and salt until smooth. Let sit for 5 minutes, then dip the top of each cookie in the glaze to coat evenly.

4. Let the iced cookies rest for about 10 minutes to set the glaze before serving. The cookies can be stored in an airtight container at room temperature for up to 5 days.

Iced Lemon Cookies

Makes 48 cookies

Cookie Dough

1 cup unsalted butter, at room temperature

1 cup powdered sugar, sifted

1 tablespoon plus 1 teaspoon finely grated lemon zest

2 tablespoons fresh lemon juice

1 teaspoon vanilla extract

2 cups all-purpose flour

1 teaspoon kosher salt

Glaze

¾ cup powdered sugar, sifted

1½ teaspoons finely grated lemon zest

2½ tablespoons fresh lemon juice

¼ teaspoon kosher salt

Sugar Cookies

Makes about 48 cookies

Cookie Dough

5 cups all-purpose flour,
plus more for dusting

1 teaspoon baking powder

1 teaspoon kosher salt

1¼ cups unsalted butter,
at room temperature

1¼ cups granulated sugar

3 ounces cream cheese,
at room temperature

1 egg, at room temperature

1 teaspoon vanilla extract

Royal Icing

2 egg whites

½ teaspoon vanilla extract

4 cups powdered sugar, sifted

2 tablespoons water

What's Mine Is Yours

To get nice clean edges
when decorating cookies, it's
always a great idea to pipe
an outline around the cookie,
let it set just slightly, and
then fill in the middle. Ice the
cookies solid white, then use
paintbrushes to paint and
decorate! You can hand-paint
the iced cookies with food
coloring slightly diluted with
any clear spirit (don't worry, the
alcohol evaporates as it dries).

I use this recipe to make cookies for basically every occasion: Christmas, Valentine's Day, Easter, Halloween, Mardi Gras, and others. I even bake saxophone cookies during Jazz Fest! These are literally an all-occasion cookie for celebrating. The recipe makes a whole lot of dough, but if you don't need it all, leftovers freeze really well and can be saved for the next holiday cooking-decorating bonanza.

1. Make the cookie dough. In a large bowl, whisk together the flour with the baking powder and salt. In the bowl of a stand mixer fitted with the paddle attachment or in a large bowl using a handheld mixer, cream the butter and sugar on medium-high speed until light and fluffy. Mix in the cream cheese until combined. Decrease the speed to low and slowly beat in the egg and vanilla, incorporating well. Stop the mixer and scrape down the sides of the bowl with a rubber spatula. Mix in the dry ingredients on low speed until a dough forms.

2. Turn the dough out onto a work surface and knead it a few times by hand. Divide the dough into two equal pieces and wrap each piece in plastic wrap. Refrigerate the dough until ready to roll out, at least 15 minutes or up to overnight. You can also freeze the dough for up to 1 month.

3. Preheat the oven to 325°F. Line two baking sheets with parchment paper or silicone liners. Remove one piece of dough from the refrigerator. Dust a work surface with flour and roll out the dough to about ⅓ inch thick. Use a 2-inch round cutter (or a cookie cutter of your choice) and cut out as many cookies as possible; transfer to the prepared baking sheets. These cookies won't really spread much, so fitting 18 to 24 on a tray is completely reasonable. Reroll the dough scraps and cut out more cookies. Bake for about 15 minutes, rotating the baking sheets after 8 minutes, until the edges of the cookies are just starting to turn lightly golden.

4. Let the cookies cool on the baking sheet as you roll out and bake the second batch. Transfer the cookies to a wire rack and continue, baking the remaining cookie dough.

5. Make the royal icing. In the bowl of a stand mixer fitted with the whisk attachment or in a large bowl using a handheld mixer, whip the egg whites and vanilla on medium-high speed until they start to froth, about 1 minute. Decrease the speed to low and slowly stream in the powdered sugar. Once incorporated, stream in the water, return the mixer to high speed, and whip until the icing is shiny and smooth. This icing should be used immediately. You can divide it up, add food coloring as desired, and fill pastry bags to decorate your cookies. If you don't have pastry bags, place the icing in heavy-duty resealable bags and cut off one corner to pipe the icing onto the cookies.

6. Let the cookies rest until the icing is set, about 1 hour. The cookies can be stored in an airtight container at room temperature for up to 3 days.

Willa Jean Chocolate Chip Cookies with Vanilla Milk

Makes about 24 cookies

1½ cups pastry flour

1½ cups bread flour

1 teaspoon baking powder

1 teaspoon baking soda

1 cup unsalted butter, at room temperature

1¼ cups firmly packed light brown sugar

¾ cup granulated sugar

2¼ teaspoons kosher salt

2 eggs, at room temperature

1½ teaspoons vanilla extract

8 ounces dark chocolate (preferably Valrhona Guanaja 70% cacao), coarsely chopped

4 ounces Valrhona Caramélia chocolate, coarsely chopped

4 ounces Valrhona Dulcey chocolate, coarsely chopped

Large-flake sea salt, for sprinkling

Tahitian Vanilla Milk (page 299)

People have very strong feelings about what a chocolate chip cookie should be. I spent every day for two and a half years figuring out what I thought it should be. Some cookies were just too thin, some were too cakey, and others were just, well, not good enough. For me, the best cookie is chewy, crispy, *and* crunchy, with ample chocolate in every bite. I start with two kinds of flour: low-protein pastry flour, which makes the cookie tender, and bread flour, which gives the cookie structure. We sell thousands of these cookies every week at Willa Jean, so I think I might be onto something.

I use a triple hit of Valrhona chocolate here: Guanaja (70% cacao), Caramélia (36%), and Dulcey (32%). Caramélia and Dulcey have pre-caramelized sugars that mimic the flavor of that brown sugar crust you get on a good cookie. Mass-produced chocolate chips are made to hold their shape (not melt) in the oven. That processing directly changes the flavor and mouthfeel of the chocolate. Valrhona isn't processed that way, so the chocolate melts into doughs and batters just the right way, causing a caramelizing effect that is 100 percent irresistible.

1. Line a large baking sheet with parchment paper. In a medium bowl, whisk together the pastry flour and bread flour with the baking powder and baking soda.

2. In the bowl of a stand mixer fitted with the paddle attachment or in a large bowl using a handheld mixer, cream the butter on medium-high speed until smooth, about 30 seconds. Add the brown sugar, granulated sugar, and salt and beat on medium-low speed until light and fluffy, about 1 minute. Stop the mixer and scrape down the sides of the bowl with a rubber spatula. Return the mixer to low speed and beat in the eggs, one at a time, beating well after each addition. Beat in the vanilla. Beat in the dry ingredients in three portions, scraping down the sides of the bowl after each addition. With the mixer on low speed, beat in the chocolate until just combined.

3. Using a 1½-ounce ice cream scoop (about 3 tablespoons), scoop slightly rounded 2-inch mounds of dough onto the prepared baking sheet, leaving a tiny bit of space between each cookie. Transfer the baking sheet to the freezer and freeze for at least 24 hours. Once frozen, the balls of dough can be transferred to resealable bags.

4. Preheat the oven to 325°F. Line three baking sheets with parchment paper or silicone liners. Transfer the frozen dough balls to the prepared baking sheets, spacing them 2 inches apart; you should have two rows of four cookies per sheet. Sprinkle with the sea salt and bake for 22 minutes, rotating the baking sheets after 11 minutes, until lightly browned.

5. Transfer the cookies to a wire rack to cool. Serve with the vanilla milk. The cookies can be kept in an airtight container at room temperature for up to 3 days.

What's Mine Is Yours

I think milk chocolate is superior in this recipe, and I highly recommend making the investment in Valrhona Caramélia milk chocolate, which is made with caramelized sugar, resulting in a really smooth, caramelly, and buttery flavor with that hint of salt. It is pure magic with peanut butter, but a good milk chocolate is delicious, too. Dark chocolate is too intense here and overwhelms the peanut butter flavor. And frankly, I think white chocolate would make the cookies too sweet.

I had a peanut butter cookie recipe I believed in, loved, and used for the better part of eighteen years. One day I handed that recipe over to Lexi Fragoso, who runs the pastry program at my restaurant, and, well, the cookie she handed me fresh from the oven was the single best peanut butter cookie I had ever eaten—she had taken some liberties with my recipe. Lexi and I had previously talked about my love of honey-roasted peanuts and the obsession I have with the peanut butter cookies at Craftsman and Wolves in San Francisco. She had done her research, had a vision for a better version of the cookie we had been making, and dove right in, as she always does. I'd be an idiot to not share with y'all the magic that is Lexi's recipe.

1. In a medium bowl, whisk together the flour and baking soda. In the bowl of a stand mixer fitted with the paddle attachment or in a large bowl using a handheld mixer, cream the butter, brown sugar, granulated sugar, and salt on medium-high speed until light and fluffy, 4 to 5 minutes. Add the peanut butter and beat until incorporated. Add the eggs, one at a time, incorporating well after each addition. Add the vanilla and scrape down the bottom and sides of the bowl with a rubber spatula. With the mixer on low speed, add the dry ingredients in three portions, mixing until fully incorporated after each addition. Stir in the chocolate and peanuts. Using a 1½-ounce ice cream scoop (about 3 tablespoons), portion the cookie dough into 26 balls, placing them on the baking sheet with a tiny bit of space between them. Place the baking sheet in the freezer for at least 4 hours and up to 1 month. Once frozen, the balls can be transferred to resealable bags.

2. Preheat the oven to 325°F. Line a baking sheet with parchment paper or a silicone liner. Transfer the frozen cookie dough balls to the prepared baking sheet, placing them about 2 inches apart, and sprinkle with the sea salt. Bake for 15 to 20 minutes, rotating the baking sheet after 8 minutes, until the cookies are golden brown around the edges and the centers are mostly set.

3. Let the cookies cool slightly on the baking sheet before eating. The cookies can be stored in an airtight container at room temperature for up to 3 days.

Lexi's Peanut Butter–Milk Chocolate Chip Cookies

Makes 26 cookies

2 cups all-purpose flour

1¼ teaspoons baking soda

½ cup plus 2 tablespoons unsalted butter, at room temperature

1¼ cups firmly packed light brown sugar

⅔ cup granulated sugar

1½ teaspoons kosher salt

1 cup peanut butter

2 eggs, at room temperature

1 teaspoon vanilla extract

4½ ounces Valrhona Caramélia chocolate, chopped

¾ cup honey-roasted peanuts, chopped

Large-flake sea salt for sprinkling

Oatmeal and All the Dried Fruits Cookies

Makes 36 cookies

1 cup dried cranberries

1 cup golden raisins

1 cup chopped dried apricots

2⅓ cups quick-cooking oats

1¾ cups all-purpose flour

2 teaspoons ground cinnamon

1 teaspoon baking soda

1 teaspoon kosher salt

1½ cups unsalted butter, at room temperature

1½ cups firmly packed light brown sugar

1 cup granulated sugar

2 eggs, at room temperature

1 teaspoon vanilla extract

Large-flake sea salt for sprinkling

After spending so much time developing that damn chocolate chip cookie (see page 92), oatmeal cookies felt hard to me. I worked through every recipe variation on the planet to find an oatmeal cookie that could confidently stand next to the chocolate chip. I love this cookie deeply. Feel free to use whatever dried fruit you want, and keep a stash of these cookies in your freezer to bake any time the mood arises.

1. In a medium bowl, combine the cranberries, raisins, and apricots and set aside. In a separate medium bowl, whisk together the oats, flour, cinnamon, baking soda, and kosher salt. In the bowl of a stand mixer fitted with the paddle attachment or in a large bowl using a handheld mixer, cream the butter with the brown sugar and granulated sugar until just mixed and light in color (mixing longer will overcream the butter and sugar, causing the cookies to spread too much). Add the eggs, one at a time, incorporating well after each addition. Decrease the speed to low and add the dry ingredients in three portions, mixing until fully incorporated after each addition. Mix in the vanilla, then the fruit.

2. Line two baking sheets with parchment paper. Using a 1½-ounce ice cream scoop (about 3 tablespoons), scoop mounds of the dough onto the prepared baking sheets, spacing them 2 inches apart. Freeze the dough for 24 hours and up to 3 months. Once frozen, the cookie dough mounds can be transferred to resealable bags.

3. Preheat the oven to 325°F. Line three baking sheets with parchment paper or silicone liners. Transfer the frozen cookie dough mounds to the prepared baking sheets, placing them 2 inches apart, and top each with a pinch of sea salt. Bake for 18 to 20 minutes, rotating the baking sheets after 10 minutes, until the cookies are very lightly browned around the edges and just set.

4. Let the cookies cool on the baking sheets for 5 minutes. Transfer the cookies to wire racks to cool completely. The cookies can be stored in an airtight container at room temperature for up to 3 days.

Mom's Haystack Cookies

Makes 24 cookies

1⅓ cups rolled oats

¾ cup granulated sugar

¼ cup unsalted butter

¼ cup unsweetened Dutch-processed cocoa powder, sifted

¼ cup evaporated milk

½ teaspoon kosher salt

1 teaspoon vanilla extract

½ cup sweetened shredded coconut

Growing up, these cookies were a staple in our house around the holidays. Incredibly quick and easy, the cookies are unbaked except for a quick toast on the rolled oats to heighten both the flavor and the texture. Haystacks keep well at room temperature, as long as your definition of room temperature is lower than 75°F.

1. Preheat the oven to 300°F. Spread the oats on a rimmed baking sheet and toast for 20 to 25 minutes, until toasty and aromatic. Remove from the oven and let cool.

2. Line two baking sheets with parchment paper. In a heavy-bottomed saucepot, combine the sugar, butter, cocoa, evaporated milk, and salt and bring to a boil while stirring. Remove from the heat and stir in the vanilla, coconut, and oats.

3. Immediately drop the warm mixture by heaping tablespoons onto the prepared baking sheets. Refrigerate to set up fully before serving. You can store the cookies in an airtight container at room temperature for up to 3 days, or in the refrigerator for up to 5 days if you prefer to enjoy these cold—or if you live in a warm climate.

Fudge cookies are one of my favorites. My dad used to purchase (and hide from us kids) a particular brand of fudge cookies that were sandwiched with chocolate cream filling. I loved those cookies, but I would eat my way around the cream filling. They're no longer on the market, so I've spent more time than I should have trying to recreate the cookie from memory. This recipe is quick and easy, with ultimate crowd-pleasing results. The edges of the cookies are nice and crunchy, with soft chewy centers. You can make this dough and keep it in the refrigerator for up to 2 days before baking.

1. Preheat the oven to 350°F. Line two baking sheets with parchment paper and lightly coat the paper with cooking spray.

2. In a medium bowl, whisk together the flour, salt, and baking soda. In a separate bowl, stir the cocoa into the butter, then stir in the granulated sugar and brown sugar. Once incorporated and sandy looking, switch to a rubber spatula and stir in the sour cream and vanilla paste, followed by the dry ingredients; stir until just combined.

3. Drop the batter onto the prepared baking sheets, using about 1 tablespoon per cookie and leaving at least 2½ inches between them to allow room for spreading. Bake for 8 to 10 minutes, rotating the baking sheets after 5 minutes, until the outer edge of each cookie is set and dry; the middle can still be slightly wet looking.

4. Let the cookies cool on the baking sheets until cooled and crispy. Store the cookies in an airtight container at room temperature for up to 5 days.

Fudge Cookies

Makes 24 cookies

1 cup all-purpose flour

½ teaspoon kosher salt

¼ teaspoon baking soda

½ cup unsweetened Dutch-processed cocoa powder, sifted

¼ cup plus 1 tablespoon unsalted butter, melted

½ cup granulated sugar

½ cup firmly packed light brown sugar

⅓ cup sour cream

1 teaspoon vanilla bean paste

These cookies are beyond words. The outside of the cookie is a perfect, thin, shattering crust, coated with powdered sugar, and the inside is an intensely rich, melty chocolate, with a little surprise of chocolate chips. It's like eating the solid version of a molten chocolate cake, but better. Make extra—you won't be able to help yourself from eating more!

As good as these cookies are, this is probably the weirdest recipe in my book 'cause the batter is so wet. You literally pour it, then you let it set up overnight. The success of this recipe rests in the temperature of the ingredients. The eggs, butter, and dry ingredients must be at room temperature. The chocolate chips should be frozen. Additionally, the melted chocolate and butter should not be so warm that they melt the chocolate chips when combined. Being extra careful with the temperature of the ingredients results in the perfect cookie. It may seem fussy, but the outcome is so good.

1. In a medium bowl, mix the flour, baking powder, and salt. In a heatproof bowl set over a pot of simmering water, melt the dark chocolate and unsweetened chocolate, stirring occasionally, until just smooth. Stir in the butter and remove from the heat.

2. In the bowl of a stand mixer fitted with the whisk attachment or in a large bowl using a handheld mixer, whip the eggs and egg yolk on high speed until foamy, then pour in the granulated sugar. Whip on high speed until thick and pale, about 10 minutes. This is called the ribbon stage, when the trail of the mixture falls from the whisk in a "ribbon" pattern and holds its shape (that is, it's not immediately absorbed into the mixture).

3. Remove the bowl from the mixer and carefully add the melted chocolate mixture in two portions, mixing well after each addition, followed by the espresso and vanilla. Using a rubber spatula, fold the dry ingredients into the egg mixture in two additions. Once fully incorporated, stir in the chocolate chips just to combine. Pour the batter into a rimmed baking sheet and place in the refrigerator to set up overnight.

4. Once the batter sets up, liberally dust powdered sugar over your countertop (to prevent sticking) and roll the dough into three logs, each approximately 1½ inches in diameter and 12 inches long. Wrap the dough in plastic wrap and freeze until solid (the logs can be frozen for up to 1 month).

continued

Dark Chocolate–Espresso Crinkle Cookies

Makes 36 cookies

⅓ cup all-purpose flour

⅔ teaspoon baking powder

¾ teaspoon kosher salt

8½ ounces dark chocolate (preferably Valrhona 64% cacao), chopped

3 ounces unsweetened chocolate, chopped

2½ tablespoons butter, at room temperature

3 eggs, at room temperature

1 egg yolk, at room temperature

1 cup granulated sugar

2 tablespoons brewed espresso or strong coffee, at room temperature

¾ teaspoon vanilla extract

1½ cups chocolate chips, frozen

Powdered sugar for rolling

continued

Dark Chocolate–Espresso Crinkle Cookies

5. Once you are ready to bake, preheat the oven to 325°F. Fill a medium bowl with powdered sugar and set aside. Line three large baking sheets with parchment paper or silicone liners and set aside.

6. Pull out one log of the frozen dough and cut it into 1-inch-thick slices. Roll each slice into a ball with your hands (you can use powdered sugar here, too, to help prevent sticking, if you're hot-handed like me). Roll each ball in the powdered sugar, covering as much of the ball as you're able to. Place on the prepared baking sheets, about 2½ inches apart, in four rows of three cookies each. Press down on each cookie JUST ENOUGH to make the bottom flat enough to not roll around, but do not flatten out the dough . . . let the oven do that work. Repeat with the remaining logs.

7. Bake for 12 to 14 minutes, rotating the baking sheets after 6 minutes, until the cookies are just set but the centers still look glossy.

8. Let the cookies cool completely on the baking sheet before removing and serving . . . if you can. The cookies can be stored in an airtight container at room temperature for up to 3 days, but they're best eaten the same day they're baked.

Madeleines are small French butter cakes, distinguished by the scalloped shape of the molds in which they're baked. With a cornbread twist, this recipe is obviously the most Southern-inspired madeleine. These are fantastic on their own, straight from the oven, but they are also great alongside custards or puddings, or even served with some fresh seasonal fruit. They require a madeleine pan, which is readily available in most kitchen supply stores. I find this recipe works very well with the 1½ by 3-inch madeleine molds, using about 1 tablespoon of batter per mold. I highly recommend using nonstick pans, but I still think it's best to butter and flour the molds before baking. If you're feeling inclined, you can substitute fine cornmeal or even raw sugar for the flour.

1. In a large bowl, whisk together the flour, fine cornmeal, coarse cornmeal, sugar, baking powder, and salt. In a separate bowl, whisk the eggs, cream, cane syrup, orange zest, and vanilla paste to combine. Add this mixture to the dry ingredients in two portions; mix with a spoon just until combined. Gradually stream in the melted butter and stir to combine. Stir in the corn kernels. Place the batter in the refrigerator to rest for about 1 hour.

2. Preheat the oven to 375°F. Liberally butter and flour a large madeleine pan. Spoon about 1 tablespoon of batter into each madeleine mold. Bake for 14 to 18 minutes, rotating the pan after 7 minutes, until the madeleines are golden brown and the middles puff. Let cool in the pan for 3 minutes before carefully removing the madeleines from the pan and transferring them to a wire rack to cool completely. (Or skip the cooling, because these are so dang good straight from the oven.) I usually use a kitchen towel or oven mitt to hold the pan as I slightly invert it and give the corner of the pan a little tap to help release the madeleines.

3. Once the pan is cool enough, liberally butter and flour it again, refill, and bake; repeat until the batter is used (it'll be three rounds of baking total).

4. Madeleines really should be eaten right after they come out of the oven (or within the hour they are baked). I do not recommend storing these, even overnight. If you insist, you can pop them in a resealable bag and store at room temperature.

Cornbread Madeleines

Makes 36 madeleines

1 cup all-purpose flour, plus more for dusting

1 cup fine cornmeal

¾ cup coarse cornmeal

¼ cup plus 1 tablespoon granulated sugar

1½ teaspoons baking powder

1 teaspoon kosher salt

3 eggs, at room temperature

2½ cups heavy cream, at room temperature

1 tablespoon cane syrup

Grated zest of 1 orange

1 teaspoon vanilla bean paste

½ cup plus 2 tablespoons unsalted butter, melted and cooled, plus more for greasing the pan

1 ear fresh corn, kernels cut from the cob

What's Mine Is Yours

This batter holds well in the fridge, so you can make it a day or two ahead and then bake when you're ready.

Moon Pies

Makes about 12 pies

Cookie Dough

1 sleeve (about 9) graham crackers, broken into pieces

1½ cups all-purpose flour, plus more for dusting

1 teaspoon kosher salt

½ teaspoon baking powder

½ teaspoon baking soda

½ teaspoon ground cinnamon

1 cup unsalted butter, at room temperature

¼ cup firmly packed light brown sugar

2 tablespoons granulated sugar

2 tablespoons cane syrup

½ teaspoon vanilla bean paste

3 tablespoons half-and-half

Marshmallow Filling

½ cup granulated sugar

¼ cup water

¼ cup light corn syrup

2 egg whites, at room temperature

½ teaspoon cream of tartar

¼ teaspoon vanilla bean paste

Chocolate Coating

1 pound dark chocolate (preferably Valrhona 70% cacao), chopped

1½ tablespoons coconut oil

Moon pies have a life of their own in the city of New Orleans. Once a year, during Mardi Gras, moon pies show up in such force that one could acquire a full year's supply from the parades in which they're thrown. Why moon pies? Well, in the early '70s, krewes (the organizations that put on the various parades during Mardi Gras) would throw boxes of Cracker Jacks from the floats, but the boxes were banned because they were hard to throw and, more importantly, those box corners hurt when they hit people in the head. The replacement became small, soft, round moon pies—much easier to throw. Forty-something years later, moon pies are still going strong.

1. Make the dough. Place the graham cracker pieces in a food processor or high-speed blender and process until they become powdery, like flour. Transfer to a large bowl and add the flour, salt, baking powder, baking soda, and cinnamon and whisk to combine.

2. In the bowl of a stand mixer fitted with the paddle attachment or in a large bowl using a handheld mixer, cream the butter, brown sugar, granulated sugar, cane syrup, and vanilla paste on medium-high speed until light and fluffy, about 3 minutes. Reduce the speed to low and add the dry ingredients in three portions, mixing until fully incorporated after each addition. Add the half-and-half and mix until the dough comes fully together. Wrap the dough in plastic wrap, flatten it with the palm of your hand, and refrigerate for at least 2 hours and up to overnight.

3. Preheat the oven to 325°F. Line a baking sheet with parchment paper or a silicone liner. On a lightly floured surface, roll out the chilled dough, to about ¼ inch thick. Using a 2½- or 2¾-inch round cookie cutter, stamp out as many rounds as possible and transfer them to the prepared baking sheet; reroll the scraps one time only to cut out more cookies. (If you reroll more than once, the dough will start to get dry and brittle.) Bake for 10 minutes, rotating the baking sheet after 5 minutes, until the outer edges of the cookies are golden but the centers are still slightly soft.

4. Let the cookies cool on the baking sheet for about 10 minutes. Transfer to a wire rack to cool completely.

5. Make the filling. In a heavy-bottomed saucepot, combine the sugar, water, and corn syrup. Do not stir, since stirring could cause crystallization of the sugar—which has no real place in marshmallow filling. Attach a candy thermometer to the rim of the pot and place the pot over high heat.

6. While the sugar starts cooking, place the egg whites and cream of tartar in the bowl of a stand mixer fitted with the whisk attachment or in a large bowl using a handheld mixer. When the sugar syrup registers 225°F

continued

continued
continued

Moon Pies

on the thermometer, turn on the mixer to medium-high speed and whip the egg whites to soft peaks, about 3 minutes. Once the sugar mixture reaches 240°F on the thermometer, turn the mixer to a moderately low speed (think 3 out of 10), remove the pot from the heat and carefully stream the hot syrup into the mixer, being very careful to stream it in along the side of the bowl—you want to avoid pouring right onto the moving whisk, which will fling molten sugar at you. Once all the sugar syrup has been added, add the vanilla paste, reduce the speed to low, and whip until cool, 6 to 8 minutes. You can store the cooled marshmallow filling in an airtight container at room temperature for about 5 days.

7. Make the coating. Place the chocolate and coconut oil in a heatproof bowl and place over a pot of simmering water. Stir with a rubber spatula until fully melted and combined. Let cool to room temperature before dipping the cookies.

8. Assemble the cookies. Line a baking sheet with parchment paper and set a wire rack on top. Fill a pastry bag with the marshmallow filling. Evenly pipe a mound of filling (about 3 tablespoons) on half of the cookies, then carefully place a second cookie on top of each mound and gently press down until even and the filling is flush with the outer edges of the cookies. Let sit for 10 to 15 minutes.

9. Dip the sandwiches into the melted chocolate, one at a time, using a fork to flip for even coating and to lift them out of the chocolate and place on the wire rack.

10. Let the moon pies set up completely before serving. If you have leftover chocolate coating, pour it onto a parchment-lined baking sheet to set up, then chop it up to use in some other cookies! The moon pies can be stored in an airtight container at room temperature for up to 5 days. If you live in a warm climate, like me, it's best to keep these in the refrigerator.

What's Mine Is Yours

If you get hot sugar on your skin, touch it immediately to cloth, be it your shirt or a kitchen towel, as you make your way to a water source. Many folks' initial reaction is to immediately stick their finger/hand/arm in their mouth, but because sugar remains so hot for so long, that will just burn your mouth, too. If you immediately touch the burn to cloth, that will lift off the sugar without burning anything else. Then you can wash the burn with cool water and apply ice if needed.

Praline Brownies

Makes 18 brownies

Pralines

1½ cups pecan pieces

1½ cups firmly packed light brown sugar

¾ cup granulated sugar

¼ cup plus 2 tablespoons unsalted butter

¾ cup heavy cream

¾ teaspoon kosher salt

¾ teaspoon vanilla extract

Brownies

2 cups all-purpose flour

1 cup granulated sugar

½ cup unsweetened cocoa powder (not Dutch-processed)

¾ cup unsalted butter

7 ounces dark chocolate (preferably Valrhona 70% cacao), finely chopped

6 eggs, at room temperature

1½ cups firmly packed light brown sugar

1 teaspoon kosher salt

This is my favorite brownie ever. It is rich and fudgy and incredibly chocolatey. Make sure to use great chocolate. The addition of crushed pralines not only adds flavor but also a fun combination of textures, from crispy and crunchy to gooey and chewy, based on how the praline melts during baking. Yes, you could omit the pralines if you feel so inclined, or you could just crush up your favorite store-bought pralines if that makes this recipe more approachable.

1. Make the pralines. Preheat the oven to 350°F. Spread the pecans on a baking sheet and toast for about 10 minutes, or until golden. Set aside to cool and leave the oven on.

2. Line a baking sheet with parchment paper. In a medium saucepot, combine the brown sugar, granulated sugar, butter, and cream. Attach a candy thermometer to the rim of the pot and place over moderate heat. Cook, stirring occasionally, until the mixture registers 230°F on the thermometer, about 8 minutes. Stir in the toasted pecans and salt. Cook, stirring occasionally, until the mixture reaches 240°F, about 2 minutes longer. Remove the pot from the heat and stir in the vanilla. Let the mixture cool down to 210°F. Stir the mixture with a wooden spoon until it stiffens and looks cloudy. Scrape the praline onto the prepared baking sheet, spread it in an even layer, and let cool until set, about 30 minutes. Transfer the sheet of praline to a work surface and coarsely chop it. You can make the praline up to 2 days ahead and store it at room temperature in an airtight container. (When stored longer, the sugar will continue to crystallize, and the praline will become brittle.)

3. Make the brownies. Coat a 9 by 13-inch baking pan with cooking spray. In a medium bowl, whisk together the flour, granulated sugar, and cocoa. In a medium saucepot set over another saucepot of gently simmering water, melt the butter with the chocolate, stirring until smooth, about 5 minutes. Set aside to cool slightly.

4. In the bowl of a stand mixer fitted with the paddle attachment or in a large bowl using a handheld mixer, combine the eggs with the brown sugar and salt and mix on medium speed for 2 minutes. Beat in the dry ingredients in four portions, mixing well after each addition. Stop the mixer and scrape down the bottom and sides of the bowl with a rubber spatula. With the mixer on low, drizzle in the chocolate mixture and beat until well combined. Stop the mixer, remove the bowl, and fold in the chopped praline.

5. Scrape the brownie batter into the prepared pan and bake for 40 minutes, rotating the pan after 20 minutes, until a cake tester comes out with a few moist crumbs attached when inserted into the center.

6. Transfer the pan to a wire rack to cool completely. Cut the brownies into 3 by 2-inch bars. The brownies can be stored in an airtight container in the refrigerator for up to 5 days. Let them come to room temperature before serving.

What's Mine Is Yours

The brownies keep in an airtight container at room temperature for up to 3 days, but they begin to dry out. I store mine in the fridge because it helps to keep them super-extra-fudgy.

Seven-Layer Bars

Makes 18 bars

Coconut-Graham Crust

1¾ cups plus 2 tablespoons all-purpose flour

2 tablespoons plus 2 teaspoons powdered sugar, sifted

¼ cup firmly packed light brown sugar

½ cup sweetened coconut flakes, toasted (see page 15)

½ teaspoon baking soda

½ teaspoon kosher salt

¼ teaspoon ground cinnamon

½ cup unsalted butter, plus 3 tablespoons melted butter

1 teaspoon honey

Magic Topping

1 (14-ounce) can sweetened condensed milk

3 ounces Valrhona Dulcey chocolate, chopped (or use whatever chocolate you fancy)

2 cups unsalted popped popcorn

7 ounces dark chocolate (preferably Valrhona 70% cacao), coarsely chopped

1 cup salted peanuts, chopped

1 cup chopped Heath bars (about 4)

1 cup sweetened coconut flakes, toasted (see page 15)

As with most things pastry, I've found that the name of these bars is really full of claims and folklore. I grew up calling these Seven-Layer Bars and learned later on in life that they're also referred to as Magic Bars (that implies a completely different experience to me). Recently, when talking to my great-aunts, I also learned they called these bars Hello, Dolly, though they couldn't say exactly why. Whatever you want to call them, they're delicious and simple. As much as it lacks any poetry, I'm going to continue calling them Seven-Layer Bars because sometimes I really enjoy being literal, and old habits die hard.

1. Make the crust. Preheat the oven to 350°F. Line a baking sheet with parchment paper. In a large bowl, combine the flour, powdered sugar, brown sugar, coconut, baking soda, salt, and cinnamon. In a 1-quart saucepot set over moderate heat, melt the ½ cup butter with the honey until fully dissolved. Pour the honey butter over the dry ingredients and mix together with a rubber spatula or gloved hands until completely incorporated. Spread the mixture loosely on the prepared baking sheet and bake for 6 minutes. Stir to break up any large chunks and bake for another 6 to 8 minutes, until the mixture is evenly golden brown, dry to the touch, and baked all the way through. Set aside to cool.

2. Once the crust mixture is completely cool, place it in a food processor in small batches and pulse until completely broken up and no large pieces remain. In a large bowl, toss the crumbs with the remaining 3 tablespoons melted butter, then press the crumb mixture evenly into the bottom of a 9 by 13-inch baking pan.

3. Make the topping. Preheat the oven to 350°F. In a medium saucepot set over low heat, warm the condensed milk with the Dulcey chocolate until melted; remove from the heat and set aside. In a large bowl, mix together the popcorn, dark chocolate chunks, peanuts, Heath bars, and coconut until well combined. Arrange the mixture in a layer on top of the graham crust. Pour over the condensed milk mixture so that it is evenly distributed. Bake for 25 to 30 minutes, rotating the baking pan after 12 minutes, until the top forms a slow, thick bubble and the edges get slightly golden.

4. Let cool to room temperature and then chill in the refrigerator until firm (Seven-Layer Bars cut best when chilled). Cut into 3 by 2-inch bars. Once cut, the bars can be stored in an airtight container for up to 4 days, either in the refrigerator or at room temperature.

Customized Seven-Layer Bars

Choose your own adventure when you make these: substitute your favorite Halloween candies, candy bars, nuts, pretzels, dried fruit, or ANYTHING you love for the Heath bars.

These bars were one of the items that always seemed to be around the house when I was growing up. Like a lot of other sweets, we stored them in the microwave, and we all cut little slivers each time we passed by. The texture of these bars is so fun to eat that I didn't even mind that it came from the coconut (that was years before I came to my senses and decided to like coconut). I love to toss chopped chocolate into the filling for extra flavor and richness.

1. Make the crust. Preheat the oven to 350°F. Lightly coat a 9 by 13-inch baking pan with cooking spray and line it with parchment paper, then lightly spray the paper.

2. In the bowl of a stand mixer fitted with the paddle attachment or in a large bowl using a handheld mixer, combine the butter, shortening, and powdered sugar and mix on medium-high speed until smooth and creamy, about 3 minutes. Stop the mixer and scrape down the sides of the bowl with a rubber spatula. Decrease the speed to low and stream in the flour. Mix until well combined. Transfer to the prepared pan, pressing the crust into an even layer on the bottom of the pan. Bake for 15 to 20 minutes, rotating the pan after 8 minutes, until the crust is golden brown and set. Let cool on a wire rack. Keep the oven on.

3. While the crust is baking, make the topping. In a medium bowl, whisk together the flour, baking powder, and salt. In a separate bowl, whisk the eggs and vanilla paste. Whisk in the brown sugar and granulated sugar. Add the dry ingredients and, using a rubber spatula or wooden spoon, mix to combine. Stir in the pecans and coconut. Spread the topping over the crust in an even layer. Return the pan to the oven and bake for 20 to 30 minutes, rotating the pan after 10 minutes, until golden brown. Transfer to a wire rack to cool for 20 minutes before glazing.

4. Make the glaze. In a medium saucepot, heat the butter over moderately high heat until it begins to smell nutty and has a brownish hue, 8 to 10 minutes. Remove from the heat and whisk in the half-and-half and vanilla paste. Whisk in the powdered sugar, until the glaze is thick enough to set up but thin enough to pour easily (like cinnamon roll icing). If the glaze gets too thick, just add a touch more half-and-half, until you reach the desired consistency. If it gets too thin, just stir in a touch more sifted powdered sugar.

5. Drizzle the glaze over the top of the still-warm coconut bars. Let cool completely before cutting into 3 by 2-inch bars. The chews can be stored in an airtight container at room temperature for 3 to 5 days.

Chocolate-Glazed Coconut Chews

Skip the brown butter glaze and drizzle the bars with melted dark chocolate (or dip them in it).

Coconut Chews

Makes 18 bars

Crust
½ cup unsalted butter, at room temperature
¼ cup vegetable shortening
¾ cup powdered sugar, sifted
1½ cups all-purpose flour

Coconut Topping
¼ cup all-purpose flour
1 teaspoon baking powder
2 teaspoons kosher salt
4 eggs, at room temperature
2 teaspoons vanilla bean paste
1½ cups firmly packed light brown sugar
½ cup granulated sugar
1½ cups pecan pieces
1½ cups sweetened coconut flakes

Brown Butter Glaze
1½ cups unsalted butter
¼ cup half-and-half
1 teaspoon vanilla bean paste
1 cup powdered sugar, sifted

This recipe is not to be confused with the ooey-gooey butter cake that is highly celebrated in St. Louis. It's certainly inspired by that cake, but I take a good deal of liberty here. I've attempted to capture my favorite parts of the ooey-gooey butter cake and combine that with my favorite parts of traditional blondies. The result is a quick and easy sweet treat that is perfect for any occasion.

1. Preheat the oven to 325°F. Lightly coat a 9 by 13-inch baking pan with cooking spray.

2. In a medium saucepot, heat the butter over moderately high heat until it begins to smell nutty and has a brownish hue, 8 to 10 minutes; remove from the heat and let cool for about 15 minutes.

3. In a large bowl, whisk together the eggs, sugar, orange zest, vanilla paste, and salt until well combined. Pour in the warm (not hot) brown butter, leaving behind any browned bits at the bottom of the saucepot. Stir to combine. Sift in the flour in two portions and stir just to combine.

4. Using a rubber spatula, transfer the batter to the prepared pan and spread it evenly. Bake for 30 to 35 minutes, rotating the pan after 15 minutes, until the bars are just set but still a little shiny right in the middle.

5. Let cool for 10 minutes before cutting into 3 by 2-inch bars and serving. You can also cool the bars completely, wrap them in plastic wrap, and store them at room temperature for up to 4 days.

Ooey-Gooey Bars

Makes 18 bars

2½ cups unsalted butter

6 eggs, at room temperature

2 cups granulated sugar

2 teaspoons finely grated orange zest

1 teaspoon vanilla bean paste

1 teaspoon kosher salt

1 cup all-purpose flour

In Louisiana, we are lucky to enjoy an abundant citrus crop every winter, and that results in all things lemon all season long. These lemon bars are perfectly tart, as I like all lemon sweets to be, but I find these even more delicious if you're lucky enough to make them with fresh, local Meyer lemons. Feel free to substitute the lemon juice with key lime, or even half yuzu juice, for an extra-fun play on a classic bar cookie.

1. Make the crust. Preheat the oven to 350°F. Lightly coat a 9 by 13-inch baking pan with cooking spray and line it with parchment paper, then lightly spray the paper.

2. In the bowl of a stand mixer fitted with the paddle attachment or in a large bowl using a handheld mixer, combine the butter, sugar, all-purpose flour, almond flour, salt, lemon zest, and vanilla and mix on medium-low speed until well incorporated, 2 to 3 minutes. Press the dough evenly into the bottom of the prepared pan. Bake for 17 to 20 minutes, rotating the pan after 8 minutes, until golden brown and set. Let cool on a wire rack. Leave the oven on.

3. Make the filling. In a large bowl, whisk together the flour, salt, and lemon zest. Whisk in the eggs, egg yolk, sugar, lemon juice, and vanilla until well combined with no lumps. Place the pan with the crust on the oven rack and carefully pour in the filling. Bake for 20 to 25 minutes, rotating the pan after 10 minutes, until the lemon custard is set in the center but jiggles in the middle when you move the pan slightly (if the surface ripples, it's not yet fully set).

4. Transfer the pan to a wire rack to cool completely, about 90 minutes. The lemon custard will set up more as the bars cool. Cut into 3 by 2-inch bars and dust with the powdered sugar before serving. The bars can be stored in an airtight container in the refrigerator for up to 5 days. Sift more powdered sugar over the top just before serving.

Lemon Bars

Makes 18 bars

Crust

1 cup unsalted butter, at room temperature

½ cup granulated sugar

1¾ cups all-purpose flour

¼ cup almond flour

1 teaspoon kosher salt

1 tablespoon finely grated lemon zest

1 teaspoon vanilla extract

Lemon Filling

⅓ cup all-purpose flour

½ teaspoon kosher salt

2 tablespoons finely grated lemon zest

6 eggs, at room temperature

1 egg yolk, at room temperature

2¼ cups granulated sugar

⅔ cup fresh lemon juice (from about 4 lemons)

1 teaspoon vanilla extract

Powdered sugar, sifted, for dusting

Raspberry-Oat Bars

Makes 18 bars

Raspberry Filling

24 ounces raspberries

½ cup granulated sugar

½ teaspoon kosher salt

2 tablespoons all-purpose flour

1 tablespoon cornstarch

1½ tablespoons fresh lemon juice

1 teaspoon vanilla bean paste

Crust

3 cups rolled oats

2 cups firmly packed
light brown sugar

1½ cups all-purpose flour

½ cup almond flour

1 teaspoon baking powder

1 teaspoon kosher salt

1 cup toasted almonds, crushed

½ cup unsalted butter,
melted and cooled

Powdered sugar for dusting

Even though raspberries are my favorite berries for this bar cookie, you could substitute blackberries, sliced strawberries, blueberries . . . or a mixture of some or all of them. These bars are acceptable to eat after all meals, in my opinion, and even better if you warm them slightly and serve with a scoop of your favorite vanilla ice cream.

1. Make the filling. In a large bowl, gently mix the raspberries, sugar, salt, flour, cornstarch, lemon juice, and vanilla paste, then set aside.

2. Make the crust. Preheat the oven to 350°F. Lightly coat a 9 by 13-inch baking pan with cooking spray and line the bottom with parchment paper, then lightly spray the paper.

3. In a large bowl, combine the oats, brown sugar, all-purpose flour, almond flour, baking powder, salt, and almonds. Stream in the butter and stir the mixture just until it resembles wet and crumbly granola. Press two-thirds of the mixture into the bottom of the prepared pan. Bake for about 15 minutes, rotating the pan after 8 minutes, until the crust is set. Remove the pan from the oven and top the crust with the raspberry filling in an even layer. Sprinkle the remaining oat crust over the top and return the pan to the oven. Bake for 25 to 30 minutes more, rotating the pan after 12 minutes, until the crust is golden brown and the fruit filling produces slow, thick bubbles.

4. Transfer to a wire rack to cool completely, about 3 hours. Cut into 3 by 2-inch bars and dust with the powdered sugar before serving. The bars can be wrapped in foil or plastic wrap and stored at room temperature for 3 to 5 days.

Puddings and Custards

Butterscotch is one of my favorite flavors, but be warned: true butterscotch is not the flavor you've grown accustomed to in popular candy. Butterscotch is simply a caramel made with brown sugar instead of granulated sugar, and every pastry chef I've had the pleasure of working with has had a version of butterscotch pudding in their repertoire.

Bourbon-Butterscotch Pudding

Makes 6 servings

¼ cup granulated sugar

¼ cup cornstarch

8 egg yolks, at room temperature

¼ cup plus 3 tablespoons unsalted butter

1 cup firmly packed dark brown sugar

2 teaspoons cane syrup

1 quart heavy cream

¼ cup delicious bourbon

1½ teaspoons vanilla bean paste

1 teaspoon kosher salt

1 pound Valrhona Dulcey chocolate, chopped

1. In a large bowl, whisk together the granulated sugar and cornstarch. Whisk in the egg yolks until smooth. Set aside.

2. In a large heavy-bottomed saucepot, combine the butter, brown sugar, and cane syrup and cook over medium-high heat until the sugar dissolves and the mixture changes from quick, small bubbles to slower, thicker bubbles. Turn off the heat and whisk in the cream, exercising extreme caution, since the sugar will hiss and steam. Return the pot to medium-high heat and bring the mixture back up to a slow boil. Cook for 3 to 5 minutes to allow the mixture to reduce a bit and for the bubbles to become a bit slower and thicker, then remove from the heat and stir in the bourbon, vanilla paste, and salt.

3. While whisking constantly, slowly stream half of the hot cream mixture into the egg yolk mixture, being careful not to cook the eggs. When half of the dairy mixture has been incorporated, pour the mixture in the bowl into the saucepot and place the pot over medium-high heat. While whisking constantly and thoroughly (get into those pot corners), return the mixture to a boil and cook for another 3 minutes, until thick and bubbling. Remove from the heat and whisk in the chocolate until smooth.

4. Divide the pudding among six 8-ounce ramekins. Place a sheet of plastic wrap directly on the surface of each custard (to prevent a skin from forming on their surface as they cool), then poke a few holes in the plastic to allow the steam to escape. Place in the refrigerator and cool completely before serving. The puddings can be covered and refrigerated for up to 5 days.

Bourbon-Butterscotch Cream Pie

You can spread this filling in a baked piecrust to make Bourbon-Butterscotch Cream Pie. Chill in the refrigerator until fully cold, about 3 hours, before serving.

Banana Pudding

Makes 6 servings

Pudding

2 cups whole milk

¼ cup unsalted butter

½ vanilla bean, split lengthwise
and seeds scraped out

2 ripe bananas, lightly mashed
or cut into 2-inch pieces, plus
2 additional bananas, sliced

½ cup granulated sugar

3 tablespoons cornstarch

3 tablespoons all-purpose flour

3 eggs

1 egg yolk

¾ teaspoon kosher salt

½ teaspoon vanilla extract

Banana Meringue

2 egg whites, at room temperature

½ cup granulated sugar

¾ teaspoon cornstarch

½ teaspoon cream of tartar

Pinch of kosher salt

½ ripe banana, pureed

Nilla wafers for assembling

Sweet Whipped Cream (page 303)
for assembling

Peanut butter powder for garnishing
(optional)

To assemble this for friends, I layer it in a trifle dish with Nilla wafers, fresh bananas, and whipped cream. Sometimes I even sprinkle peanut butter powder on top, too!

1. Make the pudding. In a large heavy-bottomed saucepot over medium-high heat, bring the milk, butter, vanilla pod, vanilla seeds, mashed bananas, and ¼ cup of the sugar to a boil. Remove from the heat and cover the top of the pot with plastic wrap; let steep for about 45 minutes.

2. While the dairy is steeping, in a small bowl, sift together the cornstarch and flour. Whisk in the whole eggs, egg yolk, and remaining ¼ cup sugar until smooth and incorporated.

3. Remove the plastic wrap from the milk mixture and discard the vanilla pod. Puree the mixture in a food processor or high-speed blender until smooth. Return the mixture to the pot and place over medium-high heat and bring to a simmer. When simmering, start streaming a small amount of the hot dairy into the egg mixture, whisking constantly to prevent the eggs from cooking. Continue whisking in the milk mixture until most of the liquid has been incorporated into the eggs. Pour the mixture in the bowl into the saucepot and place the pot over medium-high heat, again whisking constantly, until the mixture comes to a boil and thickens, 5 to 8 minutes; let boil, whisking, for about 2 minutes. Remove from the heat and stir in the salt and vanilla. Transfer to a heatproof bowl and place a piece of plastic wrap directly on the surface of the pudding (to prevent a skin from forming on the surface as it cools), then poke a few holes in the plastic to allow the steam to escape. Refrigerate the pudding.

4. Make the meringue. Preheat the oven to 225°F. Line two baking sheets with silicone liners or lightly coat the baking sheets with cooking spray and line them with parchment paper, then lightly spray the paper. In the bowl of a stand mixer fitted with the whisk attachment or in a large bowl using a handheld mixer, whip the egg whites on medium-high speed until foamy, then increase to high speed and stream in the sugar, cornstarch, cream of tartar, and salt. Whip until the whites are stiff and glossy, about 5 minutes. Remove the bowl from the mixer and gently fold in the banana puree.

5. Spread the meringue evenly over the prepared baking sheets or pipe onto the sheets in desired shapes and sizes. Bake for 1½ to 2 hours, until dehydrated and crisp (the baking time will vary with the humidity). The meringues can be stored in an airtight container at room temperature for up to 5 days.

6. In a glass trifle dish, layer the banana pudding with the Nilla wafers, sliced bananas, and whipped cream. Place the trifle in the refrigerator for a few hours (you're mostly looking for those Nilla wafers to take on some moisture to create that texture we all know and love), until set. Without the banana meringue added, the pudding can be refrigerated for up to 5 days; once added, serve right away. Break the banana meringue into shards and stick them in the trifle dish. Sprinkle some of that peanut butter powder all over the top of the pudding, if using, then serve.

Peanut Butter–Banana Pudding

If you like the idea of making your banana pudding peanutty, stir ¾ cup of peanut butter into the pudding once it has cooled.

What's Mine Is Yours

Any and all whole eggs, egg yolks, or egg whites perform best at room temperature, always. Egg whites in particular whip best when they're "aged," which helps them lose elasticity and create a more stable, stiff meringue. This process was adapted from the traditional French macaron-making technique because with all the humidity in the South, a meringue needs every head start it can get. When you're tempering eggs like this and trying to avoid scrambling them, you have to work quickly. I was taught that if you're not sweating while you're whisking, you're not doing it right.

I serve this pudding warm, y'all, but it's also super delicious served cold. When I was growing up, my mom was always baking in the kitchen, and on special occasions, she would make a chocolate–peanut butter pie with a coconut-and-pecan crust. (There used to be a box mix available at the grocery store for German chocolate cake icing that Mom used to create the piecrust out of, rather than adding the wet ingredients to make the icing. The mix has since been discontinued, and I've spent my whole career unsuccessfully trying to re-create that piecrust—I'm convinced Mom has a secret stash—but at least I've developed some of my favorite desserts in the pursuit.)

This pudding was my introduction to "cooked custards," versus that instant stuff you mix with milk straight out of the box. My brother and sister—hell, even my dad—would fight over getting to lick the spoons and run their fingers around the pot to devour every single drop of that warm pudding.

1. In a medium bowl, whisk together the sugar, cocoa, cornstarch, and salt. Add the eggs and whisk until smooth.

2. In a heavy-bottomed saucepot set over medium-high heat, combine the cream, milk, vanilla pod, and vanilla seeds. Bring to a scald (you will see bubbles around the perimeter of the liquid and a wisp of steam from the surface), then remove from the heat. Start streaming a small amount of the hot dairy into the egg mixture, whisking constantly to prevent the eggs from cooking. Continue whisking in the milk mixture until most of the liquid has been incorporated into the eggs. Pour the mixture in the bowl into the saucepot and place the pot over medium-high heat, again whisking constantly, until the mixture comes to a boil and thickens, 5 to 7 minutes. Remove from the heat and immediately whisk in the butter and chocolate; discard the vanilla pod.

3. Transfer the pudding to four bowls and serve warm. The pudding can also be refrigerated in the pan for up to 2 days and slowly reheated over medium heat, stirring constantly, until warm.

Warm Chocolate Pudding

Makes 4 servings

½ cup granulated sugar

2 tablespoons unsweetened Dutch-processed cocoa powder

2 tablespoons plus 1 teaspoon cornstarch

1 teaspoon kosher salt

2 eggs, at room temperature

1½ cups heavy cream

1½ cups whole milk

½ vanilla bean, split lengthwise and seeds scraped out

¼ cup unsalted butter, at room temperature

4 ounces dark chocolate (preferably Valrhona 70% cacao), chopped

Buttermilk Panna Cotta

Makes 8 servings

1 tablespoon plus 1 teaspoon
unflavored powdered gelatin

½ cup cold water

2½ cups heavy cream

¾ cup granulated sugar

1 teaspoon vanilla bean paste

3½ cups cold buttermilk

This panna cotta recipe is what I would call old faithful in any cook's repertoire, or like a little black dress in your wardrobe, if that's your type of thing. As long as you're using quality dairy, this panna cotta will be completely delicious and elegant. It's easily dressed up with seasonal fruit, nuts, granola, honey, your favorite sorbet, or even Champagne.

Feel free to make these up to 2 days ahead and keep them covered tightly with plastic wrap in the fridge. Otherwise, you can easily whip them up anytime, as long as you have 2 solid hours for the custards to set up.

1. In a small bowl, sprinkle the gelatin over the water. Let stand for 5 minutes to bloom, until softened.

2. In a medium saucepot set over medium heat, combine the cream, sugar, and vanilla paste. Bring to a scald (you will see bubbles around the perimeter of the liquid and a wisp of steam from the surface), then remove from the heat and let steep for 15 minutes. Return the pot to medium heat and again bring to a scald, then whisk in the gelatin mixture. Pour the buttermilk into a large bowl. Strain the cream mixture through a fine-mesh strainer into the buttermilk. Gently whisk to combine.

3. Divide the custard among eight 6-ounce ramekins. Tap the ramekins gently on the kitchen counter to release any air bubbles. Wrap the ramekins in plastic wrap and refrigerate until the panna cotta is set, at least 2 hours and up to 2 days. Serve chilled.

Large Panna Cotta with Fruit

This dessert is versatile in every way. In addition to soufflé ramekins, you can serve panna cotta in glasses or bowls and if you're feeling super adventurous—and I totally support you if you are—lightly coat a Bundt pan with cooking spray and pour in the panna cotta mixture to make one large dessert. Once set, quickly dip the bottom of the pan (which holds what will be the top of the panna cotta) in warm water and then place a serving plate over the pan and invert, letting the panna cotta release onto the serving platter. Fill the center with berries or cut fruit and watch the crowd go wild.

When I was growing up, on very special occasions, my mom would make a pudding pie with coconut, pecans, and chocolate that I've mentioned a few times in this book (yes, I loved it that much). I've still not figured out how to make that damned pie, but in all my attempts as a professional, I came up with the closest flavor and textural memory I could with this panna cotta as the main component. I like best to serve this custard with a spoonful of Warm Chocolate Pudding (page 129), candied pecans, and toasted coconut.

1. Preheat the oven to 300°F. Line a baking sheet with parchment paper or a silicone liner and coat with cooking spray.

2. Place the pecans in a medium bowl. In a small bowl, whisk together the salt and egg white, whisking until foamy and thickened, about 1 minute. Add the egg white to the pecans and, using a rubber spatula, stir to coat the nuts evenly. Add the sugar, again stirring to coat the nuts evenly. Spread the pecans on the prepared baking sheet in a single layer and bake, stirring every 10 minutes, until the nuts are aromatic and dry, about 40 minutes.

3. In a small bowl, sprinkle the gelatin over the water. Let stand for 5 minutes to bloom, until softened.

4. Place the chocolate in a large bowl. In a large heavy-bottomed saucepot over medium-high heat, combine the milk, corn syrup, and salt. Bring to a scald (you will see bubbles around the perimeter of the liquid and a wisp of steam from the surface), then remove from the heat. Whisk in the gelatin mixture until dissolved. Pour about one-third of the liquid over the chocolate and stir with a rubber spatula to melt the chocolate. Add another third of the liquid and keep stirring until smooth. Stir the remaining liquid into the chocolate until combined. Stir in the cream and vanilla.

5. Divide the custard evenly among six 8-ounce ramekins, cover tightly with plastic wrap, and refrigerate until completely set, about 2 hours. Serve chilled. The panna cotta can be stored in the refrigerator, tightly wrapped, for up to 4 days.

Blond Chocolate Panna Cotta

Makes 6 servings

Candied Pecans

1 pound pecan halves

1 teaspoon salt

1 egg white

1 cup granulated sugar

1 tablespoon plus 1 teaspoon unflavored powdered gelatin

½ cup cold water

10 ounces Valrhona Dulcey chocolate, chopped

1¼ cups whole milk

2 tablespoons light corn syrup

½ teaspoon kosher salt

2 cups heavy cream

2 teaspoons vanilla extract

What's Mine Is Yours

You can put a spin on the Candied Pecans by adding 1 teaspoon of ground spice(s)—think cinnamon, nutmeg, cardamom, or even cayenne pepper—to the nuts with the sugar.

Classic Crème Brûlée

Makes 10 servings

11 egg yolks

1 quart heavy cream

1 cup granulated sugar, plus more for dusting and torching on top

1 teaspoon kosher salt

1½ tablespoons vanilla bean paste

Few things in the pastry world make me happier than a simple yet perfectly prepared crème brûlée. I often find myself making this recipe when the world seems hectic, or I just need a reset. The elegance and simplicity of this dessert always inspires me and I love to serve it with seasonal fruit and Cornbread Madeleines (page 105).

1. Preheat the oven to 300°F. Set ten 6-ounce ramekins in a deep baking dish.

2. Set a fine-mesh sieve over a large bowl. In a medium bowl, whisk the egg yolks and set aside. In a medium saucepot, heat the cream, sugar, salt, and vanilla paste over medium-high heat. Once the sugar has fully dissolved and the cream comes to a scald (you will see bubbles around the perimeter of the liquid and a wisp of steam from the surface), remove from the heat. While whisking constantly to prevent the eggs from cooking, slowly stream the hot cream mixture into the egg yolks. Strain the custard through the sieve into the bowl.

3. Carefully divide the custard among the ramekins, about 4½ ounces per ramekin. Set the baking dish on the center rack in the oven. Fill the dish with enough hot water to match the level of the custard in the ramekins.

4. Carefully close the oven door and bake the custards for 50 to 60 minutes, until they are fully set. To test the "set" of the custards, carefully open the oven door and just gently move one corner of the baking dish to see how the liquid moves in the ramekins. If you see waves, they're not done. If the custard moves just ever so slightly, but as one unit, you're good to go! Very carefully remove the baking dish from the oven and set aside to cool until the ramekins are easily handled. If you've pulled the dish out of the oven and are a little concerned that your custards are on the side of overbaked, carefully remove the ramekins from the water bath as soon as you've taken them out of the oven. Once the custards are cool, place a piece of plastic wrap over each individual ramekin and refrigerate to cool completely or for up to 4 to 5 days.

5. To serve, remove the custards from the refrigerator and blot any condensation off the tops by gently patting the surface of each with a paper towel or clean kitchen towel. Place about 1 tablespoon sugar on the top of each custard and tilt the ramekin around to create a smooth, even layer of sugar. Dump any excess sugar onto the next ramekin, continuing until all have a sugar coating. Using a blow torch, caramelize the sugar, aiming for the inside edge of the ramekin and moving in a slow and steady circle so you don't end up with an over-brûléed center (don't point the torch at the center and keep it there). If you don't own a torch, preheat your broiler and set the custards on a baking sheet. Place the custards under the broiler, about 4 inches from the heat source, and broil just until the sugar melts and caramelizes. Serve immediately.

The use of the word "flan" here is poetic license. The defining characteristic of a flan versus other custards is that it's traditionally baked in a caramel syrup. So, we can say that all flans are custards, but not all custards are flans. This recipe uses caramelized condensed milk in place of the caramel syrup, putting it in the custard to create a phenomenally silky and slightly chewy texture. I like to serve this with condensed milk sorbet, but that's for you to decide for yourself.

1. Make the flan. Preheat the oven to 300°F. Put the chocolate in a heatproof bowl set over a pan of simmering water and stir to melt. Remove from the heat and stir in the dulce de leche; set aside.

2. In a heavy-bottomed saucepot set over medium-high heat, combine the cream, milk, salt, vanilla pod, vanilla seeds, and sugar. Bring to a scald (you will see bubbles around the perimeter of the liquid and a wisp of steam from the surface). In a medium bowl, whisk together the eggs and egg yolks. While whisking constantly, slowly stream the hot cream mixture into the eggs, being careful not to cook the eggs. Pour the egg mixture through a fine-mesh sieve into the chocolate mixture and whisk until smooth. (Rinse and dry the vanilla pod and save it for another use.) Strain the custard through the sieve again and chill immediately. Once cool, taste the custard and add salt if needed. At this point, you can store the custard in an airtight container in the refrigerator for 1 to 2 days.

3. Once ready to bake, preheat the oven to 300°F. Stir the custard and then divide it evenly among six 8-ounce ramekins. Place the ramekins in a deep baking dish and set the dish on the center rack in the oven. Fill the dish with enough hot water to match the level of the custard in the ramekins. Bake the flans for 35 to 45 minutes, until just set. Remove the baking dish from the oven and let the custards cool in the water bath for 15 to 20 minutes. Carefully remove the ramekins from the water, then place a piece of plastic wrap over each individual custard, just barely touching the top. Refrigerate until cool, about 4 hours and up to 2 days.

4. Make the sorbet. In a medium bowl, whisk together the condensed milk, water, and vanilla paste. Transfer to an ice cream machine and freeze according to the manufacturer's instructions. Serve the flans in the ramekins, topped with a scoop of the sorbet.

Chocolate-Hazelnut Flan

Makes 6 servings

Flan

6 ounces Gianduja chocolate (preferably Valrhona Azélia 35% cacao), chopped

½ cup Dulce de Leche (see page 139)

1¾ cups heavy cream

1 cup whole milk

1 teaspoon kosher salt, plus more if needed

½ vanilla bean, split lengthwise and seeds scraped out

¾ cup granulated sugar

3 eggs, at room temperature

2 egg yolks, at room temperature

Condensed Milk Sorbet

2 (14-ounce) cans sweetened condensed milk

3½ cups hot water

1 teaspoon vanilla bean paste

Dulce de Leche

Making dulce de leche is easy. Way easy. But just like my mom took it for granted that she didn't need to tell my sister to cover the potatoes with water when making mashed potatoes (spoiler alert: there was a fire and the bottom of that pot became such a permanent part of the range that we had to get a new stove), I have to stress that you HAVE TO REFILL the water in the pot and WATCH CLOSELY to make sure that the water level doesn't reduce to below the tops of the cans of sweetened condensed milk. Why, you ask? In the restaurant world, we make dulce de leche in number 10 cans—the big ones. When that water evaporates completely, the cans start to heat up. They are pressurized. They are filled with MOLTEN CARAMEL MILK. And when a can explodes . . . well, it has a nuclear reach. Not only will it cause significant bodily harm, it will haunt you from every crevice of your kitchen for months. That said, using store-bought dulce de leche is fine by me, y'all. I'm not going to judge, and I understand the value of your time. But if you fancy the challenge of patience, here you go.

Take a few cans of sweetened condensed milk (if you cook extra cans, they're good to go for as long as you don't open them—they keep at room temperature for up to the expiration date on the can—so you can always have some stored in the pantry for when the mood strikes), place them in a DEEP pot, and cover them with at least 6 inches of water. Bring the water to a boil and keep at a rolling boil for about 4 hours, replenishing the water frequently to keep the water level constant and the cans covered—if the level varies significantly, the temperature will fluctuate too much throughout the cooking process. Remove the pot from the heat and let the water cool enough that you can remove the cans. Then let the cans cool completely before opening, about 2 hours.

In 1951, the dessert scene in New Orleans was monumentally changed by the simple fact that the port was being overrun with bananas (the banana business boomed in New Orleans back then), and the city had been blessed with the quick mind of the one and only Ella Brennan. Miss Ella was managing Brennan's Restaurant at the time and was tasked rather suddenly with whipping up a dessert for a special dinner at the restaurant. She took to it, finding inspiration from a breakfast her mother had often made, and Bananas Foster was born. The contributions of Miss Ella undoubtedly shaped the New Orleans hospitality industry for decades to come, and her impact is beyond any metric of measure that I know. I highly recommend you serve this with vanilla ice cream.

1. Make the pudding. In a large heavy-bottomed saucepot, whisk together the milk, cream, bananas, sugar, salt, and cinnamon. Over medium-high heat, bring to a scald (you will see bubbles around the perimeter of the liquid and a wisp of steam from the surface). In a large bowl, whisk the eggs. Remove the saucepot from the heat and, using an immersion blender or whisk, blend the mixture until completely smooth. While whisking constantly, slowly stream the hot milk mixture into the eggs, being careful not to cook the eggs. Stir in the vanilla. Stir in the bread, cover, and let soak at room temperature for 30 minutes or in the refrigerator overnight.

2. Preheat the oven to 325°F. Grease a 9 by 13-inch baking pan with butter and pour in the bread mixture. Bake for 65 to 75 minutes, until golden brown and set in the middle. Set aside to cool while you prepare the sauce (which is best made right before serving).

3. Make the sauce. In a large skillet, melt the butter over medium-high heat. Stir in the brown sugar, cinnamon, and salt and cook for about 1 minute. Remove the skillet from the heat and pour in the liqueur, then return the pan to the heat and cook, stirring continuously, until the sugar dissolves completely, about 1½ minutes. Place the banana slices in the pan, flat-side up, and cook until the bananas start to soften, about 2 minutes, then flip. Remove the skillet from the heat once more and pour in the rum. Return the pan to high heat and very carefully ignite the alcohol using a long lighter or the flame from the stove. Gently shake the pan until the flame is gone. Remove from the heat.

4. To serve, spoon the pudding into bowls. Spoon the sauce and the bananas over the top and finish with vanilla ice cream, if using. This pudding can be covered with plastic wrap and kept in the refrigerator for up to 3 days; serve it at room temperature or pop it in a 325°F oven for 10 minutes to warm it through.

Bananas Foster Bread Pudding

Makes 8 to 10 servings

Bread Pudding

1 quart whole milk

2 cups heavy cream

2 ripe bananas, mashed

1 cup granulated sugar

1 teaspoon kosher salt

1½ teaspoons ground cinnamon

5 eggs, at room temperature

1 teaspoon vanilla extract

6½ cups Banana Bread (page 38), torn into 1½-inch pieces

Butter for greasing the pan

Sauce

½ cup unsalted butter

2 cups firmly packed dark brown sugar

1 teaspoon ground cinnamon

½ teaspoon kosher salt

¼ cup banana liqueur

6 ripe but not mushy bananas, peeled, halved crosswise, then halved lengthwise

½ cup dark rum

Vanilla ice cream for serving (optional)

Made with a whole lot of milk, cream, and eggs, this bread pudding really exemplifies the custard category. I enjoy it the most in late spring and early summer, eaten with berries and stone fruit. I'll grab ripe peaches or blackberries and allow them to macerate all day in a bit of sugar (use vanilla sugar if you have it on hand; see page 22) and some bourbon. If I'm serving the bread pudding warm, which is almost always, I'll warm up the fruit with its juices, throw on a scoop of ice cream (butter pecan, vanilla, peach, blackberry, cherry, whatever . . .), and then pour the fruit and its juices right over the top. A pro move, no doubt.

1. Make the cornbread. Preheat the oven to 350°F. Butter or lightly spray an 8-inch square baking pan. In a medium bowl, whisk together the flour, cornmeal, sugar, baking powder, and salt. In a large bowl, whisk the eggs with the buttermilk; stir in the dry ingredients until combined. Stir in the butter. Scrape the batter into the prepared pan. Bake for 25 minutes, rotating the pan halfway through baking, until golden. Transfer the cornbread to a wire rack to cool, about 30 minutes.

2. Once the cornbread is cool, tear or cut it into roughly 1-inch pieces and place it in a large bowl.

3. Make the custard. In a medium saucepot set over medium heat, warm the milk with ¾ cup of the sugar. In a large bowl, whisk the eggs and the remaining ¾ cup sugar. Once the milk comes to a scald (you will see bubbles around the perimeter of the liquid and a wisp of steam from the surface), slowly stream the hot milk mixture into the eggs while whisking constantly, being careful not to cook the eggs. Add the cream and vanilla. Pour the custard over the cornbread and let sit at room temperature for at least 30 minutes or in the refrigerator overnight.

4. Preheat the oven to 350°F. Butter a 9 by 13-inch baking pan. Pour the bread pudding mixture into the pan and bake for about 45 minutes, rotating the pan after 25 minutes, until springy and golden.

5. You can serve this pudding immediately, or not—the choice is yours. The pudding can be refrigerated for up to 3 days and brought to room temperature before heating in a 325°F oven to warm it through. To serve, scoop into bowls and spoon caramel sauce over the top. Don't forget the ice cream!

Cornbread Bread Pudding

Makes 8 to 10 servings

Bread Pudding Cornbread

Butter for greasing the pan

1½ cups all-purpose flour

1½ cups fine or coarse cornmeal (or a mixture of both)

½ cup granulated sugar

1½ tablespoons baking powder

1 teaspoon kosher salt

3 eggs, at room temperature

1½ cups buttermilk, at room temperature

¼ cup plus 2 tablespoons unsalted butter, melted

Custard

1 quart whole milk

1½ cups granulated sugar

9 eggs, at room temperature

2 cups heavy cream, at room temperature

¾ teaspoon vanilla extract

Caramel Sauce (page 298) for serving

Ice cream for serving

New Orleans–Style Bread Pudding

Makes 8 to 10 servings

Bread Pudding

1 quart whole milk

2 cups heavy cream, cold

1 cup granulated sugar

1½ teaspoons ground cinnamon

1 teaspoon vanilla extract

Grated zest of 1 orange

5 eggs, at room temperature

6½ cups torn stale crustless white bread (about 12 slices, torn into 1½-inch pieces)

Butter for greasing the pan

Sauce

½ cup unsalted butter

½ cup light corn syrup

1 cup granulated sugar

¾ cup dark rum

¾ cup heavy cream

1 teaspoon vanilla extract

½ teaspoon kosher salt

Bread pudding is a rite of passage for pastry chefs in New Orleans. I would go so far as to say that when pastry chefs are applying for jobs in New Orleans, making bread pudding is a key part of the application process. Making this version is pure muscle memory for me. Even though it came well after childhood, I cut my teeth and "grew up," professionally speaking, making this recipe almost daily. Use a dark rum you like to drink for the sauce, as we do in New Orleans, 'cause this sauce is a lil boozy.

1. Make the pudding. In a large bowl, whisk together the milk, cream, sugar, cinnamon, vanilla, orange zest, and eggs. Stir in the bread pieces, cover, and let soak at room temperature for 30 minutes or refrigerate overnight.

2. Preheat the oven to 325°F. Grease a 9 by 13-inch baking pan with butter and pour in the bread mixture. Bake for 65 to 75 minutes, rotating the pan after 35 minutes, until golden brown and set in the middle. Set aside.

3. Make the sauce. In a saucepot set over medium heat, cook the butter until it turns a light brown color with a rich, nutty aroma, about 5 minutes. Add the corn syrup, sugar, rum, cream, vanilla, and salt. Simmer and reduce the sauce until it thickens enough to coat the back of a spoon, about 15 minutes. Remove from the heat.

4. Scoop a large spoonful of warm bread pudding onto serving plates. Ladle the sauce over the pudding and serve.

New Orleans–Style Bread Pudding Lite

Because I am incapable of leaving things alone, I love to make this recipe, but I substitute 3 cups Japanese panko (bread crumbs) for 3 cups of the torn bread. This version has the same flavor as the original recipe but a phenomenally smooth texture.

What's Mine Is Yours

In New Orleans, the tradition is to use leftover French bread for bread pudding. Understand that French bread in New Orleans is unlike what the rest of the world knows French bread to be, mostly because in New Orleans, it's baked with rice flour. That being said, any light, fluffy "white" bread or combination of breads will work well.

You can absolutely make this recipe ahead of time. The pudding can be refrigerated for 4 to 5 days and reheated in a 350°F oven until just warm. The sauce can be refrigerated for up to 2 weeks and gently reheated to serve. If you make the whole dish ahead of time and are serving it family style, score the bread pudding (cut it across the top), top with the cold sauce, and place it in the oven to reheat.

I have to confess that I spent the first half of my life not loving cheesecake. I just didn't understand it. Then, lo and behold, at the farmers' market in New Orleans, I was introduced to cheesecake made with Creole Cream Cheese.

1. Make the crust. Preheat the oven to 375°F. In a medium bowl, stir together the graham cracker crumbs, granulated sugar, brown sugar, salt, and butter to combine. Pat the mixture into a 10-inch springform pan, pressing the crumbs firmly in an even layer on the bottom and making sure they come at least halfway up the side of the pan. Bake for 7 to 10 minutes, until the crust is fragrant, dry, and toasty. Let cool, then wrap the entire outside of the pan tightly in two layers of foil, all the way to the top.

2. Make the filling. In the bowl of a stand mixer fitted with the paddle attachment or in a large bowl using a handheld mixer, cream the plain cream cheese and sugar on medium-high speed for about 4 minutes, until incredibly smooth and light. Stop the mixer and scrape down the bottom and sides of the bowl with a rubber spatula. Add the Creole Cream Cheese and vanilla paste and beat on medium-high speed for about 2 minutes, scraping down the bowl once more. Decrease the speed to medium and beat in the eggs, one at a time, incorporating each one before adding the next. Mix just until the batter is smooth and uniform. Continuing to mix past that point, even though the batter won't look different, only incorporates extra air, which will cause the cheesecake to bubble excessively and the surface to crack as that air tries to escape during the baking process.

3. Decrease the oven temperature to 350°F. Pour the batter into the prepared crust and tap the pan gently on the counter a few times to remove any large air bubbles. Place the springform pan in a large baking or roasting pan (just big enough for the springform pan to fit in) and set the pan on the middle rack in the oven. Fill the pan with enough hot water to reach the rim of the springform pan. Bake for about 1 hour, or until the sides of the custard are set and the middle is still just slightly wobbly. Generally, if the entirety of the custard is fully set, your cheesecake is overbaked. Don't panic—it'll still be delicious, and you'll do better next time!

4. Let the cheesecake cool in the water until it is about room temperature. (You don't want to have to try to grab the pan out of hot water if you can help it.) However, if you're worried that your cheesecake might be slightly overbaked, you'll want to pull it out rather quickly, and let it cool at room temperature. Refrigerate for at least 3 hours before slicing. The cake can be refrigerated, covered, for up to 4 days.

continued

Creole Cream Cheesecake

Makes one 10-inch cheesecake

Crust

2 cups graham cracker crumbs (about 16 whole crackers)

3 tablespoons granulated sugar

3 tablespoons firmly packed light brown sugar

¼ teaspoon kosher salt

½ cup unsalted butter, melted

Filling

2 pounds cream cheese, at room temperature

1 cup granulated sugar

1⅓ cups Creole Cream Cheese (page 305)

1 teaspoon vanilla bean paste

2 eggs, at room temperature

continued
Creole Cream Cheesecake

Sour Cream–Creole Cream Cheesecake with Roasted Strawberries in Their Own Sauce

You can substitute 1 cup sour cream mixed with ¼ cup buttermilk for the 1⅓ cups Creole Cream Cheese. Top the cake with Roasted Strawberries in Their Own Sauce (page 302).

What's Mine Is Yours

In my professional opinion, springform pans are a giant pain in the ass. If they're dropped, or even washed too hard, they can bend, which will compromise the integrity of everything you'll ever try to bake in them again. They're sometimes leaky and uneven for the same reason, even if you can't actually see where the pan has shape-shifted. I prefer to use a 9-inch round cake pan with sides that are 4 inches high. I lightly spray the pan, then cut a round of parchment paper the size of the pan, place it on the bottom, and lightly spray it again before carrying on with the crust step.

The real challenge of this approach comes when it's time to unmold the cake. If you're smarter than I am, you'll give yourself enough time to throw the entire pan in the freezer for a few hours before you're ready to unmold the cheesecake. When you are ready, run a spatula or a knife (use the dull side of the knife to lead the way; that way you're not accidentally cutting into the cake) around the circumference of the cake. Place a plate over the pan, invert the cake onto the plate, and remove the pan. If the cake is extra cold, lightly rub and tap the bottom of the pan (or use a blow torch just because you have one!) to create enough heat to release the cake. Very quickly place another plate on top of the cake and carefully invert the cake onto the plate, so it is right side up. Voilà!

Pumpkin Cheesecake

Makes one 9-inch cheesecake

Crust

2 cups finely ground gingersnap cookies (approximately thirty-five 2-inch cookies)

¼ teaspoon cayenne pepper

¼ cup plus 2 tablespoons unsalted butter, melted

Filling

2¼ pounds cream cheese, at room temperature

1½ cups firmly packed light brown sugar

1 (28-ounce) can pure pumpkin puree (2½ cups)

1 tablespoon plus 1 teaspoon ground espresso

1 teaspoon ground cinnamon

1 teaspoon kosher salt

4 eggs, at room temperature

2 egg yolks, at room temperature

This recipe is yet another result of my dislike of pumpkin pie (see my Pumpkin Pie with Roasted White Chocolate Cream, page 184). This cheesecake is really an innocent bystander in my attempt to make something at Thanksgiving that I would actually want to eat. The combination of pumpkin and espresso is like peanut butter and chocolate; they should just be together.

1. Make the crust. Preheat the oven to 350°F. Lightly coat a 9-inch springform pan with cooking spray and cut a piece of parchment paper to fit the bottom of the pan. Lightly spray the paper. Wrap the entire outside of the pan tightly in two layers of foil, all the way to the top. In a medium bowl, combine the gingersnaps and cayenne. Stir in the butter until evenly incorporated. Press the mixture into the bottom of the prepared pan and up the sides as far as you are able. Bake the crust for 10 minutes, or until golden and aromatic. Remove from the oven and set aside. Reduce the oven temperature to 325°F.

2. Make the filling. In the bowl of a stand mixer fitted with the paddle attachment or in a large bowl using a handheld mixer, whip the cream cheese with the brown sugar until very smooth, stopping the mixer and scraping down the bottom and sides of the bowl with a rubber spatula several times. Once the mixture is completely smooth, add the pumpkin, espresso, cinnamon, and salt and mix on medium-low speed until combined. Beat in the eggs and egg yolks, one at a time, incorporating well after each addition, just until evenly mixed. Continuing to mix past that point, even though the batter won't look different, only incorporates extra air, which will cause the cheesecake to bubble excessively and the surface to crack as that air tries to escape during the baking process.

3. Set a roasting pan on the center rack in the oven. Pour the filling into the prepared crust and set the springform pan in the roasting pan. Carefully fill the roasting pan with hot water so it's a little over halfway up the side of the springform pan. Bake the cheesecake for 1 to 1½ hours, until the filling is set and slightly puffy. Once done, carefully remove the roasting pan from the oven and let the cheesecake cool before removing it from the water bath. (You don't want to try to grab the pan out of hot water if you can help it.) However, if you're worried that your cheesecake might be slightly overbaked, you'll want to pull it out rather quickly and let it cool at room temperature. Refrigerate for at least 3 hours before slicing. The cake can be refrigerated, covered, for up to 5 days.

Chocolate-Espresso Cheesecake

Makes one 9-inch cheesecake

Crust

2 cups graham cracker crumbs
(about 16 whole crackers)

3 tablespoons granulated sugar

3 tablespoons firmly packed
light brown sugar

¼ teaspoon kosher salt

½ cup unsalted butter, melted

Filling

8½ ounces dark chocolate
(preferably Valrhona
70% cacao), chopped

1½ pounds cream cheese,
at room temperature

1 cup granulated sugar

3 eggs, at room temperature

1½ tablespoons instant
espresso powder

1 teaspoon finely grated lemon zest

1 teaspoon vanilla bean paste

1 teaspoon kosher salt

¾ cup sour cream,
at room temperature

This is a light and silky chocolate cheesecake. I make this often as a gift for party hosts, neighbors, and friends, since it's a classic crowd-pleaser. You'll want to make the chocolate topping at least a day ahead (it'll actually hold in an airtight container in the refrigerator for up to 3 days) so it has time to rest before you whip it to serve.

1. Make the crust. Preheat the oven to 375°F. Lightly coat a 9-inch springform pan with cooking spray and line the bottom with a piece of parchment paper cut to fit. Lightly spray the paper. Wrap the entire outside of the pan tightly in two layers of foil, all the way to the top.

2. In a medium bowl, stir together the graham cracker crumbs, granulated sugar, brown sugar, salt, and butter until combined. Press the mixture into the bottom of the prepared pan and up the sides as far as you are able. Bake for 7 to 10 minutes, until fragrant, dry, and toasty. Remove from the oven and set aside. Let cool completely before filling. Decrease the oven temperature to 300°F.

3. Make the filling. Put the chocolate in a microwave-safe bowl and melt in 20-second intervals, stirring after every 20 seconds, until completely smooth. Set aside.

4. In the bowl of a stand mixer fitted with the paddle attachment or in a large bowl using a handheld mixer, whip the cream cheese and sugar on medium speed until completely smooth, about 4 minutes. Stop the mixer and scrape down the bottom and sides of the bowl with a rubber spatula to ensure there are no lumps. Add the eggs, one at a time, mixing well after each addition. Decrease the speed to low and mix in the espresso, lemon zest, vanilla paste, and salt. Stir the sour cream into the melted chocolate, then add to the cream cheese mixture, mixing on low speed until the chocolate is fully incorporated and the batter is not streaky. Stop the mixer, scrape down the bottom and sides of the bowl with a rubber spatula again, and mix just long enough to ensure a uniform batter.

5. Scrape the batter into the prepared pan, using a rubber spatula to get every bit. Tap the pan gently on the counter a few times to release any large air bubbles from the batter. Place the pan in a deep baking dish or roasting pan and set it on the center rack in the oven. Fill the baking dish with as much hot water as it will hold. Bake the cheesecake for 70 to 80 minutes, until the top of is dry and the center is just slightly set. Remove the pan from the oven and let cool for 15 minutes before carefully removing the cheesecake from the water bath. However, if you're worried that your cake might be slightly overbaked, you'll want to pull it out rather quickly and let it cool at room temperature. Refrigerate for at least 3 hours before slicing. The cake can be refrigerated, covered, for up to 5 days.

6. Make the topping. In a medium saucepot, combine ¾ cup of the cream with the corn syrup and espresso and bring to a boil. Cover and remove from the heat. Let steep for 15 minutes.

7. In a large stainless-steel bowl set over a pan of barely simmering water, melt the dark chocolate and milk chocolate. While the chocolate is melting, strain the cream through a fine-mesh sieve into a bowl. Return the cream to the saucepot and bring to a bare simmer. Remove the chocolate from the heat and, using a large rubber spatula, stir about one-quarter of the warm cream into the chocolate; it will look kind of broken, but keep stirring to emulsify. Add the remaining warm cream in three portions, mixing well after each addition. The sauce will start to thicken and get glossy. Whisk in the remaining 1 cup heavy cream, then cover and refrigerate overnight or for up to 3 days.

8. Transfer the chilled ganache to the bowl of a stand mixer fitted with the whisk attachment or use a handheld mixer. Beat on medium speed for about 10 seconds, then increase the speed to high and beat until barely stiff, about 45 seconds longer. Transfer to a piping bag or a resealable bag with a bottom corner snipped off. Pipe dollops of the ganache all over the unmolded cheesecake (alternatively, you can spread the ganache over the top of the cake). Dust with cocoa and serve. The cheesecake can be stored wrapped in plastic wrap or in an airtight container in the refrigerator for 4 to 5 days.

Ganache Topping

1¾ cups heavy cream

1 tablespoon light corn syrup

2 teaspoons instant espresso powder

3¼ ounces dark chocolate (preferably Valrhona 70% cacao), chopped

1¾ ounces milk chocolate (preferably Valrhona Jivara 40% cacao), chopped

Unsweetened cocoa powder for dusting

Cobblers, Crisps, Galettes, Pies, and Tarts

My mom made this cobbler for us just about every summer weekend when I was growing up. She is, and always has been, an avid gardener, growing as much produce in her garden as she can handle. We were also always packing up the car and heading to farmers' markets and pick-your-own farms to collect as much as we were able. This cobbler is so quick and easy that I have a feeling she whipped it up to calm and satiate the family, so she could quietly get to work on the rest of the meal.

1. Preheat the oven to 350°F.

2. Make the filling. In a medium bowl, combine the peaches, blackberries, sugar, bourbon, and vanilla paste and toss until combined. Scrape into an 8 by 12-inch glass or ceramic baking dish.

3. Make the topping. In a medium bowl, whisk together the flour, sugar, and milk until no lumps remain. Pour evenly over the fruit and bake for 50 to 60 minutes, rotating the baking dish after 25 minutes, until the top is golden brown and nice, slow, thick bubbles form around the edges.

4. Serve warm. The cobbler can be stored, uncovered, at room temperature for up to 3 days; warm in a 300°F oven before serving.

My Mom's Peach, Blackberry, and Bourbon Cobbler

Makes 8 to 10 servings

Filling

5 cups peeled peach wedges

4 cups blackberries

¾ cup granulated sugar

¼ cup bourbon (or use more, if you prefer)

1½ teaspoons vanilla bean paste

Topping

1½ cups self-rising flour

1½ cups granulated sugar

1½ cups whole milk

What's Mine Is Yours

Southern bakers love their self-rising flour, but I know that's not everyone's cup of tea. If that includes you, for 1½ cups self-rising flour, substitute 1½ cups all-purpose flour, whisked together with 2½ teaspoons baking powder and a rounded ¼ teaspoon salt.

Fruit Crisp with Pecan Streusel

Makes 6 to 8 servings

Streusel Topping

2 cups pecans

⅔ cup granulated sugar

⅔ cup all-purpose flour

1 teaspoon kosher salt

Grated zest of ½ orange

½ cup unsalted butter, melted

Filling

⅓ cup granulated sugar

⅓ cup firmly packed
light brown sugar

¾ teaspoon ground cinnamon

¼ cup all-purpose flour

½ teaspoon kosher salt

Grated zest of ½ lemon

4 cups peeled, cored, and diced
apples (about 3, preferably a mix
of Honeycrisp, Crispin, and/or
Granny Smith)

4 cups peeled, cored, and diced
Bosc pears (about 3)

1½ tablespoons fresh lemon juice

2 tablespoons cold unsalted
butter, diced

The following recipe is incredibly flexible and forgiving (as in, if you mess up, it's still really delicious 99 percent of the time). This version includes apples and pears, but you can have a lot of fun with other fruit throughout all the seasons of the year. This crisp is great with quince, peaches, rhubarb, and kumquats, and any type of berry you feel passionate about. (If you use berries, increase the volume to about 10 cups to account for shrinkage during baking.) Just go have fun!

1. Make the topping. Preheat the oven to 300°F. Spread the pecans on a large rimmed baking sheet and toast for 15 to 20 minutes, or until crunchy and fragrant. Set aside to cool and increase the oven temperature to 350°F. Transfer the pecans to a food processor and pulse until coarsely chopped. Add the sugar, flour, salt, and orange zest and pulse just to combine. With the processor on low speed, stream in the butter until clumps form. You can make this topping up to 2 days in advance and store it in an airtight container in the refrigerator. Bring to room temperature before using.

2. Make the filling. In a large bowl, whisk the granulated sugar and brown sugar with the cinnamon to prevent clumps. Add the flour, salt, and lemon zest. Add the apples and pears, sprinkle with the lemon juice, and toss to combine. Add the butter and toss again; you still want to see small chunks of butter throughout the mixture.

3. Scrape the filling into a 9-inch square baking pan or cast-iron skillet; don't be afraid to mound the apples and pears high—they will shrink during baking. Top with the streusel and bake for 55 to 60 minutes, rotating the pan after 30 minutes, until the filling is thick and bubbling and the topping is golden. You are looking for small bubbles that don't pop; this happens when the moisture has evaporated and the sugar starts to caramelize.

4. Let the crisp cool slightly before serving. The crisp can be kept at room temperature for up to 3 days; reheat slightly to serve.

What's Mine Is Yours

As a rule, I think nuts are best toasted low and slow, which allows the natural oils to release and makes them smell and taste crazy-good.

My most favorite apple to bake with (and eat) is Honeycrisp. Their amazing texture holds up in almost all baking I've tried. Granny Smiths are another easy, accessible variety that bake well and deliver a pop of tart flavor. Crispin apples, while not nearly as tart as Granny Smiths, hold up beautifully in baking, making them a great choice for pies, cobblers, and crisps. For fun, mix up all three to create a dynamic play on texture and flavor.

When baking with pears, I tend to stick to Bosc exclusively, since they hold their structure better than most any other variety (not to mention that they're generally the most accessible). It's important to remember the short life of a perfectly ripe pear and to seize that moment. Pears ripen from the inside out, and off the tree, which makes it a challenge; look for pears that are soft at the top, right where the stem is, but not soft anywhere else. Baking with overripe pears will result in pockets of mushy pear.

You can approach and execute this galette with (or without) as much attention to detail as you choose. The results will be stunning and delicious no matter how masterfully you place each piece of fruit . . . or don't place it, as the case may be. The most important thing, I find, is that you taste your fruit and adjust the sugar, lemon juice, and salt accordingly, based on the flavor of that day's bounty. Berries work great here, as do figs, apples, pears, and all of the stone fruits. If you want to get a little crazy, spread a thin layer of pastry cream over the dough before adding the fruit and baking.

1. Preheat the oven to 400°F. In a large bowl, whisk together the granulated sugar and cornstarch. Add the berries, ginger, lemon juice, vanilla paste, and salt. Toss until the fruit is well coated.

2. Line a rimmed baking sheet with parchment paper. On a lightly floured surface, roll the prepared pie dough into an even round, about 14 inches in diameter and a little less than ¼ inch thick. Transfer the dough to the center of the prepared baking sheet and mound the fruit on top, leaving a 2-inch border around the edge. Alternatively, arrange the fruit in a pinwheel pattern, starting in the middle and forming concentric circles, leaving a 2-inch border around the edge. Fold the border of the pie dough up over the fruit. Crimp the dough to itself to seal. Make sure you have enough dough over the fruit to catch all that delicious fruity, saucy jamminess that is going to be created. Lightly brush the dough with the egg white and sprinkle with the raw sugar. Let rest in the refrigerator for about 20 minutes.

3. Bake the galette in the center of the oven for 35 to 40 minutes, rotating the baking sheet after 18 minutes, until the fruit filling is bubbling and the crust is nice and golden brown.

4. Let the galette cool for about 20 minutes before serving. Store at room temperature for up to 2 days, if for some reason it lasts that long.

Berry Galette

Makes one 10-inch galette

½ cup granulated sugar

2 tablespoons cornstarch

4 cups berries (blueberries, blackberries, hulled and sliced strawberries, or whatever)

¼ teaspoon ground ginger

1 teaspoon fresh lemon juice

1 teaspoon vanilla bean paste

Pinch of kosher salt

All-purpose flour for dusting

1 recipe Single-Crust Pie Dough (page 308), prepared through step 1

1 egg white, beaten

2 tablespoons raw sugar

Stone Fruit Galette

Makes one 10-inch round galette

4 cups sliced stone fruit (sliced peaches, halved cherries, sliced plums, sliced nectarines, or halved apricots)

½ cup granulated sugar

½ cup crushed toasted almonds (optional)

2 tablespoons honey

2 tablespoons cornstarch

¼ teaspoon ground ginger

1 teaspoon fresh lemon juice

1 teaspoon vanilla bean paste

Pinch of kosher salt

1 recipe Single-Crust Pie Dough (page 308), prepared through step 1

1 egg white, beaten

2 tablespoons raw sugar

Galettes are one of my favorite ways to dessert. They are such a simple pleasure to produce, made even better by sharing the experience with friends and family. Summer stone fruit galettes could be the singular excuse for keeping piecrust in your freezer, honestly. When summer delivers that first batch of perfect peaches, this recipe is one of the best ways to let them shine. One of my favorite cooking memories is of spending a week with eleven friends in Tuscany picking baskets of stone fruit from the property's gardens to make daily galettes (we of course called them crostatas since we were in Italy). Depending on what is available in the season, you can vary the stone fruit. The key is to cut the fruit about the same size.

1. Preheat the oven to 400°F. In a large bowl, combine the fruit with the granulated sugar, almonds (if using), honey, cornstarch, ginger, lemon juice, vanilla paste, and salt. Toss until the fruit is well coated.

2. Line a rimmed baking sheet with parchment paper. On a lightly floured surface, roll the prepared pie dough into an even round, about 14 inches in diameter and a little less than ¼ inch thick. Transfer the dough to the center of the prepared baking sheet and arrange the fruit on top in a pinwheel pattern, starting in the middle and forming concentric circles, leaving a 2-inch border around the edge. Alternatively, just mound that fruit up evenly in the middle of the dough, leaving a 2-inch border around the edge. Fold the border of the pie dough up over the fruit. Crimp the dough to itself to seal. Make sure you have enough dough over the fruit to catch all that delicious fruity, saucy jamminess that is going to be created. Lightly brush the dough with the egg white and sprinkle with the raw sugar. Let rest in the refrigerator for about 20 minutes.

3. Bake the galette in the center of the oven for about 40 minutes, rotating the baking sheet after 20 minutes, until the fruit filling is bubbling and the crust is nice and golden brown.

4. Let the galette cool for about 20 minutes before serving. Store at room temperature for up to 2 days.

Fruit Prep Talk

The most important rule is to cut the produce as evenly as possible to ensure even baking.

Fresh cherries: Cut in half and pit.

Strawberries: Wash, dry, hull, and cut in half.

Raspberries, blackberries, and blueberries: Just rinse, pat dry, and use.

Peaches and plums: Cut in half, pit, and slice each half evenly. Shingle the halves over the filling. If your peaches are large, adjust accordingly.

Figs: Wash, dry, and cut in half. I like to drizzle a little cane syrup on mine before and after baking.

Apples and pears: I recommend poaching apple and pear halves first and then slicing. (See Basic Poaching Liquid, page 298.)

Tomatoes: Use a handful of halved cherry tomatoes or slice a large tomato into ⅓-inch-thick slices and shingle. Season with salt and pepper.

I love the uncomplicated simplicity of fruit galettes and how they provide a wonderful way to showcase fruit and piecrust in a quick and simple execution. For this galette, you can use your favorite baking apple. I really enjoy using a mixture of Granny Smiths and Honeycrisps for varying textures and a balance of sweet-tart flavors. I will also sometimes spread a layer of pastry cream or even apple butter on the pie dough before topping with the apples and baking, for a little more depth.

Apple Galette

Makes one 10-inch galette

1. Preheat the oven to 400°F. In a large bowl, combine the apples with the granulated sugar, honey, cornstarch, ginger, cinnamon, cardamom, cloves, nutmeg, lemon juice, vanilla paste, and salt. Toss until the fruit is well coated.

2. Line a rimmed baking sheet with parchment paper. On a lightly floured surface, roll the prepared pie dough into an even round, about 14 inches in diameter and a little less than ¼ inch thick. Transfer the dough to the center of the prepared baking sheet and arrange the apples on top in a pinwheel pattern, starting in the middle and forming concentric circles, leaving a 2-inch border around the edge. Alternatively, just mound the apples up evenly in the middle of the dough, leaving a 2-inch border around the edge. Fold the border of the pie dough up over the fruit. Crimp the dough to itself to seal. Make sure you have enough dough over the fruit to catch all of that delicious fruity, saucy jamminess that is going to be created. If you find that you have leftover liquid from the apples in the bowl, you can pour it right over the apples just before you put the galette in the oven.

3. Lightly brush the dough with the egg white and sprinkle with the raw sugar. Let rest in the refrigerator for about 20 minutes.

4. Bake the galette in the center of the oven for about 40 minutes, rotating the baking sheet after 20 minutes, until the fruit filling is bubbling and the crust is nice and golden brown.

5. Let the galette cool for about 20 minutes before serving. Store at room temperature for up to 2 days.

4 cups peeled, cored, and sliced apples, sliced ⅛ inch thick (about 3, preferably a mix of Honeycrisp, Crispin, and/or Granny Smith)

½ cup granulated sugar

2 tablespoons honey

2 tablespoons cornstarch

¼ teaspoon ground ginger

½ teaspoon ground cinnamon

¼ teaspoon ground cardamom

⅛ teaspoon ground cloves

⅛ teaspoon ground nutmeg

1 teaspoon fresh lemon juice

1 teaspoon vanilla bean paste

Pinch of kosher salt

All-purpose flour for dusting

1 recipe Single-Crust Pie Dough (page 308), prepared through step 1

1 egg white, beaten

2 tablespoons raw sugar

Blueberry Pie

Makes one 10-inch single-crust pie

2 tablespoons unsalted butter, at room temperature

½ cup granulated sugar

1 egg, at room temperature

4 cups blueberries

1 tablespoon all-purpose flour

1½ tablespoons cornstarch

1 teaspoon finely grated lemon zest

1 teaspoon fresh lemon juice

½ teaspoon kosher salt

1 recipe Tart Dough (page 312), chilled

¼ cup powdered sugar

I sometimes cook down half the blueberries on the stovetop before mixing them with the rest of the fresh blueberries and adding them to this pie. There's absolutely no real reason to do this, but I really love the different textures of the blueberries when I do this extra step. Serve this pie slightly warm with your favorite ice cream or a dollop of whipped cream, or even with Whipped Cranberry Cream Cheese (page 306).

1. Preheat the oven to 375°F. In the bowl of a stand mixer fitted with the paddle attachment or in a large bowl using a handheld mixer, beat the butter with the granulated sugar and egg until smooth and creamy. Fold in the blueberries and flour, then fold in the cornstarch, lemon zest, lemon juice, and salt.

2. Spoon the filling into the prepared tart shell. Line a rimmed baking sheet with parchment paper or foil. Place the pie on the baking sheet and bake in the center of the oven for about 40 minutes, rotating the pie after 20 minutes, until the crust is golden brown and the filling is bubbling thick and slow.

3. Let the pie cool to room temperature, about 3 hours. Dust with the powdered sugar, slice, and serve. The pie can be stored at room temperature, uncovered or loosely tented with foil, for up to 3 days.

For this pie, it's important to note that I do not like to combine all the filling ingredients until the very moment before they go into the pie shell, for maximum flavor and a jammy pie situation. I also really like a whole crust on the top of my strawberry pie because it allows me to create the biggest pie possible, and it also evens out the filling-to-crust ratio, which is very important to me. Lattice is not my jam.

1. Make the egg wash: In a small bowl, whisk together the egg, milk, and salt.

2. Preheat the oven to 425°F. Spread the pastry cream evenly across the prepared pie shell. In a medium bowl, toss together the rhubarb, strawberries, kumquats, lemon juice, vanilla paste, granulated sugar, cornstarch, and salt. Carefully spoon the filling into the pie shell. Brush the overhanging pie dough of the bottom crust with a thin layer of the egg wash.

3. Drape the dough for the top crust over the filling. Press the bottom and top crusts together to seal, then fold the edge of the crust and tuck it under itself so it rests on the lip of the pie pan. Using your fingers, pinch the top of the fold evenly all the way around the pie to seal. Trim any overhanging dough, then crimp the dough decoratively (see page 177).

4. Make a few cuts in the top crust for venting. Be as creative and artistic (or not at all) as you wish. Brush the entire surface of the pie with the egg wash and sprinkle with the raw sugar, if using.

5. Line a rimmed baking sheet with parchment paper or foil. Place the pie on the prepared baking sheet and put a foil collar around the edge of the pie (see page 24). Position the pie in the center of the oven and decrease the oven temperature to 375°F. Bake for about 1½ hours, rotating the pan after 45 minutes, until the crust is golden brown and the juices seeping through your possibly artistic vents are thick and creating large, slow bubbles.

6. Let the pie cool for 10 minutes before removing the foil collar, and then for at least 5 hours before serving. The pie can be stored well wrapped or in an airtight container at room temperature for up to 2 days.

Strawberry Pie

Makes one 9-inch double-crust pie

Egg wash
1 egg
1 teaspoon milk
¼ teaspoon kosher salt

1 cup Pastry Cream (page 303)
1 recipe Double-Crust Pie Dough (page 310)
4 cups chopped fresh or thawed frozen rhubarb (cut into ½-inch pieces)
2 cups strawberries, hulled and halved
¼ cup kumquats, sliced and seeded
1 tablespoon fresh lemon juice
1 teaspoon vanilla bean paste
¾ cup granulated sugar
¼ cup cornstarch
Pinch of kosher salt

Raw sugar for sprinkling (optional)

What's Mine Is Yours

Seeding kumquats is tedious, I admit, but oh-so-worth it. I love kumquats for their tart, bitter sweetness and for their texture when cooked. They add so much depth of flavor to this pie.

Peach Pie

Makes one 9-inch double-crust pie

Egg Wash

1 egg

1 teaspoon water

Pinch of kosher salt

8 cups peeled sliced peaches

½ cup granulated sugar

½ cup firmly packed
light brown sugar

⅓ cup cornstarch, sifted

2 tablespoons fresh lemon juice

½ teaspoon vanilla extract

1 teaspoon kosher salt

1 recipe Double-Crust Pie Dough
(page 310), bottom crust edge
not folded under

Raw sugar for sprinkling
(optional)

This pie . . . I don't even know what to say. I love it so dearly. It's a time machine back to every summer of my childhood. I can recall specific moments in my life—where I was, whom I was with, how I felt in the world, the weather, and every single first bite of peach pie throughout the years as peach season rolled along. The rules are simple: find the most perfectly ripe peaches and do as little to them as possible, because they shine on their own. Feel free, as the season continues, to add any amount of other stone fruit you want to the mix, but I'll be a peach pie purist for life.

1. Make the egg wash: In a small bowl, whisk together the egg, water, and salt. Brush the entire surface of the pie shell with the egg wash and sprinkle with the raw sugar, if using.

2. Preheat the oven to 425°F. In a large bowl, toss together the peaches, granulated sugar, brown sugar, cornstarch, lemon juice, vanilla, and salt. Spoon the filling into the prepared pie shell. Brush the edge of the crust with egg wash.

3. Drape the dough for the top crust over the filling. Press the bottom and top crusts together to seal. Trim any overhanging dough, then press with the tines of a fork to seal the dough decoratively (see right).

4. Make a few cuts in the top crust for venting. Be as creative and artistic (or not at all) as you wish.

5. Line a baking sheet with parchment paper or foil. Place the pie on the prepared baking sheet and put a foil collar around the edge of the pie (see page 24). Position the pie in the center of the oven and decrease the oven temperature to 375°F. Bake for about 1½ hours, rotating the pan after 45 minutes, until the crust is golden brown and the juices seeping through your possibly artistic vents are thick and creating large, slow bubbles.

6. Let the pie cool on a wire rack for 10 minutes before removing the foil collar and then for 5 hours before serving. The pie can be stored tented with foil or in an airtight container at room temperature for up to 3 days.

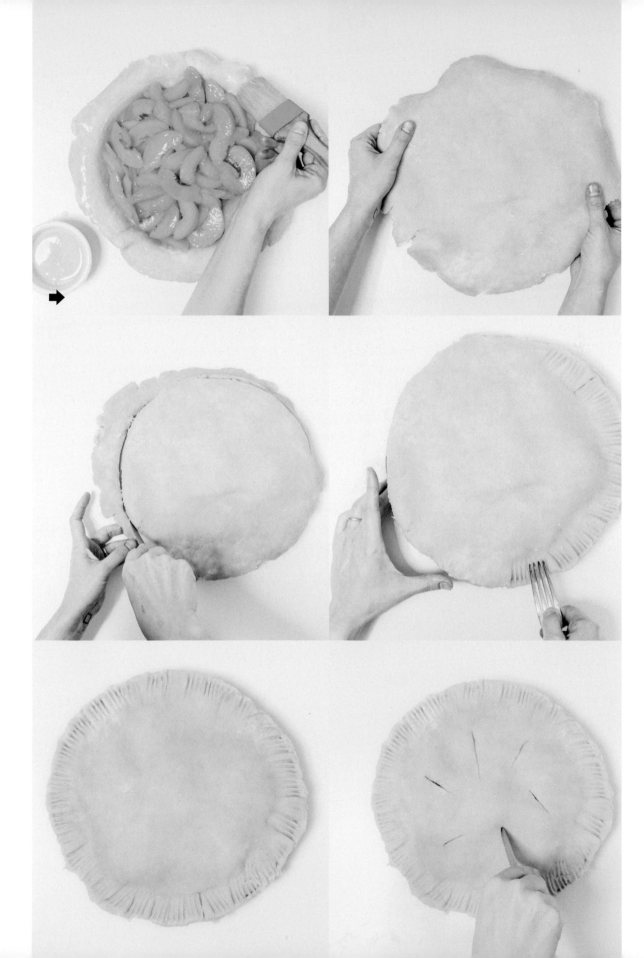

Crimp School

Crimping and decorating pies has become an entire lifestyle with the birth and popularity of social media. There are more how-to suggestions and intimidating, intricate pie suggestions on the internet than I could possibly count. Don't be intimidated or hold yourself to some postable standard. Your pie should be delicious. Period.

My personal rules for pie crimping are simple: First, try to bake in a pie pan that has a little bit larger lip around the edge. Second, keep your dough as cold as possible. This may mean that you put your pie back in the fridge more than once while you are rolling the crust and assembling it. I promise it will pay off. Third, if you're preparing a double-crust pie, be sure the seal between the top and the bottom crust is secure. Brush it well with water or egg wash to glue the two together. Fourth, once you've crimped your pie, place it in the freezer and let it get as cold as possible before you bake it. The cooler it is, the more likely it will be to hold its shape during baking.

I like a standard finger crimp, using my index fingers and thumbs to create a zig-zag all the way around the pie. Using your dominant hand's index finger (or a different finger, based on the size of crimp you want and the size of your fingers), press outward from the inside of the piecrust. Using the index finger and thumb of your nondominant hand, lightly pinch the outside dough around the dominant hand's finger to create a V- or U-shape. Rotate the pie as you work your way around. If this feels like too much work, that's okay. You can literally just use the prongs of a fork and indent the lip of the crust all the way around. That also looks pretty great when baked.

Most times I prefer a streusel crust to a double piecrust. It's a really great opportunity to add more textures and flavors to your pie (making it even better with ice cream!). I add pecans and a touch of orange zest here, but any tree nut will do.

1. Make the topping. Preheat the oven to 300°F. Spread the pecans on a large rimmed baking sheet and toast for 15 to 20 minutes, or until crunchy and fragrant. Set aside to cool and increase the oven temperature to 400°F. Transfer the pecans to a food processor and pulse until coarsely chopped. Add the sugar, flour, salt, and orange zest and pulse just to combine. With the processor at low speed, stream in the butter until clumps form. You can make this mixture up to two days in advance and store it in an airtight container in the refrigerator. Bring to room temperature before using.

2. Make the filling. In a medium bowl, combine the granulated sugar, brown sugar, flour, cinnamon, ginger, nutmeg, and cardamom. In a large bowl, toss the apples with the lemon juice and honey. Add in the dry ingredients and toss to combine.

3. Fill the prepared piecrust with the fruit mixture; this will feel overfilled, but apples lose a ton of mass while baking. Top generously with the streusel topping. Bake in the center of the oven for 15 minutes. Lower the oven temperature to 350°F and bake for 35 to 45 minutes more, rotating the pie after 16 minutes, until the streusel is golden brown and the filling has large, thick bubbles.

4. Let the pie cool completely before eating. The pie can be kept, loosely tented with foil, at room temperature for up to 3 days.

Apple-Streusel Pie

Makes one 9-inch single-crust pie

Streusel Topping

2 cups pecans

⅔ cup granulated sugar

⅔ cup all-purpose flour

1 teaspoon kosher salt

Grated zest of ½ orange

½ cup unsalted butter, melted

Filling

½ cup granulated sugar

½ cup firmly packed light brown sugar

2 tablespoons all-purpose flour

1 teaspoon ground cinnamon

¼ teaspoon ground ginger

¼ teaspoon ground nutmeg

⅛ teaspoon ground cardamom

8 cups peeled, cored, and sliced apples (6 to 8 apples, preferably a mix of Granny Smith and Honeycrisp)

1 tablespoon fresh lemon juice

1 tablespoon honey

1 recipe Single-Crust Pie Dough (page 308), parbaked

Double-Crust Apple Pie

Make one 9-inch double-crust pie

½ cup granulated sugar

½ cup firmly packed
light brown sugar

2 tablespoons all-purpose flour

1 teaspoon ground cinnamon

¼ teaspoon ground ginger

¼ teaspoon ground nutmeg

⅛ teaspoon ground cardamom

8 cups peeled, cored, and
sliced apples (6 to 8 apples,
preferably a mix of Granny
Smith and Honeycrisp)

½ cup huckleberries,
cranberries, blueberries,
elderberries, mulberries,
dewberries, or mayhaws

1 tablespoon fresh lemon juice

1 tablespoon honey

1 recipe Double-Crust Pie Dough
(page 310)

Egg Wash

1 egg

1 teaspoon milk

¼ teaspoon kosher salt

Raw sugar for sprinkling
(optional)

Growing up, we would take a trip to North Carolina every October for a family reunion. My mom would refuse to leave until we'd visited multiple farms, as well as the farmers' market, and picked out the perfect apples. She bought them ALL. That meant that over the following days and weeks, our house was filled with the smells of warm spices and baked goods. We would bake my grandmother's apple cake (page 235) and make apple bread, apple muffins, applesauce, apple pie, apple butter, and any other thing that might be slightly delicious with apple in it. It took me longer than I'd like to admit to really appreciate a good slice of pie (ironic that I'm now writing this, eh?), but a double-crust apple pie has always, *always* had a special place in my heart. The combination of apples and huckleberries (a nod to the places my mom lived growing up in an Air Force family) and the play of textures, flavors, and tartness always keeps me interested in what the next bite will bring. Huckleberries are dear to me 'cause my mom used them all the time when baking for our family, but you could substitute other berries based on availability.

1. Preheat the oven to 425°F. In a medium bowl, combine the granulated sugar and brown sugar with the flour, cinnamon, ginger, nutmeg, and cardamom and set aside. In a large bowl, toss the apples and huckleberries with the lemon juice and honey. Add the dry ingredients and toss to combine.

2. Fill the prepared pie shell with the fruit mixture; this will feel overfilled, but apples lose a ton of mass while baking. Brush the overhanging pie dough of the bottom crust with a thin layer of the egg wash.

3. Quickly drape the dough for the top crust over the filling. Press the bottom and top crusts together to seal, then fold the edge of the crust and tuck it under itself so it rests on the lip of the pie pan. Using your fingers, pinch the top of the fold evenly all the way around the pie to seal. Trim any overhanging dough, then crimp the dough decoratively (see page 177). Make a few cuts in the top crust to allow venting. Be as creative and artistic (or not at all) as you wish. Brush the entire surface of the pie with the egg wash and sprinkle with the raw sugar, if using. Pop the pie into the freezer and let it sit for 20 to 30 minutes.

4. Line a rimmed baking sheet with parchment paper or foil. Place the pie on the baking sheet and bake in the center of the oven for 15 minutes. Decrease the oven temperature to 350°F and bake for 35 to 45 minutes, rotating the pie after 16 minutes, until the crust is golden brown and the filling is bubbling thick and slow.

5. Let the pie cool. Serve warm, at room temperature, or cold—for breakfast, lunch, dinner, tea, with ice cream, with cheese . . . however you prefer to pie! The pie can be kept at room temperature for 3 to 5 days.

Pumpkin Pie with Roasted White Chocolate Cream

Make one 9-inch pie

Roasted White Chocolate Cream

8 ounces white chocolate
(preferably Valrhona),
finely chopped

1 cup chilled heavy cream

¼ teaspoon unflavored
powdered gelatin

½ cup whole milk

Pinch of kosher salt

Filling

1 (15-ounce) can pure
pumpkin puree

3 eggs, at room temperature

¾ cup firmly packed
light brown sugar

½ teaspoon kosher salt

½ teaspoon ground cinnamon,
plus more for dusting

1 teaspoon ground ginger

¼ teaspoon ground cloves

¼ teaspoon ground nutmeg

1½ cups heavy cream

1 recipe Single-Crust Pie Dough
(page 308), parbaked

I legit despise pumpkin pie. I tried it every Thanksgiving as a kid, but it never worked out. The overuse of too many warm spices in baking when I was growing up made me averse to things like cinnamon and cloves. As an adult, I made it my mission to make a pumpkin pie I enjoy eating . . . by covering it in something I really like: white chocolate cream. I can almost eat a full slice of this pie.

1. Make the white chocolate cream. Preheat the oven to 275°F. Line a baking sheet with parchment paper or a silicone liner. Spread the chocolate evenly on the prepared baking sheet and place in the oven. Once the chocolate melts for a few minutes, remove the baking sheet from the oven and stir the chocolate using a clean, dry rubber spatula. Continue to cook the chocolate, stirring every 5 minutes, until the chocolate is golden brown, about 20 minutes total. (Bear in mind that the chocolate will go through a phase of looking lumpy and will lose its melty quality. I assure you, it's just a phase, so keep going.) This step can be done days in advance; the roasted chocolate will keep in a clean bowl, covered, at room temperature.

2. In a small bowl, combine 1½ teaspoons of the cream with the gelatin. Let sit for about 5 minutes until the gelatin softens. If the chocolate is not mostly melted, place it in a clean, dry heatproof bowl over a pot of simmering water to melt, stirring often with a spatula (it's okay if it is a little bit chunky or pasty—the hot milk and blending will do the rest of the work). In a heavy-bottomed saucepot over medium-high heat, bring the milk and salt to a scald (you will see bubbles around the perimeter of the liquid and a wisp of steam from the surface). Stir in the gelatin mixture, then remove from the heat. In two portions, add the milk mixture to the melted white chocolate, stirring well with a spatula after each addition. The chocolate will take on that lumpy, seized quality again, but keep stirring; it'll smooth out. Once all the milk has been added to the chocolate, blend with an immersion blender (or use a food processor) for 45 seconds to 1 minute, until smooth. Then, while blending, slowly pour in the remaining chilled cream until fully incorporated. Refrigerate overnight.

3. Make the filling. Preheat the oven to 375°F. In a large bowl, whisk together the pumpkin, eggs, brown sugar, salt, cinnamon, ginger, cloves, and nutmeg until incorporated. Stir in the cream until well combined.

4. Pour the filling into the prepared piecrust and bake for about 1 hour, rotating the pie after 30 minutes, until the center is set.

5. Place the pie on a wire rack to cool completely. Top the pie with the cream in any way you see fit—I pile it in the center—and dust with cinnamon. Cut and serve! The pie can be loosely tented with foil and refrigerated for up to 4 days; bring to room temperature to serve.

What's Mine Is Yours

If you want to get fancy, shave
extra white chocolate over the
pie before serving it.

This is one good lookin' pie. Once it's baked and cooled, you can top it in a variety of ways: pile the marshmallow topping in the center, using a piping bag and decorating tip to decorate, or just place a dollop on each slice. The marshmallow Fluff–like consistency and stickiness make it difficult to get intricate decorating with pastry tips, but you could just pipe a mound on top of the pie and use an offset spatula to create spikes. I also like to use a plain tube tip to pipe nice even lines all across the pie. Once you're satisfied with the marshmallow coverage, use a blowtorch to toast that fluff right up. You could also place it under a broiler, but that's far less fun and controllable.

1. Make the crust. Preheat the oven to 350°F. Wrap the entire outside of a 9-inch springform pan tightly in two layers of foil, all the way to the top. In a medium bowl, combine the gingersnaps and cayenne. Stir in the melted butter until evenly incorporated. Press the mixture into the bottom of the prepared pan and up the sides as far as you are able. Bake the crust for 10 minutes, or until golden and aromatic. Remove from the oven and set aside on a wire rack. Keep the oven on.

2. Make the filling. Using a fork, poke holes in the sweet potatoes and roast on a baking sheet for about 45 minutes, or until a bubbly liquid begins to leak out of the skins. Remove from the oven and cool for 5 minutes. Carefully peel the potatoes and pass the flesh through a potato ricer into a medium bowl. Alternatively, in the bowl of a stand mixer fitted with the paddle attachment or in a large bowl using a handheld mixer, beat the flesh to smooth it into a puree. Set aside to cool.

3. In a medium bowl, whisk together the condensed milk, whole milk, pineapple juice, whole eggs, and egg yolk. Stir this mixture into the sweet potato puree until smooth. Whisk in the sugar and salt, followed by the butter. Scrape the filling directly into the crust and bake in the center of the oven for 10 minutes. Decrease the oven temperature to 300°F and bake for 50 to 60 minutes longer, rotating the pie after 25 minutes, until the pie is just set in the middle. Let the pie cool completely.

4. Make the topping. In a heavy-bottomed saucepot, combine the sugar, honey, and water. Attach a candy thermometer to the rim of the pot and bring the mixture to a simmer over high heat. While the sugar is cooking, in the bowl of a stand mixer fitted with the whisk attachment or in a large bowl using a handheld mixer, whip the egg whites on medium-high speed until foamy. Reduce the speed to moderately low and mix in the cream of tartar. When the sugar syrup reaches 230°F on the thermometer, adjust the mixer to high speed. When the sugar syrup reaches 240°F, remove the

continued

Sweet Potato and Toasted Honey Marshmallow Pie

Makes one 9-inch pie

Crust
2 cups finely ground gingersnap cookies (approximately thirty-five 2-inch cookies)
¼ teaspoon cayenne pepper
¼ cup plus 2 tablespoons unsalted butter, melted

Filling
3 sweet potatoes
½ cup sweetened condensed milk
½ cup whole milk
½ cup pineapple juice
2 eggs, at room temperature
1 egg yolk
½ cup granulated sugar
½ teaspoon kosher salt
¼ cup unsalted butter, melted

Honey Marshmallow Topping
1 cup granulated sugar
¼ cup honey
¼ cup water
¼ cup egg whites, at room temperature
½ teaspoon cream of tartar

continued

Sweet Potato and Toasted Honey Marshmallow Pie

pan from the heat, turn the mixer to moderate speed, and very carefully pour the sugar syrup into the egg white mixture, pouring it down the inside of the bowl; do not hit the whisk, as it will send molten sugar flying through the air. Once the sugar syrup is fully incorporated, increase the mixer speed to high and whip until the mixture is cool, about 10 minutes. Transfer the marshmallow topping to a pastry bag, if you have one, or leave it in the bowl. You can make the marshmallow up to 1 day ahead and keep it in an airtight container in the refrigerator.

5. Preheat the broiler. Top the cooled pie with the marshmallow topping and brown it under the broiler to your heart's content. Alternately, use a blowtorch to brown the top before serving. The pie can be loosely tented with foil and refrigerated for up to 3 days. You might want to blast the marshmallow with a torch to refresh it a bit before serving.

These days, I find coconut cream pie a more accessible staple of the American South's baking repertoire than the coconut layer cake. It has become widely available at Southern bakeries and restaurants throughout the region and beyond. If you're serving this pie a few slices at a time over a few days, I highly recommend you hold off on placing the toasted coconut on top until you serve, so it keeps its crunchy, crispy texture.

1. Make the filling. In a heavy-bottomed saucepot, whisk together the cream and milk over medium-high heat. Meanwhile, in a medium bowl, whisk together the sugar, cornstarch, flour, and salt. Whisk in the egg yolks. Once the cream mixture comes to a scald (you will see bubbles around the perimeter of the liquid and a wisp of steam from the surface), whisk about 1 cup of it into the yolk mixture, whisking constantly to prevent the eggs from cooking. Pour the mixture in the bowl into the saucepot and place the pot over medium-high heat. Bring to a boil, whisking constantly, and cook for 1 minute.

2. Remove the saucepot from the heat and stir in the butter, coconut, and vanilla. Scrape the mixture into a heatproof bowl and place a piece of plastic wrap directly on the surface (to prevent a skin from forming on the surface as it cools), then poke a few holes in the plastic to allow the steam to escape. Transfer to the refrigerator to cool.

3. Make the topping. Place the cream in the bowl of a stand mixer fitted with the whisk attachment and whip the cream on high speed until it becomes frothy. Stream in the sugar, followed by the vanilla. Continue whipping until soft peaks form.

4. Spread the topping all the way to the edges of the crust to seal in the filling. Garnish with the toasted coconut, if serving immediately, reserving any unused coconut for serving leftovers. This pie can be loosely tented with foil and refrigerated for up to 3 days (top with the reserved coconut just before serving).

Coconut Cream Pie

Makes one 9-inch single-crust pie

Filling
1 cup heavy cream
1 cup whole milk
½ cup granulated sugar
3 tablespoons cornstarch
1 tablespoon all-purpose flour
½ teaspoon kosher salt
5 egg yolks
¼ cup unsalted butter, at room temperature
1¼ cups sweetened shredded coconut
1 tablespoon vanilla extract
1 recipe Single-Crust Pie Dough (page 308)

Topping
2 cups heavy cream
¼ cup granulated sugar
1 teaspoon vanilla extract
1 cup sweetened coconut flakes, toasted (see page 15)

This recipe is a great way to mix up the classic coconut cream pie. I can remember clearly the first time I experienced both cajeta (caramelized goat's milk) and perfectly prepared flan; both tiny yet impactful revelations in my food experiences. I've always wanted a way to showcase and share my love for flan in a more portable and sharable way than just baking a flan in a ramekin. So, I did the true Southern thing and put it in a crust, of course.

1. Preheat the oven to 325°F. Spread ½ cup of the cajeta over the bottom of the prepared crust.

2. In a large bowl, whisk together the condensed milk, coconut milk, evaporated milk, eggs, vanilla paste, and salt. Pour the mixture directly into the crust. Bake in the center of the oven for 80 to 90 minutes, rotating the pie after 40 minutes, until the custard is mostly set but still jiggles ever so slightly in the center.

3. Let the pie cool for 45 minutes. Refrigerate for 2 hours to cool completely.

4. Drizzle the top of the pie with the remaining ½ cup cajeta and sprinkle with the toasted coconut just before serving, reserving any unused coconut for serving leftovers. This pie can be loosely tented with foil and refrigerated for up to 3 days (top with the reserved coconut just before serving).

Baked Coconut Flan

If for some reason you bought this book and don't actually like pie, I see you. Feel free to bake this filling in ramekins or even in a Bundt pan that you've lightly coated with cooking spray and then cajeta. If you use a 9-cup Bundt pan, double the recipe. Place the ramekins or Bundt pan in a roasting pan and add hot water to the roasting pan to come three-quarters of the way up the outside of your ramekins or Bundt pan. Bake for 40 minutes if using ramekins or 55 minutes in a Bundt, until the center is mostly set but still jiggles a bit when you shake the pan.

Baked Coconut Flan Pie

Makes one 9-inch pie

1 cup Cajeta (page 302) or Dulce de Leche (see page 139; this will be a little sweeter)

1 recipe Single-Crust Pie Dough (page 308), parbaked

2½ cups plus 2 tablespoons sweetened condensed milk

¾ cup plus 2 tablespoons sweetened coconut milk

¾ cup evaporated milk

3 eggs, at room temperature

1 teaspoon vanilla bean paste

½ teaspoon kosher salt

½ cup sweetened coconut flakes, lightly toasted (see page 15)

Lemon Meringue Pie

Makes one 9-inch pie

7 eggs, at room temperature, separated

1¾ cups granulated sugar

¼ cup cornstarch

1½ tablespoons all-purpose flour

¾ teaspoon kosher salt

Finely grated zest and juice of 6 lemons (about ¾ cup juice)

1½ cups water

3 tablespoons unsalted butter

1 recipe Single-Crust Pie Dough (page 308)

¼ teaspoon cream of tartar

I dislike citrus desserts that don't taste like citrus. I often find that lemon desserts, in particular, are loaded with cream and sugar that mellow out the tart brightness of the lemon flavor. Lemon is delicious and should be celebrated! This pie is best made with fresh lemons and lemon juice, and if you're lucky enough to live in an area where Meyer lemons grow, be sure to give those a try in this recipe as well.

1. Place the egg yolks in a medium bowl and beat with a whisk; set aside. In a heavy-bottomed saucepot set over medium heat, whisk 1 cup of the sugar with the cornstarch, flour, and salt. Stir in the lemon zest, lemon juice, and water. Cook, whisking the entire time, until the mixture thickens and starts to bubble, 4 to 6 minutes. Remove from the heat and whisk in the butter.

2. Very gradually whisk about ¾ cup of the hot liquid into the egg yolks, whisking constantly to prevent the eggs from cooking. Pour the mixture in the bowl into the saucepot and place over medium heat, again whisking constantly, until the mixture comes to a boil. Cook until it is thick enough that your whisk leaves trails in the mixture as you're stirring, 3 to 5 minutes. Remove from the heat and immediately pour into the prepared pie shell.

3. Place a piece of plastic wrap directly on top of the custard (to prevent a skin from forming on the surface as it cools), then poke a few holes in the plastic to allow the steam to escape. Cool completely in the refrigerator before topping with the meringue, at least 90 minutes.

4. Preheat the oven to 350°F. In the bowl of a stand mixer fitted with the whisk attachment or in a large bowl using a handheld mixer, whip the egg whites until foamy, about 1 minute. On medium speed, slowly stream in the remaining ¾ cup sugar and the cream of tartar. Increase the speed to high and whip until stiff peaks form (the whites should hold their points when you pull the whisk out of the meringue), about 3 minutes. Using a rubber or offset spatula, immediately spread the meringue all the way to the edges of the crust to seal in the custard.

5. Bake the pie for 12 to 15 minutes, until the meringue is a nice toasty golden brown. Serve right away or let cool completely, cover, and store in the refrigerator for up to 3 days.

This is my great-aunt Jean's recipe. Her name, as it turns out, is Wilma Jean—a fact I didn't know until after I had opened Willa Jean, and my great-aunt joked with me that I'd spelled her name incorrectly. Jean is from Hendersonville, North Carolina, and she grew up in Appalachia during the Great Depression. During that time, graham crackers were too costly to buy for piecrust, so she learned to make piecrust with saltine crackers. I love this piecrust, but I know it's not fancy. It was Chef Bill Smith of Crook's Corner in North Carolina who taught me that it's totally okay to be myself and do what I do (who would've thought?). He was the one who made me appreciate how damn good this crust is. Bill also serves a lemon saltine pie, and eating his food encouraged me to embrace my highbrow *and* lowbrow food memories. He did so unknowingly, as I just sat at the bar counter one night, my head exploding with the reminder that food just needs to be good. Period.

1. In a small bowl, sprinkle the gelatin over the ice water and let stand until softened, about 5 minutes. In a medium bowl, using a whisk, beat the egg yolks until thick and lemon-colored, about 1 minute. Transfer to a medium saucepot and add 1 cup of the sugar along with the lemon zest, lemon juice, and salt; stir until smooth. Cook over low heat, stirring constantly with a whisk, until thickened (be careful not to turn this into scrambled eggs), about 5 minutes. Remove from the heat and stir in the gelatin mixture until dissolved. Let cool for 1 hour, then transfer to a large bowl.

2. In a clean bowl, using a whisk or a handheld mixer on medium speed, beat the egg whites until foamy; gradually beat in the remaining ½ cup sugar, 1 tablespoon at a time. Increase the speed to high and beat until soft peaks form, about 3 minutes. Whisk about 1 cup of the beaten egg whites into the lemon mixture, then use a spatula to fold in the remaining egg whites and half the whipped cream, each in two portions; do not wait for the egg whites and cream to be fully incorporated before adding the rest, or the eggs might deflate. Spoon the filling into the prepared crust. Refrigerate until set, about 1 hour. Garnish with the remaining whipped cream and the lemon slices, if using. The pie can be loosely tented with foil and stored in the refrigerator for up to 3 days.

Lemon Meringue Pie with Graham Cracker Crust

If saltines aren't your thing, you can make this pie using my homemade Graham Cracker Crust (page 313). You can also buy premade graham cracker crusts; just note that this recipe makes enough filling for two store-bought graham cracker crusts (they run smaller and shallower than my from-scratch crust).

Aunt Jean's Lemon Chiffon Pie

Makes one 9-inch pie

1 (¼-ounce) envelope unflavored powdered gelatin

¼ cup ice cold water

4 eggs, separated, at room temperature

1½ cups granulated sugar

1½ teaspoons finely grated lemon zest

½ cup fresh lemon juice

¾ teaspoon kosher salt

1 cup heavy cream, whipped in two batches, ½ cup at a time

1 recipe Saltine Piecrust (page 313)

Lemon slices for serving (optional)

Key Lime Pie with Whipped White Chocolate Cream

Makes one 9-inch pie

Filling

3 (14-ounce) cans sweetened condensed milk

Finely grated zest of 2 limes

1 cup key lime juice

1 egg, at room temperature

2 egg yolks, at room temperature

1 recipe Graham Cracker Crust (page 313)

Whipped White Chocolate Cream

7 ounces white chocolate (preferably Valrhona), chopped

2 teaspoons unflavored powdered gelatin

1 tablespoon cold water

½ cup heavy cream

2 teaspoons vanilla bean paste

I love the tart sweetness of this pie, and I really love to highlight the richness by adding white chocolate to the whipped topping. The addition of the white chocolate also acts as a stabilizer for the cream, allowing it to stay whipped longer. The white chocolate cream is a double delicious recipe that I recommend keeping around and whipping up not only for this recipe but for any other desserts you top with whipped cream.

1. Make the filling. Preheat the oven to 350°F. In a medium bowl, whisk together the condensed milk, lime zest, key lime juice, whole egg, and egg yolks until smooth. Pour the batter into the prepared crust and bake for 35 to 45 minutes, rotating the pie after 20 minutes, until the filling is set and the center doesn't jiggle when you move the pan. Let the pie cool completely.

2. Make the white chocolate cream. Put the chocolate in a heatproof medium bowl and fill a large bowl with ice water. In a small bowl, combine the gelatin and water and let stand until the gelatin has softened, about 5 minutes. In a small saucepot, bring the cream and vanilla paste to a simmer over medium heat, then whisk in the gelatin mixture. Remove from the heat. Strain the mixture through a fine-mesh sieve into the chocolate, whisking continuously as the chocolate melts. Continue to whisk until fully combined and uniform, then transfer the bowl to the ice bath.

3. Using a handheld mixer, whip the white chocolate cream on high speed until stiff peaks form. Before adding the cream to the pie, make sure there's not a lot of condensation on top of the pie. If there is, very lightly dab it with a kitchen towel. Dollop, spread, pipe, or spike the white chocolate cream on top of the pie and serve. This pie can be stored in an airtight container or covered well with foil or plastic wrap in the refrigerator for up to 4 days.

To me, buttermilk pie is in the same category as chess pie or vinegar pie. They're all pies that really showcase the resourcefulness of the Southern baker. They're not precious or fussy, just simple and delicious, and they use what is readily available. The key to success is as basic as using the best buttermilk you can find.

1. Preheat the oven to 350°F. In the bowl of a stand mixer fitted with the paddle attachment or in a large bowl using a handheld mixer, beat the eggs and sugar on medium-high speed until frothy, about 3 minutes. Beat in the butter and flour until smooth. Decrease the speed to low and slowly pour in the buttermilk, vanilla, lemon zest, and lemon juice, beating until just incorporated. Once you add the buttermilk, the filling may look slightly separated, but not to worry; it'll bake great. Pour the filling directly into the prepared pie shell.

2. Place the pie shell on a rimmed baking sheet and bake in the center of the oven for 45 to 60 minutes, rotating the pie after 30 minutes, until the top of the pie is set and the center is just firm to the touch (light touch; don't go poking it).

3. Transfer to a wire rack and cool completely before serving. This pie can be stored in an airtight container or well wrapped in plastic wrap in the refrigerator for up to 3 days.

Buttermilk Pie

Makes one 9-inch pie

3 eggs, at room temperature

1¼ cups granulated sugar

½ cup unsalted butter, at room temperature

¼ cup all-purpose flour

1¼ cups buttermilk

1 teaspoon vanilla extract

Grated zest of 1 lemon

1 tablespoon fresh lemon juice

1 recipe Single-Crust Pie Dough (page 308), prepared through step 2

Ice Box Pie

Makes one 9-inch pie

8 ounces cream cheese, at room temperature

1 (14-ounce) can sweetened condensed milk

2 teaspoons finely grated lemon or lime zest

⅓ cup fresh lemon juice or lime juice

¼ teaspoon kosher salt

1 recipe Graham Cracker Crust (page 313)

This is another one of those pies I consider too easy. As a result, I've tried countless times to make it more complicated, but I've never created a version that is just as simple and delicious as this recipe. By all means, take any liberties you see fit, such as subbing key limes, yuzu, or any other citrus. Just let me know what you come up with.

1. In the bowl of a stand mixer fitted with the paddle attachment or in a large bowl using a handheld mixer, beat the cream cheese on medium-high speed until light, smooth, and fluffy, 4 to 5 minutes. Stop the mixer and scrape down the bottom and sides of the bowl with a rubber spatula a couple of times. With the mixer on medium-low speed, add the condensed milk, lemon or lime juice and zest, and salt. Increase the speed to medium-high speed and mix until smooth.

2. Scrape the filling into the prepared crust, smooth the top with a rubber or offset spatula, and refrigerate until completely set before serving, 4 to 5 hours. This icebox pie can be kept in the refrigerator for up to 4 days.

Chess pie has multiple origin stories, oral histories, and influences. Despite the differences in these stories, the one thing that rings true in all of them is that this pie comes from a place of scarcity, preservation, and ingenuity. Lisa Donovan, one of the greatest pastry chefs and writers of our time, did some digging and learned that the name "chess pie" may actually have originated from the use of chestnut flour, which would've been widely available in the United States before the American chestnut tree contracted a blight and every last one was wiped out. Over the years, and throughout communities, this pie evolved with the availability, or lack thereof, of resources and ingredients, along with the influence of the cultures of the actual pie makers. It is singular, to me, in its pure expression of pastry in the American South: the richness, sweetness, simplicity, ease, and the nuances of baking in a region with so many histories.

Chess Pie

Makes one 9-inch single-crust pie

2 eggs, at room temperature

6 egg yolks, at room temperature

1 cup granulated sugar

1 cup heavy cream

1 cup evaporated milk

⅓ cup fine cornmeal

1 tablespoon finely grated lemon zest

¼ cup cold unsalted butter, cut into 3 pieces

2 teaspoons kosher salt

2 teaspoons fresh lemon juice

1 recipe Single-Crust Pie Dough (page 308), parbaked

1. Preheat the oven to 350°F. In a large bowl, whisk together the eggs, egg yolks and ½ cup of the sugar.

2. In a heavy-bottomed saucepot set over medium-high heat, combine the cream, evaporated milk, cornmeal, lemon zest, and the remaining ½ cup sugar. While whisking constantly, bring the mixture to a full boil. Continue cooking, whisking vigorously, until the mixture is thick and bubbling, 4 to 5 minutes. Remove from the heat and whisk in the butter, salt, and lemon juice. While whisking constantly, carefully pour a small amount of the hot cornmeal mixture into the eggs; keep whisking to prevent the eggs from cooking. Pour the egg mixture into the cornmeal mixture and whisk well.

3. Pour the custard into the prepared pie shell and bake in the center of the oven for 45 to 60 minutes, rotating the pie after 30 minutes, until the center of the pie is just set.

4. Transfer the pie to a wire rack to cool completely before serving. The pie can be stored loosely tented with foil at room temperature for up to 3 days.

Chess Pie with Fruit Topping

You may top this pie with fruit compote (any kind you like), fresh fruit, lightly whipped cream, or brûléed citrus.

Chocolate Chess Pie with Whipped Chocolate–Mint Ganache

Makes one 9-inch pie

Whipped Mint Ganache

3½ cups heavy cream

2 tablespoons light corn syrup

15 mint leaves

6½ ounces dark chocolate (preferably Valrhona 70% cacao), chopped

3¼ ounces milk chocolate (preferably Valrhona), chopped

1 cup heavy cream

1 cup evaporated milk

1 cup granulated sugar

⅓ cup coarse cornmeal

¼ cup unsalted butter, chilled

6 eggs, at room temperature

6 egg yolks, at room temperature

8 ounces dark chocolate (preferably Valrhona 70% cacao), finely chopped

1½ teaspoons kosher salt

1 recipe Single-Crust Pie Dough (page 308), parbaked

Unsweetened cocoa powder, sifted, for dusting

I've made this humble pie slightly more involved, creating a rich, chocolatey custard filling using dark chocolate instead of cocoa powder. Finishing with sweet whipped cream (see page 303) is always an option, but top this pie with whipped chocolate ganache to add another dimension of chocolate deliciousness and texture. Make the topping a day ahead, so it has time to set up before you whip it.

1. Make the ganache. In a medium saucepot, combine 1¼ cups of the heavy cream with the corn syrup and mint and bring to a boil. Cover and remove from the heat. Let steep for 15 minutes.

2. In a large stainless-steel bowl set over a pan of barely simmering water, melt the dark chocolate and milk chocolate. While the chocolate is melting, strain the cream mixture through a fine-mesh sieve into a bowl and discard the mint. Return the cream to the saucepot and bring to a bare simmer. Remove the chocolate from the heat and, using a large rubber spatula, stir about one-quarter of the warm cream into the chocolate; it will look kind of broken but keep stirring to emulsify. Add the remaining warm cream in three portions, stirring well after each addition. The sauce will start to thicken and get glossy. Whisk in the remaining 2¼ cups heavy cream, cover, and refrigerate overnight.

3. Preheat the oven to 425°F. In a medium saucepot, bring the cream, evaporated milk, ½ cup of the sugar, and the cornmeal to a boil over moderately high heat, whisking constantly. Reduce the heat to low and simmer, whisking, until the mixture thickens and starts to get bubbly, about 5 minutes. Whisk in the butter until combined.

4. Meanwhile, in a large bowl, whisk together the whole eggs, egg yolks, and the remaining ½ cup sugar until combined. Working quickly and carefully, whisk the hot cornmeal mixture into the egg mixture, being sure to whisk vigorously to prevent the eggs from cooking. Whisk in the chocolate and then add the salt.

5. Pour the filling into the prepared piecrust and bake for 8 minutes, then decrease the oven temperature to 325°F and bake for about 45 minutes longer, rotating the pie after 20 minutes, until the filling is firm and glossy. The pie has a habit of cracking on the surface, but don't worry. A bit of personality is beautiful and we're putting whipped ganache all over the top anyway. Transfer the pie to a wire rack to cool for at least 4 hours. At this point, you can cover the pie and refrigerate overnight, if desired.

6. Transfer the chilled ganache to the bowl of a stand mixer fitted with the whisk attachment or use a handheld mixer. Beat on medium speed for about 10 seconds, then increase the speed to high and beat until barely stiff, about 45 seconds longer. Transfer to a piping bag or a resealable plastic bag with one corner snipped off and pipe dollops of the ganache all over the pie. Alternatively, you can spread the ganache on the top of the pie. Dust with the cocoa and serve. The pie can be loosely tented with foil and refrigerated for up to 4 days.

What's Mine Is Yours

A little rule of thumb: don't let granulated sugar sit on top of your egg yolks or it'll start cooking the eggs.

Kentucky Derby pie is something I discovered in high school. There was a small Greek restaurant in the town where I grew up that, for some reason, had Kentucky Derby pie on its menu. I was absolutely hooked the first time I tried it, and it has been one of my favorites ever since. Traditionally, this pie is made with walnuts because Kentucky is covered with walnut trees. We're not so lucky down here in Louisiana when it comes to walnuts, but we do grow some really beautiful pecans. And, luckily enough, pecans taste pretty perfect with bourbon, too.

Kentucky-ish Derby Pie

Makes one 9-inch single-crust pie

1 cup unsalted butter, melted and cooled

¾ cup firmly packed light brown sugar

¼ cup granulated sugar

½ teaspoon kosher salt

2 eggs, at room temperature

¼ cup bourbon

½ teaspoon vanilla bean paste

½ cup all-purpose flour

½ cup pecans (or walnuts, if you're a purist)

6 ounces Valrhona Caramélia chocolate, chopped

1 recipe Single-Crust Pie Dough (page 308), parbaked

Ice cream for serving (optional)

1. Preheat the oven to 350°F. In the bowl of a stand mixer fitted with the paddle attachment or in a large bowl using a handheld mixer, combine the butter, brown sugar, granulated sugar, and salt and mix on medium speed until well mixed. Add the eggs, one at a time, mixing well after each addition, followed by the bourbon and vanilla paste. Mix in the flour, pecans, and chocolate until just combined.

2. Pour the mixture directly into the prepared pie shell. Bake for about 45 minutes, rotating the pie after 25 minutes, until the surface of the pie is completely set in the center and the crust is golden brown.

3. Let the pie cool completely before cutting. I do enjoy this pie served warm with a scoop of ice cream and a sip or two of that same bourbon. The pie can be stored at room temperature or in the refrigerator for about 4 days—if it lasts that long.

What's Mine Is Yours

Any chocolate chips or chunks of chocolate can be substituted for the Caramélia. Using a dark chocolate will result in a deeper and more bitter flavor but will be delicious. Just use quality chocolate.

Bourbon-Chocolate Pecan Pie

Makes one 9-inch single-crust pie

2 cups pecan halves

4½ ounces dark chocolate (preferably Valrhona 64% cacao), chopped

1 recipe Single-Crust Pie Dough (page 308), parbaked

3 eggs, at room temperature

1 cup granulated sugar

1 cup cane syrup

Pinch of kosher salt

½ cup unsalted butter, melted

2 tablespoons bourbon

You will want to let this pie chill before you eat it so that it sets up and slices well. I'm a big fan of warming it, one slice at a time, and serving it with vanilla ice cream. If you ever come visit me in New Orleans, we can go to Camellia Grill and watch them slather their pecan pie with deliciously weird fake butter and then griddle it to perfection.

1. Preheat the oven to 350°F. In a medium bowl, toss together the pecans and chocolate and spread in the prepared pie shell.

2. In a large bowl, whisk the eggs with the sugar, cane syrup, and salt until fully combined. Stir in the butter and bourbon. Pour the mixture over the chocolate and pecans in the pie shell, filling it as full as you're able without overflowing the crust.

3. Place the pie on a baking sheet and bake in the center of the oven for 45 to 60 minutes, rotating the pie after 30 minutes, until the center is just set. Remove from the oven and allow to cool completely on a wire rack before serving. The pie can be stored at room temperature for up to 5 days.

Bourbon and Nut Pie

I don't know why you would want to, but you can leave the chocolate out of this pie and replace it with an additional ¾ cup of other nuts.

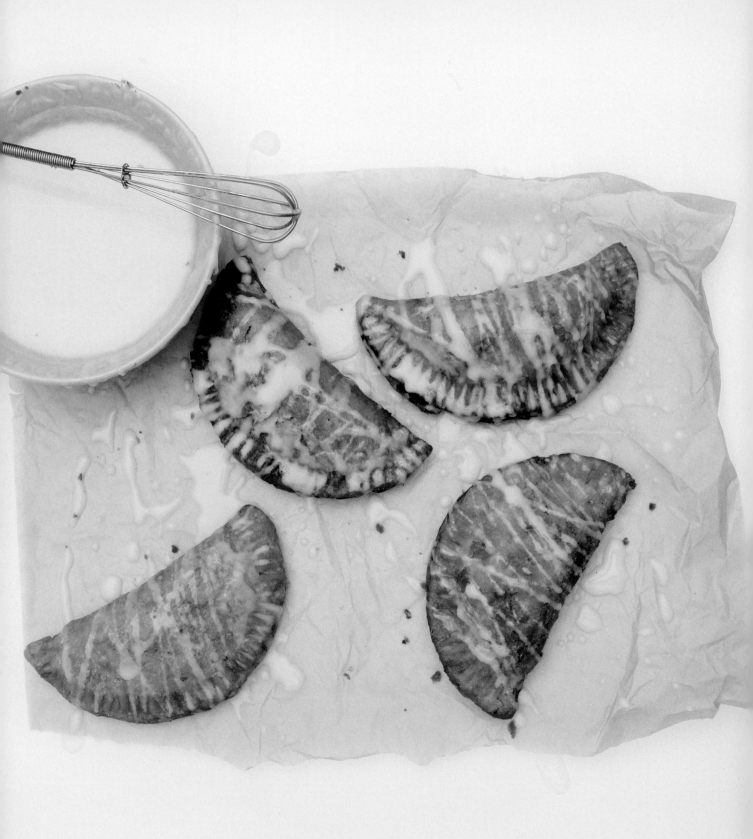

How to Hand Pie

Hand pies are a Southern staple, found at church gatherings, bake sales, family reunions, and just about everywhere else, honestly. New Orleans, as long as I've known her, has had Hubig's Pies in every store in the city. They were so plentiful and available that I took them for granted for my first ten years living here (rumors go so far as to say that if you were arrested in New Orleans, a Hubig's Pie was served at the Orleans Parish Prison). During my post-Katrina travels outside New Orleans, I fell in love with hand pies, or, as they are called in other parts of the world, pasties (in Scotland) or simply meat pies (in New Zealand). I found a small shop in the depths of the South Island of New Zealand (which was by far my favorite pie shop) where even the fruit pies were casually referred to as meat pies, despite their sweet fillings.

I love hand pies, meat pies, pasties, or whatever you want to call them, and generally whatever they're filled with. I will eat them in every town and country I can, and I've collected memories of eating hand pies all over the world. To this day, I still crave some of the ones I've tasted over the years.

When I returned to New Orleans in 2010, I used our restaurant staff's family meal as a place to learn how to make the things I had eaten during my years of traveling. My obsession with hand pies continued, but it took a solid year for me to dive into a Hubig's. Then one day, I witnessed a very heated debate on the best flavor of Hubig's among a group of cooks at the restaurant; it spilled over into the dining room staff and continued for hours. Coconut won out as not only the best flavor but also the most difficult to find (perhaps part of why it was the favorite?). Unable to participate in the debate in any meaningful way, I started my quest to procure every damn flavor of Hubig's Pies (full disclosure: I found only nine of ten flavors rumored to exist) and to learn, once and for all, why they are so legendary.

My experiment led me to love the chocolate, peach, and blueberry hand pies the most. Admittedly, it's not my favorite crust of all time, but nostalgia leaves room for that, right? The experience of eating one of those pies in this great city is worth more than the less-than-optimal crust. Unfortunately, the Hubig's facility suffered a devastating five-alarm fire in 2012, and the city has been without Hubig's Pies since. (The company has announced that they are rebuilding and will eventually reopen.)

Generally speaking, hand pies are deep-fried rather than baked. They're often coated in a sweet icing afterward; this preserves the pie as much as contributing to the overall flavor. There are a bunch of different ways to hand pie, but I find the simplest pleasure is sticking to a perfect pie dough, a simple seasonal filling, and a small drizzle of icing to top it off. You can adapt all the fruit pie filling recipes in this chapter to the hand pie approach.

Blueberry Hand Pies

Makes about 24 hand pies

Blueberry Filling

3½ cups fresh blueberries
(or frozen, if that's all you have)

½ cup granulated sugar

1 tablespoon all-purpose flour

1½ tablespoons cornstarch

1 teaspoon finely grated lemon zest

1 teaspoon fresh lemon juice

½ teaspoon kosher salt

All-purpose flour for dusting

1 recipe Double-Crust Pie Dough
(page 310), prepared through step 1

Egg Wash

1 egg

1 teaspoon water

Vegetable, peanut, or canola oil
for frying

Icing

1½ cups powdered sugar, sifted

¼ cup plus 1 tablespoon whole milk

½ teaspoon vanilla extract

¼ teaspoon kosher salt

We have such a generous and delicious blueberry season in the South, and every year I am stunned by how much I love blueberries. This is my favorite way to ring in the season after a day spent foraging the berries off wild bushes on the outskirts of the city. If you're short on time, or blueberries, you can always fill these hand pies with your favorite blueberry preserves.

1. Make the filling. In a heavy-bottomed saucepot set over medium-high heat, combine 2 cups of the blueberries with the sugar, flour, cornstarch, lemon zest, lemon juice, and salt and cook until the mixture bubbles and thickens like jam, about 10 minutes. Remove from the heat and stir in the remaining 1½ cups blueberries. Allow the filling to cool completely in the refrigerator before assembling the pies. The filling can be stored in an airtight container in the refrigerator for up to 3 days.

2. Line a baking sheet with parchment paper. On a lightly floured surface, using a lightly floured rolling pin, roll out each piece of dough to about ⅛ inch thick. Using a 4-inch round cookie cutter, cut out as many rounds as you're able; place the rounds on the prepared baking sheet and transfer to the refrigerator as you work. Gather and roll out the scraps and cut out as many additional rounds as possible, transferring those rounds to the refrigerator as well. After that second roll-out, the dough just gets tough and dry, so discard the remaining scraps (or you can drop them in the fryer when you're frying your pies and then toss them in cinnamon sugar).

3. In a small bowl, whisk together the egg and water. Work with only one or two dough rounds at a time. Using your hand, lightly stretch the middle of the round just slightly and fill with about 3 tablespoons of the filling. Brush one side of the round with egg wash and fold the dough over so that both sides meet evenly. Press lightly to seal. Using a fork dipped in flour, indent the edges of the pie to create an even seal all the way around.

4. Freeze the pies, stored in an airtight container or tightly wrapped in plastic wrap, for at least 30 minutes and up to 2 weeks before frying.

5. Line a baking sheet with paper towels. If you have a home fryer, heat the oil in it to 365°F. If you don't have a home fryer, fill a deep pot halfway with oil and attach a kitchen thermometer to the rim of the pot. Heat the oil to 365°F. Carefully place four frozen pies into the hot oil and cook for 3 to 4 minutes on each side, until golden brown. You don't want to fry more than four pies at a time, since you'll bring down the oil temperature too quickly and that will cause the pies to take longer to cook, giving the dough extra time to just soak in oil (not delicious). Carefully remove the pies from the hot oil and place on the prepared

continued

Blueberry Hand Pies

baking sheet to drain. Let the pies cool for 10 minutes. Repeat to fry the remaining pies. (Alternatively, you can bake the hand pies; see below.)

6. Make the icing. In a medium bowl, whisk together the powdered sugar, milk, vanilla, and salt until smooth.

7. If you like that thin, fully iced look, dip your hand pies in the icing while they're still on the warm side and let them set up on a wire rack. Alternatively, you can use the end of a whisk to drizzle the icing over the pies. Let the pies cool for at least 5 minutes and then serve warm or completely cooled. They're best eaten the day they're made, but they can be stored in an airtight container at room temperature and eaten the next day if you really, really want one for breakfast.

Baked Hand Pies

To bake rather than fry your hand pies, preheat the oven to 400°F and line a baking sheet with parchment paper or a silicone liner. Arrange the hand pies on the baking sheet and, using a paring knife, make a few vents in the sides of the pies to allow steam to escape. Bake for 25 to 30 minutes, rotating the baking sheet after 15 minutes, until the pies are golden brown on all sides. Remove from the oven and let cool for at least 15 minutes before icing and/or eating.

Apple Hand Pies

Makes about 24 hand pies

Apple Filling

3 tablespoons unsalted butter

¼ cup granulated sugar

¼ cup firmly packed
light brown sugar

½ teaspoon ground cinnamon

⅛ teaspoon ground ginger

⅛ teaspoon ground nutmeg

⅛ teaspoon ground cardamom

½ teaspoon kosher salt

3½ cups peeled, cored, and
diced apples (about 3, preferably
a mix of Honeycrisp, Crispin,
and/or Granny Smith)

2 teaspoons fresh lemon juice

1 teaspoon vanilla extract

2 teaspoons honey

All-purpose flour for dusting

1 recipe Double-Crust Pie Dough
(page 310), prepared through step 1

Egg Wash

1 egg

1 teaspoon water

Vegetable, peanut, or canola oil
for frying

Icing

1½ cups powdered sugar, sifted

¼ cup plus 1 tablespoon whole milk

½ teaspoon vanilla extract

¼ teaspoon kosher salt

Absolutely nothing on earth makes me feel cozier than an apple hand pie at the beginning of fall. The smell, the warmth of the pie in my hand, and even the aroma of the escaping steam after the first bite take me back to the mountains of Asheville, North Carolina, every single time.

1. Make the filling. In a large skillet, melt the butter over moderately high heat. Stir in the granulated sugar, brown sugar, cinnamon, ginger, nutmeg, cardamom, and salt and cook for 1½ to 2 minutes, until the sugar dissolves completely. Remove the skillet from the heat and add the apples, then return to the heat and cook, stirring continuously, until the apples are well coated and slightly translucent, about 1½ minutes. Stir in the lemon juice, vanilla, and honey and cook until the apples are just tender. Remove from the heat and cool completely before assembling the hand pies. You can make this filling up to 3 days ahead of time and store it in an airtight container in the refrigerator until ready to assemble.

2. On a lightly floured surface, using a lightly floured rolling pin, roll out each piece of dough to about ⅛ inch thick. Using a 4-inch round cookie cutter, cut out as many rounds as you're able; place the rounds on a baking sheet and transfer to the refrigerator as you work. Gather and roll out the scraps and cut out as many additional rounds as possible, transferring those rounds to the refrigerator as well. After that second roll-out, the dough just gets tough and dry, so discard the remaining scraps (or you can drop them in the fryer when you're frying your pies and then toss them in cinnamon sugar).

3. In a small bowl, whisk together the egg and water. Work with only one or two dough rounds at a time. Using your hand, lightly stretch the middle of the round just slightly and fill with about 3 tablespoons of the filling. Brush one side of the round with egg wash and fold the dough over so that both sides meet evenly. Press lightly to seal. Using a fork dipped in flour, indent the edges of the pie to create an even seal all the way around.

4. Freeze the pies, stored in an airtight container or tightly wrapped in plastic wrap, for at least 30 minutes and up to 2 weeks before frying.

5. Line a baking sheet with paper towels. If you have a home fryer, heat the oil in it to 365°F. If you don't have a home fryer, fill a deep pot halfway with oil and attach a kitchen thermometer to the rim of the pot. Heat the oil to 365°F. Carefully place four frozen pies into the hot oil and cook for 3 to 4 minutes on each side, until golden brown. You don't want to fry more than four pies at a time, since you'll bring down the oil temperature too quickly and that will cause the pies to take longer to cook, giving the dough extra time to just soak in oil (not delicious). Carefully remove the pies from the hot oil and place on the prepared baking sheet to drain. Let the pies cool for 10 minutes. Repeat to fry the remaining pies. (Alternatively, you can bake the hand pies; see page 213.)

6. Make the icing. In a medium bowl, whisk together the powdered sugar, milk, vanilla, and salt until smooth.

7. If you like that thin, fully iced look, dip your hand pies in the icing while they're still on the warm side and let them set up on a wire rack. Alternatively, you can use the end of a whisk to drizzle the icing over the pies. Let the pies cool for at least 5 minutes and then serve warm or completely cooled. They're best eaten the day they're made, but they can be stored overnight in an airtight container at room temperature and eaten the next day if you really, really want one for breakfast.

Strawberry-Rhubarb Hand Pies

Makes about 24 hand pies

All-purpose flour for dusting

1 recipe Double-Crust Pie Dough (page 310), prepared through step 1

Strawberry-Rhubarb Filling

2 cups fresh or frozen and thawed rhubarb, cut into ½-inch pieces

2 cups strawberries, hulled and halved

¼ cup kumquats, sliced and seeded

2 teaspoons fresh lemon juice

¾ teaspoon vanilla bean paste

½ cup granulated sugar

2 tablespoons cornstarch

Pinch of kosher salt

Egg Wash

1 egg

1 teaspoon water

Vegetable, peanut, or canola oil for frying

Icing

1½ cups powdered sugar, sifted

¼ cup plus 1 tablespoon whole milk

½ teaspoon vanilla extract

¼ teaspoon kosher salt

Make the filling for these hand pies right before you assemble them, or the ingredients will start weeping, and you'll lose all that delicious strawberry-rhubarb flavor.

1. On a lightly floured surface, using a lightly floured rolling pin, roll out each piece of dough to about ⅛ inch thick. Using a 4-inch round cutter, cut out as many rounds as you're able; place the rounds on a baking sheet and transfer to the refrigerator as you work. Gather and roll out the scraps and cut out as many additional rounds as possible, transferring those rounds to the refrigerator as well. After that second roll-out, the dough just gets tough and dry, so discard the remaining scraps (or you can drop them in the fryer when you're frying your pies and then toss them in cinnamon sugar).

2. Make the filling. In a medium bowl, toss together the rhubarb, strawberries, kumquats, lemon juice, vanilla paste, sugar, cornstarch, and salt.

3. In a small bowl, whisk together the egg and water. Work with only one or two dough rounds at a time. Using your hand, lightly stretch the middle of the round just slightly and fill with about 3 tablespoons of the filling. Brush one side of the round with egg wash and fold the dough over so that both sides meet evenly. Press lightly to seal. Using a fork dipped in flour, indent the edges of the pie to create an even seal all the way around.

4. Freeze the pies, stored in an airtight container or tightly wrapped in plastic wrap, for at least 30 minutes and up to 2 weeks before frying.

5. Line a baking sheet with paper towels. If you have a home fryer, heat the oil in it to 365°F. If you don't have a home fryer, fill a deep pot halfway with oil and attach a kitchen thermometer to the rim of the pot. Heat the oil to 365°F. Carefully place four frozen pies into the hot oil and cook for 3 to 4 minutes on each side, until golden brown. You don't want to fry more than four pies at a time, since you'll bring down the oil temperature too quickly and that will cause the pies to take longer to cook, giving the dough extra time to just soak in oil (not delicious). Carefully remove the pies from the hot oil and place on the prepared baking sheet to drain. Let the pies cool for 10 minutes. Repeat to fry the remaining pies. (Alternatively, you can bake the hand pies; see page 213.)

6. Make the icing. In a medium bowl, whisk together the powdered sugar, milk, vanilla, and salt until smooth.

7. If you like that thin, fully iced look, dip your hand pies in the icing while they're still on the warm side and let them set up on a wire rack. Alternatively, you can use the end of a whisk to drizzle the icing over the pies. Let the pies cool for at least 5 minutes and then serve warm or completely cooled. They're best eaten the day they're made, but they can be stored overnight in an airtight container at room temperature and eaten the next day if you really, really want one for breakfast.

Turnovers are a surefire way to impress yourself and your friends or houseguests. I like to assemble turnovers and keep them in my freezer, ready to pull out and bake at any time, for a breakfast with friends or even to satisfy a midafternoon sweet tooth. That being said, you can make this dough, cut it, and freeze it for another day, or you could fully assemble the turnovers and freeze them (wrapped well) for up to a month. If you have puff pastry in your freezer, but not enough time or patience to make the filling, substitute your favorite jam or marmalade.

1. Make the filling. In a large heavy-bottomed sauté pan, heat the butter until melted. Stir in the granulated sugar, brown sugar, and honey and let cook until bubbling. Add the apples and toss to coat. Stir in the lemon zest, lemon juice, salt, cinnamon, cardamom, and ginger; stir to combine. Cook for about 4 minutes, or until the apples just start to soften. Remove from the heat, stir in the vanilla, and transfer to a bowl to cool completely before use. The filling can be made up to 3 days ahead of time and stored in an airtight container in the refrigerator.

2. Make the dough. Line a 9 by 13-inch baking pan with plastic wrap, leaving about 8 inches of overhang on either end. Spread the 3 cups of room-temperature butter evenly in the pan, so it forms a 9 by 13-inch sheet. Fold the plastic wrap over the butter and refrigerate for a minimum of 1 hour. Thirty minutes before you are about to start the lamination process, allow the butter to sit at room temperature until pliable. If you notice it is not very pliable or bendy, using the plastic wrap as a sling, lift the butter out of the pan, place it on your work surface, and beat it with a rolling pin until it has softened slightly.

3. Meanwhile, in the bowl of a stand mixer fitted with the dough hook or a large bowl using a wooden spoon, combine the bread and cake flours with the sugar and salt. Add the cold cubed butter and mix until the dough resembles coarse meal. Slowly stream in the water, lemon juice, and egg yolks. Mix until the dough comes together just enough to leave the sides of the bowl clean. Remove the dough from the bowl and press it into a 9 by 13-inch rectangle. Wrap the dough in plastic wrap and let rest in the refrigerator for at least 20 minutes and up to 2 days.

4. Dust a work surface with all-purpose flour. Unwrap the dough and dust it with flour until the dough is no longer sticky. With a lightly floured rolling pin, applying even pressure, roll out the dough lengthwise to a 12 by 20-inch rectangle. Unwrap the butter, then carefully place it diagonally in the middle of the dough. Fold the four edges of the dough up over the butter so the points meet, encasing it. Roll out the dough until it is 10 by 28 inches. Fold the dough over itself in thirds, like a letter. Rotate the

continued

Caramel-Apple Turnovers

Makes 16 pastries

Caramel-Apple Filling

3¾ tablespoons unsalted butter

¾ cup granulated sugar

¼ cup firmly packed light brown sugar

1½ tablespoons honey

4 cups peeled, cored, and evenly chopped Granny Smith apples (about 7)

1½ teaspoons finely grated lemon zest

1 tablespoon fresh lemon juice

¾ teaspoon kosher salt

¾ teaspoon ground cinnamon

⅓ teaspoon ground cardamom

⅓ teaspoon ground ginger

1 teaspoon vanilla extract

Turnover Dough

3 cups unsalted butter, at room temperature, plus ¾ cup plus 3 tablespoons cold unsalted butter, cubed

5¼ cups bread flour

5¼ cups cake flour

¼ cup granulated sugar

3 tablespoons kosher salt

3 cups cool water

2 teaspoons fresh lemon juice

3 egg yolks, at room temperature

All-purpose flour for dusting

Egg Wash

1 egg

1 teaspoon water

Raw sugar for sprinkling (optional)

Icing

2 cups powdered sugar, sifted

About 3 tablespoons whole milk

1 teaspoon vanilla extract

continued

Caramel-Apple Turnovers

dough 90 degrees and repeat this process, rolling out the dough to 10 by 28 inches. Fold the dough over itself again in thirds. Wrap the dough in plastic wrap and refrigerate for 20 minutes.

5. Take the dough out of the refrigerator and, with the creased side facing you; roll it out until the dough is approximately 9 by 32 inches. Trifold the dough, wrap in plastic wrap, and refrigerate for 30 minutes. You can keep this in the refrigerator, wrapped well in plastic wrap, for up to 3 days. If you want to keep it longer, you'll need to move the dough to the freezer, since it will start to oxidize and change color. Keep it well wrapped and freeze for up to 1 month. When you're ready to use the dough, thaw it overnight in the refrigerator or for 1 hour at room temperature, still wrapped (you don't want to expose the dough to the air for any length of time, since it will create a "skin" that will ultimately prevent the dough from rising to its fullest potential).

6. To use, lightly flour a work surface and a rolling pin. Dusting with flour as you work, roll out the dough to about ¾ inch thick. Cut it into 5-inch squares using a sharp knife or a pastry wheel. At this point, you can stack the squares between sheets of parchment paper in an airtight container and freeze them. If you're going to form the pastries now, place the dough squares in the refrigerator and work only with one or two at a time.

7. Make the egg wash. In a small bowl, whisk together the egg and water.

8. Using your hand, lightly stretch the middle of a dough square just enough to fill it with your desired filling, while still allowing all of the corners to meet. Place about 3 tablespoons of the filling on the stretched middle of the dough and brush one corner with the egg wash. Fold the dough over the filling to form a triangle and press the edges lightly to seal. Using a fork dipped in flour, indent and seal the two sides where the dough meets.

9. Brush the pastry with the egg wash, sprinkle with the raw sugar and prick a few small holes at the top of the thickest point of the filling to vent steam. Rest in the freezer for at least 30 minutes before baking.

10. Preheat the oven to 375°F. Line a baking sheet with parchment paper and arrange the turnovers on it. Bake on a rack positioned slightly above center in your oven for 35 to 40 minutes, rotating the baking sheet after 15 minutes, until golden brown.

11. Transfer the turnovers to a wire rack to cool for 10 to 15 minutes before icing. (If you're opting out of icing, serve the turnovers immediately.)

12. Make the icing. In a medium bowl, whisk together the powdered sugar, milk, and vanilla until smooth. Drizzle over the warm turnovers and serve. These are best eaten the day they're baked, but they can be stored overnight in an airtight container at room temperature.

Feel free to switch up your peaches and do a mix of peach varieties, cherries, or even cleaned and sliced strawberries for a fun, summery turnover. You just need a total of 4½ cups of fruit here—that's the rule.

1. Make the filling. In a large bowl, combine the peaches, brown sugar, cinnamon, ginger, and amaretto (if using) in a bowl and toss to coat.

2. Make the dough. Line a 9 by 13-inch baking pan with plastic wrap, leaving about 8 inches of overhang on either end. Spread the 3 cups of room-temperature butter evenly in the pan, so it forms a 9 by 13-inch sheet. Fold the plastic wrap over the butter and refrigerate for a minimum of 1 hour. Thirty minutes before you are about to start the lamination process, allow the butter to sit at room temperature until pliable. If you notice it is not very pliable or bendy, using the plastic wrap as a sling, lift the butter out of the pan, place it on your work surface, and beat it with a rolling pin until it has softened slightly.

3. Meanwhile, in the bowl of a stand mixer fitted with the dough hook or a large bowl using a wooden spoon, combine the bread and cake flours with the sugar and salt. Add the cold cubed butter and mix until the dough resembles coarse meal. Slowly stream in the water, lemon juice, and egg yolks. Mix until the dough comes together just enough to leave the sides of the bowl clean. Remove the dough from the bowl and press it into a 9 by 13-inch rectangle. Wrap the dough in plastic wrap and let rest in the refrigerator for at least 20 minutes and up to 2 days.

4. Dust a work surface with all-purpose flour. Unwrap the dough and dust it with flour until the dough is no longer sticky. With a lightly floured rolling pin, applying even pressure, roll out the dough lengthwise to a 12 by 20-inch rectangle. Unwrap the butter, then carefully place it diagonally in the middle of the dough. Fold the four edges of the dough up over the butter so the points meet, encasing it. Roll out the dough until it is 10 by 28 inches. Fold the dough over itself in thirds, like a letter. Rotate the dough 90 degrees and repeat this process, rolling out the dough to 10 by 28 inches. Fold the dough over itself again in thirds. Wrap the dough in plastic wrap and refrigerate for 20 minutes.

5. Take the dough out of the refrigerator and, with the creased side facing you; roll it out until the dough is approximately 9 by 32 inches. Trifold the dough, wrap in plastic, and refrigerate for 30 minutes. You can keep this in the refrigerator, wrapped well in plastic wrap, for up to 3 days. If you want to keep it longer, you'll need to move the dough to the freezer, since it will start to oxidize and change color. Keep it well wrapped and freeze for up to 1 month. When you're ready to use the dough, thaw it overnight in the refrigerator or for 1 hour at room

continued

Peach Turnovers

Makes 16 pastries

Peach Filling

4½ cups peeled, pitted, and diced peaches, same or mixed varieties (about 8)

3 tablespoons firmly packed light brown sugar

¾ teaspoon ground cinnamon

¾ teaspoon ground ginger

1½ tablespoons amaretto (optional)

Turnover Dough

3 cups unsalted butter, at room temperature, plus ¾ cup plus 3 tablespoons cold unsalted butter, cubed

5¼ cups bread flour

5¼ cups cake flour

¼ cup granulated sugar

3 tablespoons kosher salt

3 cups cool water

2 teaspoons fresh lemon juice

3 egg yolks, at room temperature

All-purpose flour for dusting

Egg Wash

1 egg

1 teaspoon water

Raw sugar for sprinkling (optional)

Icing

2 cups powdered sugar, sifted

About 3 tablespoons whole milk

1 teaspoon vanilla extract

Cobblers, Crisps, Galettes, Pies, and Tarts

Peach Turnovers

temperature, still wrapped (you don't want to expose the dough to the air for any length of time, since it will create a "skin" that will ultimately prevent the dough from rising to its fullest potential).

6. To use, lightly flour a work surface and a rolling pin. Dusting with flour as you work, roll out the dough to about ¾ inch thick. Cut it into 5-inch squares using a sharp knife or a pastry wheel. At this point you can stack the squares between sheets of parchment paper in an airtight container and freeze them. If you're going to form the pastries now, place the dough squares in the refrigerator and work only with one or two at a time.

7. Make the egg wash. In a small bowl, whisk together the egg and water.

8. Using your hand, lightly stretch the middle of a dough square just enough to fill it with your desired filling, while still allowing all of the corners to meet. Place about 3 tablespoons of the filling on the stretched middle of the dough and brush one corner with the egg wash. Fold the dough over the filling to form a triangle and press the edges lightly to seal. Using a fork dipped in flour, indent and seal the two sides where the dough meets.

9. Brush the pastry with egg wash, sprinkle with the raw sugar (if using) and prick a few small holes at the top of the thickest point of the filling to vent steam. Rest in the freezer for at least 30 minutes before baking.

10. Preheat the oven to 375°F. Line a baking sheet with parchment paper and arrange the turnovers on it. Bake on a rack positioned slightly above center in your oven for 35 to 40 minutes, rotating the baking sheet halfway after 15 minutes, until golden brown.

11. Transfer the turnovers to a wire rack to cool for 10 to 15 minutes before icing. (If you're opting out of icing, serve the turnovers immediately.)

12. Make the icing. In a medium bowl, whisk together the powdered sugar, milk, and vanilla until smooth. Drizzle over the warm turnovers and serve. These are best eaten the day they're baked, but they can be stored overnight in an airtight container at room temperature.

Cheese Turnovers

Makes 16 pastries

Cheese Filling

3 cups crumbled feta cheese

1½ cups ricotta cheese

1 cup grated Parmesan cheese

3 eggs

1 tablespoon freshly ground
black pepper

Turnover Dough

3 cups unsalted butter, at room
temperature, plus ¾ cup plus
3 tablespoons cold unsalted
butter, cubed

5¼ cups bread flour

5¼ cups cake flour

¼ cup granulated sugar

3 tablespoons kosher salt

3 cups cool water

2 teaspoons fresh lemon juice

3 egg yolks

All-purpose flour for dusting

Egg Wash

1 egg

1 teaspoon water

For a little savory turnover, I like to make these, which were inspired by eating bourekas during my travels through the Middle East. I like to use sheep's-milk cheese that is packaged in brine, but any feta will make for a delicious filling. I like to sprinkle a little extra grated Parmesan on top of these turnovers when they bake, but if you want to sprinkle them with sesame seeds, you'll be a little more in line with how bourekas are traditionally served.

1. Make the filling. In a large bowl, combine the feta, ricotta, and Parmesan with the eggs and pepper and mash together until smooth-ish. Cover and store in the refrigerator until ready to use. This mixture can be made up to a day ahead of time.

2. Make the dough. Line a 9 by 13-inch baking pan with plastic wrap, leaving about 8 inches of overhang on either end. Spread the 3 cups of softened butter evenly in the pan, so it forms a 9 by 13-inch sheet. Fold the plastic wrap over the butter and refrigerate for a minimum of 1 hour. Thirty minutes before you are about to start the lamination process, allow the butter to sit at room temperature until pliable. If you notice it is not very pliable or bendy, using the plastic wrap as a sling, lift the butter out of the pan, place it on your work surface, and beat it with a rolling pin until it has softened slightly.

3. Meanwhile, in the bowl of a stand mixer fitted with the dough hook or a large bowl using a wooden spoon, combine the bread and cake flours with the sugar and salt. Add the cold cubed butter and mix until the dough resembles coarse meal. Slowly stream in the water, lemon juice, and egg yolks. Mix until the dough comes together just enough to leave the sides of the bowl clean. Remove the dough from the bowl and press it into a 9 by 13-inch rectangle. Wrap the dough in plastic wrap and let rest in the refrigerator for at least 20 minutes and up to 2 days.

4. Dust a work surface with all-purpose flour. Unwrap the dough and dust it with flour until the dough is no longer sticky. With a lightly floured rolling pin, applying even pressure, roll out the dough lengthwise to a 12 by 20-inch rectangle. Unwrap the butter, then carefully place it diagonally in the middle of the dough. Fold the four edges of the dough up over the butter so the points meet, encasing it. Roll out the dough until it is 10 by 28 inches. Fold the dough over itself in thirds, like a letter. Rotate the dough 90 degrees and repeat this process, rolling out the dough again to 10 by 28 inches. Fold the dough over itself again in thirds. Wrap the dough in plastic wrap and refrigerate for 20 minutes.

5. Take the dough out of the refrigerator and, with the creased side facing you, roll out until the dough is approximately 9 by 32 inches. Trifold the dough, wrap in plastic, and refrigerate for 30 minutes. You can keep this in the refrigerator, wrapped well in plastic wrap, for up to 3 days. If you want to keep it longer, you'll need to move the dough to the freezer, since it will start to oxidize and change color. Keep it well wrapped and freeze for up to 1 month. When you're ready to use the dough, thaw it overnight in the refrigerator or for 1 hour at room temperature, still wrapped (you don't want to expose the dough to the air for any length of time, since it will create a "skin" that will ultimately prevent the dough from rising to its fullest potential).

6. To use, lightly flour a work surface and a rolling pin. Dusting with flour as you work, roll out the dough to about ¾ inch thick. Cut it into 5-inch squares using a sharp knife or a pastry wheel. At this point you can stack the squares between sheets of parchment paper in an airtight container and freeze them. If you're going to form the pastries now, place the dough squares in the refrigerator and work with only one or two at a time.

7. Make the egg wash. In a small bowl, whisk together the egg and water.

8. Using your hand, lightly stretch the middle of a dough square just enough to fill it with your desired filling, while still allowing all of the corners to meet. Place about 3 tablespoons of the filling on the stretched middle of the dough and brush one corner with the egg wash. Fold the dough over the filling to form a triangle and press the edges lightly to seal. Using a fork dipped in flour, indent and seal the two sides where the dough meets.

9. Brush the pastry with the egg wash and prick a few small holes at the top of the thickest point of the filling to vent steam. Rest in the freezer for at least 30 minutes before baking.

10. Preheat the oven to 375°F. Line a baking sheet with parchment paper and arrange the turnovers on it. Bake on a rack positioned slightly above center in your oven for 35 to 40 minutes, rotating the baking sheet after 15 minutes, until golden brown. Serve immediately. These are best eaten the day they're baked, but they can be stored overnight in an airtight container at room temperature.

This recipe equates to the best version of a Fig Newton cookie that I could possibly imagine. I love figs, and we're lucky enough to have a very fruitful fig season in Louisiana every summer. This tart can be made with any variety of fresh fig you prefer. I tend to use Celeste, Brown Turkey, and even LSU purple figs, since they grow everywhere around southern Louisiana. Just make sure to use whatever is local and delicious, though you can easily substitute the figs for any seasonal fruit, except melons.

1. Preheat the oven to 350°F. Arrange the figs in the prepared tart shell in a circular formation so they slightly overlap. Place in the freezer while you make the filling.

2. In a small saucepot, cook the butter until it turns a light brown color with a rich nutty aroma, about 5 minutes; remove from the heat and cool for about 15 minutes.

3. In a medium bowl, whisk the sugar with the flour and salt. In another medium bowl, whisk together the eggs, orange zest, and vanilla paste. Whisk in the dry ingredients in two portions, whisking until just incorporated. Stream in the brown butter and stir to combine. Pour the custard mixture over the figs and spread evenly with a rubber spatula.

4. Bake the tart for 30 to 40 minutes, rotating it after 15 minutes, until the crust is golden brown and the custard has nearly set in the center. Transfer the tart to a wire rack to cool and let it have some airflow around it, about 10 minutes. This tart is BEYOND delicious, served fresh and hot out of the oven (it doesn't cut neatly, but who cares?), but it's also equally great once it has cooled fully. The tart can be kept at room temperature for up to 5 days, but it'll be best if you can rewarm it for 5 minutes in a 300°F oven before you eat it.

Fig and Brown Butter Custard Tart

Makes one 10-inch tart

2 pints fresh figs, quartered or halved

1 recipe Tart Dough (page 312)

½ cup unsalted butter

1 cup granulated sugar

½ cup all-purpose flour

Pinch of kosher salt

3 eggs, beaten, at room temperature

1 teaspoon finely grated orange zest

1 teaspoon vanilla bean paste

What's Mine Is Yours

You can substitute a parbaked bottom crust (see page 308) for the tart shell if you prefer.

A slice of a simple chocolate tart is one of the most perfect experiences in life, in my opinion. The success of this recipe relies on the quality and flavor of the chocolate, and therefore it's most important to use a really great chocolate. This recipe is so adaptable to adding and experimenting with different layers of flavor within the tart. You can steep flavors into the chocolate filling or even add layers of nut butters, caramel, or cajeta to the bottom of the crust. I also like to garnish with a few flecks of sea salt on each slice when serving, just to turn up the volume.

1. Make the dough. In the bowl of a stand mixer or in a medium bowl, sift together the cocoa and powdered sugar. Add the butter and, using the paddle attachment or a handheld mixer, mix on medium-high speed until smooth, about 3 minutes. Stop the mixer and scrape down the sides of the bowl with a rubber spatula. With the mixer on low speed, beat in the egg yolks, one at a time, mixing well after each addition. Add the vanilla paste and mix to combine.

2. Decrease the speed to low and stream in the flour and salt. Mix until a dough starts to form. Remove the bowl from the mixer and, using your hand, turn the dough a few times in the bowl to bring it all together. Form the dough into a disk, wrap in plastic wrap, and let rest in the refrigerator for at least 45 minutes or up to overnight.

3. Preheat the oven to 375°F. Lightly dust a work surface with cocoa powder. Remove the dough from the refrigerator and roll it out to an 11-inch round to about ¼ inch thick. Carefully place the dough over a 9-inch nonstick tart pan and press it into the bottom and up the sides, making sure the dough is uniform and even. Trim off any extra dough that may be overhanging the rim of the pan by rolling your rolling pin across the top of the tart. Use dough trimmings to reinforce weak spots and to patch holes. Refrigerate for 15 to 30 minutes. If it is especially warm where you're making this, you can also roll the dough between two sheets of parchment paper and chill before transferring to the tart pan. The dough is temperamental in the heat.

4. Remove the tart from the refrigerator and use a fork or paring knife to "dock" the bottom crust, pricking holes all the way around and in the center of the dough to keep it from bubbling up and becoming uneven during baking. Lay a sheet of parchment paper over the dough and weight it down with about 2 cups granulated sugar, dried beans, or pie weights (enough to fill the tart shell three-quarters full). Bake for 15 minutes, or until the dough looks set; remove the parchment and sugar, beans, or pie weights. Return the tart to the oven and bake for

Chocolate Tart

Makes one 9-inch tart

Chocolate Sable Tart Shell

2½ tablespoons unsweetened Dutch-processed cocoa powder, plus more for dusting

½ cup powdered sugar

½ cup unsalted butter, at room temperature

2 egg yolks, at room temperature

½ teaspoon vanilla bean paste

1½ cups all-purpose flour

½ teaspoon kosher salt

¼ cup chopped dark chocolate (preferably Valrhona 70% cacao) for coating the bottom of the shell

Ganache Filling

15 ounces dark chocolate (preferably Valrhona 70% cacao), chopped

1¾ cups heavy cream

1 tablespoon honey

1 teaspoon kosher salt

3 tablespoons unsalted butter, diced, at room temperature

1 teaspoon vanilla bean paste

2 teaspoons sea salt flakes

continued

continued
Chocolate Tart

12 to 15 minutes, until the crust is fully baked. Remove from the oven and cool to room temperature.

5. In a microwave-safe medium bowl, melt the ¼ cup dark chocolate in the microwave, stirring every 15 seconds, until melted and smooth. Using a pastry brush, paint the melted chocolate on the bottom and up the side of the prepared tart shell, leaving the top ¼ inch of the side uncoated.

6. Make the ganache. Put the 15 ounces dark chocolate in a heatproof medium bowl and set it over a saucepot of simmering water. Melt, stirring until smooth. (You can also melt the chocolate in a microwave, heating it for 15 seconds, stirring, and repeating until melted.) In a medium saucepot, bring the cream, honey, and salt to a boil over moderately high heat. Remove from the heat and, mixing vigorously with a rubber spatula, stream one-third of the dairy mixture into the melted chocolate, adding more of the liquid as you incorporate. The mixture will reach a point where it looks broken or separated, but keep going. I promise it'll come back together! Continue stirring and adding the cream until all of it has been incorporated into the chocolate.

7. Let the mixture cool for about 5 minutes, then add the butter and vanilla paste, mixing with an immersion blender for 30 seconds (be careful not to introduce air bubbles into the ganache by blending too close to the surface) or whisk by hand. Let the ganache cool for 5 to 10 minutes, then pour the ganache directly into the prepared tart shell. Refrigerate for at least 2 hours, then serve at room temperature. The tart can be stored in an airtight container and kept at room temperature for up to 3 days.

Flavored Chocolate Tarts

Add 1 tablespoon finely grated lemon or orange zest to the cream in step 6 (use a Microplane to grate the zest; if you don't, the cream will need to be strained).

Add 1 tablespoon instant coffee powder to the cream in step 6.

Replace ¼ cup of the cream in step 6 with ¼ cup of any desired liquor, such as bourbon, Bailey's, or Grand Marnier, or any flavor that will stand up to the chocolate.

Spread the cooled crust with 1 cup peanut, sunflower, almond, cashew, or macadamia nut butter before adding the ganache.

Spread the cooled crust with Caramel Sauce (page 298) or Cajeta (page 302), so it becomes like a Rolo candy; be sure to let the ganache cool and set before adding.

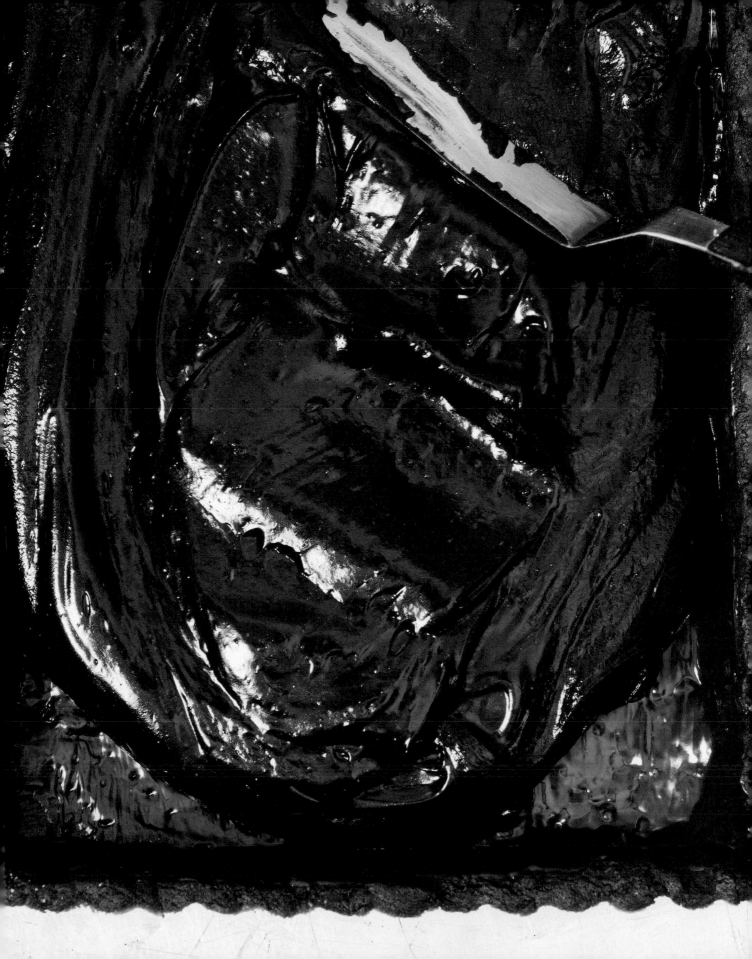

Cakes

This cake was always a hit with my grandpa's coworkers when my grandmother made it—and she made it almost every other day during apple season! My grandmother grew up in Appalachia, so she used the apples indigenous to that area; I tend to use Honeycrisps or Granny Smiths. I also prefer walnuts to pecans in this recipe. The cake is a bit sweet, but it balances really beautifully with the tang of the buttermilk sauce.

Grandma Mac's Apple Cake

Makes one 10-inch cake

1. Make the cake. Preheat the oven to 325°F. Liberally butter and lightly flour every crevice of a 10-cup tube or Bundt pan.

2. In a medium bowl, whisk the flour, baking soda, and cinnamon. In the bowl of a stand mixer fitted with the paddle attachment or in a large bowl using a handheld mixer, combine the sugar, eggs, oil, orange juice, and vanilla and beat on medium speed until well blended. Add the dry ingredients and mix until incorporated. Fold in the apples, nuts, and coconut. Spoon into the prepared pan. Bake for about 1½ hours, rotating the pan after 45 minutes, until the top springs back when lightly pressed with a fingertip. Transfer to a wire rack and let the cake cool in the pan for 15 minutes.

3. While the cake is cooling, make the sauce. In a medium saucepot, combine the sugar, butter, buttermilk, and baking soda. Cook over medium heat, whisking constantly, until the mixture boils for at least 1 full minute. The sauce may look a bit separated, but continue whisking; it will come together.

4. Place a serving plate with a raised edge over the pan, and invert the cake onto the plate, then remove the pan. Puncture the top of the cake all over with a skewer or even a table knife. Spoon the hot sauce over the warm cake, continuing until the cake has absorbed most of the sauce. This will look like too much sauce at first, but the cake will absorb most of it while it cools. Let the cake stand for at least 1 hour before serving. The cake is even better the next day. Store it in an airtight container at room temperature.

Apple Cake

Butter for greasing the pan

2 cups all-purpose flour, plus more for flouring the pan

1 teaspoon baking soda

1 teaspoon ground cinnamon

2 cups granulated sugar

3 eggs, at room temperature

1¼ cups vegetable oil

¼ cup fresh orange juice

1 teaspoon vanilla extract

2 cups peeled grated Honeycrisp or Granny Smith apples (about 4)

1 cup chopped walnuts or pecans

1 cup sweetened coconut flakes

Buttermilk Sauce

1 cup granulated sugar

½ cup unsalted butter

½ cup buttermilk

½ teaspoon baking soda

Jam Cake

Makes one 9-cup Bundt cake

Jam Cake

1 cup unsalted butter, at room temperature, plus more for greasing the pan

3½ cups all-purpose flour, plus more for flouring the pan

1 teaspoon ground cloves

1½ teaspoons ground nutmeg

2½ teaspoons ground cinnamon

1 teaspoon ground cardamom

1½ teaspoons kosher salt

2 cups granulated sugar

8 eggs, at room temperature

2 teaspoons baking soda

2 tablespoons tepid water

2 cups seedless blackberry jam

1 cup buttermilk, at room temperature

1½ cups pecan pieces

Icing

¼ cup plus 2 tablespoons unsalted butter

½ cup firmly packed light brown sugar

¼ cup whole milk

1 cup powdered sugar, sifted

My maternal grandmother's family was scattered around the South, from Kentucky throughout Appalachia and down into Florida. As a result, this jam cake was adapted along the way by the women of my family. Much like the Kentucky-ish Derby pie on page 205, by the time it made its way into my repertoire, the traditional black walnuts had been replaced with pecans. It had also been converted into a Bundt cake, drizzled with caramel frosting, rather than the original layers of cake and icing. My guess is a great-aunt who didn't have much of a sweet tooth wanted to minimize the sweetness; I can't blame her. I'm fortunate enough to have grown up with a mother who believes in preserving the seasons, so I use whatever she made in her last batch, but blackberry jam is my favorite and also what the original recipe called for.

1. Make the cake. Preheat the oven to 350°F. Liberally butter and flour every crevice of a 9-cup Bundt pan and lightly dust with flour.

2. In a medium bowl, sift together the flour, cloves, nutmeg, cinnamon, cardamom, and salt. In the bowl of a stand mixer fitted with the paddle attachment or in a large bowl using a handheld mixer, beat the butter and sugar on medium-high speed until light and fluffy, about 5 minutes. Beat in the eggs, one at a time, mixing well after each addition. Stir the baking soda into the water and add to the bowl, followed by the jam. Add the dry ingredients in three portions, alternating with the buttermilk, beginning and ending with the dry ingredients. Mix until just combined. Stir in the pecans.

3. Using a rubber spatula, scrape the batter into the prepared pan. Bake for about 90 minutes, rotating the pan after 45 minutes, until the cake is golden and a cake tester comes out clean when inserted into the center of the cake.

4. Let the cake cool for 10 minutes. Place a plate over the cake pan, invert the cake onto the plate, and remove the pan. Cool completely before icing.

5. Make the icing. In a medium saucepot, melt the butter over moderately high heat. Add the brown sugar and bring to a boil, allowing the sugar to completely dissolve. Carefully whisk in the milk; be mindful that the mixture may hiss, steam, and bubble up. Remove the mixture from the heat and transfer to the bowl of a stand mixer fitted with the whisk attachment or to a medium bowl and use a handheld mixer. With the mixer on medium speed (not so high that the whisk flings hot sugar on you), stream in the powdered sugar. Remove the whisk attachment from the mixer and use it or a spoon to drizzle the icing over the cake in whichever way you see fit. This cake can be stored at room temperature for 3 to 4 days if well covered or in an airtight container.

Dried Fruit Jam Cake

Inspired by the delicious spice flavor of this cake, around the holidays I often add dried fruit to make a more palatable fruitcake of sorts. Feel free to add raisins, chopped dried apricots, dried cranberries, dried cherries, any dried berries, or a combination of any or all of these for a total of 1½ cups. Just stir them in with the pecans.

What's Mine Is Yours

Depending on the humidity where you are, the icing may come out slightly loose or too thick for your preference. If it's a little loose, sift additional powdered sugar and whisk it into the icing until it is the desired consistency. If it's a little thick, add a teaspoon of milk and whisk until it thins to your liking.

Angel Food Cake

Makes one 10-inch cake

1¾ cups egg whites,
at room temperature

¾ cup granulated sugar

½ teaspoon kosher salt

1½ teaspoons cream of tartar

1 cup cake flour, sifted

2 tablespoons vanilla extract

2 tablespoons fresh lemon juice

4 ounces white chocolate
(preferably Valrhona), grated

4 ounces dark chocolate
(preferably Valrhona
70% cacao), grated

This recipe was inspired by Alan Carter, a pastry chef I got to work with for a too-short time while I was living in San Francisco. He made a tall and phenomenal angel food cake with chocolate grated into the batter. It was a revelation to me—how to make something so delicious and beautifully light with chocolate in it. You can completely leave the chocolate out of this recipe, but why would you? You need a 10-inch, two-piece angel food cake pan for this recipe, y'all. In the South, your mom's angel food cake pan is just as valuable an heirloom as her cast-iron skillet.

1. Preheat the oven to 375°F. DO NOT grease the angel food cake pan. In the bowl of a stand mixer fitted with the whisk attachment or in a large bowl using a handheld mixer, whip the egg whites on medium speed until they become foamy. Once foamy, slowly add the sugar and salt, followed by the cream of tartar. Increase the speed to high and whip until the egg whites form stiff peaks (the whites should hold their points when you pull the whisk out), about 5 minutes.

2. Remove the bowl from the mixer and, using a rubber spatula, fold in the flour in two portions, followed by the vanilla and lemon juice. Be sure to fold in everything at the bottom and along the sides of the bowl, where the flour likes to hide and clump. Stir in the white chocolate and dark chocolate.

3. Spoon the batter evenly into the angel food cake pan. Run a knife or spatula through the batter in the pan to try to eliminate any potential air pockets. Bake for 35 to 45 minutes, rotating the pan after 15 minutes, until the top springs back when gently pressed with your fingertip. Remove from the oven and immediately place a wire rack over the pan and invert the cake onto the rack, but do not remove the pan. Let the cake cool completely.

4. To unmold the cake, turn the pan over, carefully run a knife along the inside, and then firmly spank the sides of the pan. Place the wire rack over the cake pan, invert the cake onto the rack again, and remove the pan. Place a serving plate on top of the cake and invert it again so the cake is right side up. Slice with a serrated knife and serve. The cake can be kept covered at room temperature for up to 3 days.

Crispy Angel Food Cake

One of my favorite things to do with this cake (and pound cakes) is to slice it and lightly fry it up in a sauté pan in clarified butter until it's golden brown and crispy. I top the warm, crispy, pan-fried cake slice with chopped fresh fruit or a scoop of ice cream.

What's Mine Is Yours

You have to sift the cake flour in this recipe so it doesn't weigh down the batter and cause it to lose all the volume you create with the egg whites—and so you don't get big ol' clumps of flour in your cake.

I like to freeze my cheese grater and chocolate before grating. Grating the chocolate on the largest holes of the grater allows me to add chocolate to the batter without weighing down the cake. The cake looks awesomely speckled when baked, and the chocolate adds a delightful moisture.

What's Mine Is Yours

For an extra-tasty treat in the morning (or anytime, really), go ahead and get yourself a slice of cake, butter each side, and griddle it in a skillet until it's golden brown, as you would for a grilled cheese sandwich. I was taught this pro tip by none other than the marvelous food journalist Jennifer V. Cole on a camping-ish trip on a lake in Alabama, and hopefully she won't mind me sharing the goods with y'all.

It's key to buy great almond paste for this recipe. It's an expensive ingredient for a reason, and you get what you pay for. If you make this with inexpensive almond paste, you will end up with a cake that tastes cheap. To pick a great almond paste, try to find one with almonds, not sugar, listed as the first ingredient.

1. Make the cake. Preheat the oven to 350°F. Liberally butter and lightly flour every crevice of a 10-cup Bundt pan.

2. In a medium bowl, whisk together the flour, baking powder, and salt. In another bowl, whisk the eggs with the lemon zest, orange zest, and vanilla.

3. In the bowl of a stand mixer fitted with the paddle attachment or in a large bowl using a handheld mixer, cream the butter, sugar, and almond paste on medium-high speed until light and fluffy, 4 to 5 minutes. Stop the mixer and scrape down the bottom and sides of the bowl with a rubber spatula to ensure the mixture is as smooth as possible. With the mixer on medium speed, add the egg mixture in several portions, fully incorporating after each addition. Decrease the speed to low and mix in the dry ingredients in two portions, mixing until just incorporated; you do not want to overbeat the batter.

4. Using a rubber spatula, scrape the batter into the prepared pan. Place in the center of the oven and bake for 45 to 60 minutes, rotating the pan after 30 minutes, until the cake is golden brown and a cake tester comes out clean when inserted into the middle of the cake.

5. While the cake is baking, make the syrup. Heat the water and sugar in a medium saucepot over medium-high heat. Bring to a boil, stirring until the sugar is fully dissolved. Remove from the heat, stir in the orange juice and lemon juice, and keep warm. (This syrup can be made ahead of time and stored in the refrigerator. However, you'll want to heat it back up before you apply it to the cake, since it is best absorbed when both the syrup and the cake are warm.)

6. Transfer the cake to a wire rack and let cool in the pan for 10 minutes. Place a serving plate over the pan, invert the cake onto the plate, and remove the pan. Using a pastry brush, brush the cake all over with the syrup. Let the cake cool completely before topping with powdered sugar and almonds, if using. This cake will keep well in an airtight container at room temperature for about 4 days, and in my opinion, it's best on days two and three.

Almond Pound Cake

Makes one 10-cup Bundt cake

Almond Cake

1 cup unsalted butter, at room temperature, plus more for greasing the pan

1 cup all-purpose flour, plus more for flouring the pan

½ teaspoon baking powder

¼ teaspoon kosher salt

5 eggs, at room temperature

1 teaspoon finely grated lemon zest

1 teaspoon finely grated orange zest

¼ teaspoon vanilla extract

1 cup granulated sugar

1½ cups plus 1 tablespoon almond paste

Citrus Soaker Syrup

½ cup water

¼ cup granulated sugar

¼ cup fresh orange juice

¼ cup fresh lemon juice

Powdered sugar for garnish (optional)

Crushed sliced almonds for garnish (optional)

Glazed Lemon-Cornmeal Cake

Makes one 9-inch cake

Lemon-Cornmeal Cake

1¼ cups all-purpose flour

¼ cup corn flour

⅓ cup coarse yellow cornmeal

¾ cup granulated sugar

1 tablespoon baking powder

1 teaspoon kosher salt

2 eggs, at room temperature

1 cup buttermilk,
at room temperature

1½ tablespoons finely grated
lemon zest

1 tablespoon fresh lemon juice

1 teaspoon vanilla extract

½ cup unsalted butter, melted
and cooled

Glaze

1 cup powdered sugar, sifted

2 tablespoons fresh lemon juice

1 teaspoon heavy cream or milk
(or even water will work)

This is one of the easiest and quickest cakes I've ever had the pleasure of getting to know. I think it's even easier to make than my Glazed Lemon-Cornmeal Muffins (page 50). It's a bit lighter and sweeter than the muffins and is a perfect pairing for any late spring or summer fruit.

1. Make the cake. Preheat the oven to 350°F. Lightly coat a 9-inch round cake pan with cooking spray, then line the bottom of the pan with parchment paper and lightly spray the paper. In a medium bowl, whisk together the all-purpose flour, corn flour, cornmeal, sugar, baking powder, and salt. In a separate bowl, whisk together the eggs, buttermilk, lemon zest, lemon juice, and vanilla. Using a rubber spatula, make a well in the middle of the dry ingredients and pour in the buttermilk mixture, followed by the butter. Stir just until evenly incorporated.

2. Transfer the batter to the prepared pan and spread it into an even layer. Bake for 25 to 35 minutes, rotating the pan after 15 minutes, until the cake is slightly golden and a cake tester comes out clean when inserted into the center of the cake.

3. Meanwhile, make the glaze. In a medium bowl, combine the powdered sugar, lemon juice, and cream and whisk together until smooth. You can adjust the consistency by adding more of each liquid, or more sugar to thicken, based on your personal taste. Set aside.

4. Transfer the cake to a wire rack and let cool in the pan for 5 minutes. Run a knife along the inside of the pan, place a plate over the pan, carefully invert the cake onto the plate (it will still be hot), and remove the pan. Peel off the parchment paper. Gently place a serving plate on top of the cake and carefully invert it onto the serving plate so the cake is right side up.

5. While still warm, spread the glaze over the top of the cake. This cake is equally delicious served warm or at room temperature. It will keep for about 3 days if wrapped airtight and stored at room temperature.

Lemon Pound Cake

Makes one 10-cup Bundt cake

Lemon Pound Cake

1 cup unsalted butter,
at room temperature, plus
more for greasing the pan

3 cups all-purpose flour,
plus more for flouring the pan

½ teaspoon baking soda

1 teaspoon kosher salt

1 packet (about 1½ teaspoons)
lemonade powder (not sugar-free)

2 cups granulated sugar

3 eggs, at room temperature

2 tablespoons finely grated
lemon zest

2 tablespoons fresh lemon juice

1 cup buttermilk, at room
temperature

Soaker Syrup

¼ cup water

¼ cup plus 1 tablespoon
granulated sugar

1 tablespoon fresh lemon juice

Glaze

1 cup powdered sugar, plus
more as needed

2 tablespoons fresh lemon juice
plus more as needed

Damn, y'all, I love lemon pound cake beyond words. At one of my first restaurant jobs, a gracious woman would drop by every so often, bringing her lemon pound cake for the pastry kitchen staff. It was incredible. I asked her for the better part of a year what her secret was. She'd just giggle, saying I would never guess, giving me a wink. I became obsessed and eventually figured it out . . . lemonade powder. She was shocked and delighted, and I've never made it any other way since.

1. Preheat the oven to 325°F. Liberally butter and lightly flour every crevice of a 10-cup Bundt pan.

2. Make the cake. In a medium bowl, whisk together the flour, baking soda, salt, and lemonade powder. In the bowl of a stand mixer fitted with the paddle attachment or in a large bowl using a handheld mixer, cream the butter and sugar on medium-high speed until light and fluffy, about 4 minutes. Stop the mixer and scrape down the bottom and sides of the bowl with a rubber spatula. Return the mixer to medium-high speed, and beat in the eggs, one at a time, incorporating well after each addition. Decrease the speed to low and beat in the lemon zest and lemon juice. Alternately beat in the dry ingredients and the buttermilk, beginning and ending with the dry ingredients. Mix just until the ingredients are fully incorporated.

3. Using a rubber spatula, scrape the batter into the prepared pan and smooth it out as evenly as you're able. Place the cake on the center rack of your oven and bake for 60 to 80 minutes, rotating after 30 minutes, until the cake is golden brown and a cake tester comes out clean when inserted into the center of the cake.

4. While the cake bakes, make the soaker syrup. In a small saucepot, combine the water and sugar over high heat. Bring to a boil and cook until the sugar has fully dissolved. Remove from the heat and stir in the lemon juice. (The soaker syrup can be made ahead of time and stored in the refrigerator. Just warm it up before you brush it on the cake, since it absorbs better if both the syrup and the cake are warm.)

5. Make the glaze. Sift the powdered sugar into a large bowl. Whisk in the lemon juice. This ratio might change a bit depending on the humidity. If it is a bit thin, add a touch more sifted powdered sugar. If it's a bit thicker than you'd like, add a touch more lemon juice. Don't make the glaze more than 30 minutes in advance because it will continue to thicken as it sits.

6. Transfer the cake to a wire rack and let cool in the pan for 10 minutes. Place a serving plate over the pan, invert the cake onto the plate, and remove the pan. Using a pastry brush, immediately soak the cake with the syrup by brushing it on the top and sides. Let the cake cool completely and then, using a spoon, drizzle the glaze over the top. This cake will keep in an airtight container at room temperature (or just store it in your microwave like my mom used to do) for several days. It is great on day one but even better on day two, in my honest opinion.

The first coconut cake recipe appeared in the cookbook *What Mrs. Fisher Knows About Old Southern Cooking* in 1881. Since then, coconut cake has been wildly popular across the American South. It's the state dessert of South Carolina, if you can believe such a thing. Growing up around Charleston meant years of exposure to coconut layer cakes, since they're on almost every dessert menu and are served at any and all occasions. Per usual, I obsessed over developing my own version of this cake. To inspire me, I ventured outside my childhood experiences and found my personal coconut cake North Star in none other than pastry chef Dolester Miles. Dols prepares all of the desserts for Frank Stitt's restaurants in Birmingham, Alabama, as she's done for the past thirty-plus years. Do yourself a favor and never pass up the opportunity to stop on in and have a slice of her unbelievable coconut cake.

This cake is really a two-day affair because the filling needs to chill overnight and the cake is best when it has had several hours to set up in the fridge.

1. Make the filling. Place the cream, sugar, and butter in a large saucepot and bring to a boil over medium-high heat, stirring occasionally, until the sugar has dissolved. Meanwhile, in a small bowl, mix together the cornstarch, vanilla, and water. Add to the cream mixture and bring to a boil. Simmer until thickened, about 1 minute.

2. In a food processor, pulse the coconut until finely chopped. Stir the coconut into the warm cream mixture until well combined. Transfer to a large baking dish and let cool. Cover the filling with plastic wrap and refrigerate overnight.

3. Make the cake. Preheat the oven to 325°F. Lightly coat two 10-inch round cake pans with cooking spray, line with parchment paper, and spray the paper. Set aside.

4. In a large bowl, whisk together the flour, baking powder, and salt. In a small bowl, mix together the cream, vanilla, and coconut extract. In the bowl of a stand mixer fitted with the paddle attachment or in a large bowl using a handheld mixer, cream the butter and sugar on medium speed until light and fluffy, 5 to 6 minutes. Add the eggs, one at a time, and beat until creamy, occasionally stopping the mixer and scraping down the bottom and sides of the bowl with a rubber spatula. Decrease the speed to low. Alternate beating in the dry ingredients and the cream mixture, beginning and ending with the dry; mix until just combined. Note that this cake batter will be a bit thicker than most cake batters.

continued

Coconut Cake

Makes one 10-inch layer cake

Coconut Filling

3¾ cups heavy cream

2¼ cups granulated sugar

1½ cups unsalted butter

3 tablespoons cornstarch

¾ teaspoon vanilla extract

2 tablespoons water

6¾ cups sweetened shredded coconut

White Cake

4½ cups all-purpose flour

1½ tablespoons baking powder

½ teaspoon kosher salt

1½ cups heavy cream, at room temperature

1½ tablespoons vanilla extract

1 teaspoon coconut extract

2 cups unsalted butter, at room temperature

3 cups granulated sugar

6 eggs, at room temperature

Coconut Simple Syrup

1¼ cups granulated sugar

1¼ cups water

2 teaspoons coconut extract (optional, but it's real good)

Cream Cheese Frosting

1 cup unsalted butter, at room temperature

8 ounces cream cheese, at room temperature

1 teaspoon vanilla bean paste

5 cups powdered sugar, sifted

2 cups sweetened coconut flakes for garnish

continued
Coconut Cake

5. Divide the batter evenly between the prepared cake pans (about 5 cups per pan). Using an offset spatula, spread the batter as evenly as you're able. Bake for 40 to 45 minutes, rotating the pans after 20 minutes, until a cake tester comes out clean when inserted into the center of each cake. Let the cakes cool completely in the pans on a wire rack.

6. Make the syrup. In a heavy-bottomed saucepot set over medium-high heat, bring the sugar and water to a boil. Once the sugar has fully dissolved, boil the syrup for 45 seconds, then remove from the heat and set aside to cool. Stir in the coconut extract, if using.

7. Make the frosting. In the bowl of a stand mixer fitted with the paddle attachment or in a large bowl using a handheld mixer, beat the butter and cream cheese on medium-high speed until light and fluffy, about 3 minutes. Decrease the speed to low and slowly add the vanilla paste and powdered sugar. Continue beating until smooth and creamy, about 3 minutes.

8. Preheat the oven to 375°F. Line a baking sheet with parchment paper. Spread the coconut flakes in an even layer on the baking sheet. Bake for 5 to 7 minutes, until golden; set aside to cool.

9. Build the cake. Place the filling in the bowl of a stand mixer fitted with the paddle attachment or use a handheld mixer and beat on medium-high speed until smooth and creamy, 4 to 5 minutes. Remove the cakes from the pan and discard the parchment. Using a serrated knife, trim the domed tops of the cakes so they're flat; save the scraps for snacking. Cut each cake horizontally into three even layers. Place one layer on a cake plate or stand. Brush with about one-fifth of the simple syrup. Top with 1½ cups of the filling, leaving a ¼-inch border around the perimeter. Place a second layer on top. Repeat the process with the next four layers. Top with the remaining cake layer and brush the top with the simple syrup.

10. Spread the top and sides of the cake with the frosting. Refrigerate the cake for at least 5 hours and up to 5 days. Bring to room temperature before serving. Press the toasted coconut into the sides of the cake, cut, and serve.

I've been on a professional quest for the perfect yellow cake recipe for twenty years. Yes, twenty years. Then Stella Parks wrote her phenomenal book *Brave Tart* and put a perfect recipe out in the world as if it were really no big deal . . . as she does. I honestly don't know a better recipe, so I asked to collaborate, as pastry-minded folks, and she graciously agreed. (But, seriously, go buy her book. You'll see she really digs into the beautifully nerdy side of pastry, which, as a science nerd, I greatly appreciate.) She makes this amazingly perfect yellow cake, and I don't think anyone should make any other yellow cake recipe (sorry, all other folks). Despite my goal to make baking far less intimidating, I recommend you follow this recipe to the dot. You will not be disappointed, and frankly, your cake game will be unbeatable.

I've tried my best to make this cake even more irresistible by turning it into the ultimate strawberry shortcake, with a rich, tangy cream and strawberries soaked in elderflower liqueur—my personal favorite.

1. Make the cake. Adjust the oven rack to the lower-middle position and preheat to 350°F. Line two 8-by-3-inch anodized aluminum pans with parchment paper and coat with cooking spray (the cakes will brown more and rise less in 2-inch pans). Sift the flour (if using a cup measure, spoon into the cup and level with a knife before sifting) and set aside.

2. Combine the butter, sugar, baking powder, potato flour, and salt in the bowl of a stand mixer fitted with a paddle attachment or using a handheld mixer. Mix on low to moisten, then increase to medium and cream until fluffy and light, about 5 minutes, pausing to scrape the bowl and beater halfway through. With the mixer running, add the egg yolks one at a time, mixing well after each addition, followed by the vanilla. Reduce the speed to low and sprinkle in one-third of the flour, followed by a third of the milk. Alternate between the two, allowing each addition to be roughly incorporated before adding the next. Once it is smooth, fold the batter with a flexible spatula to ensure it's well mixed from the bottom up. Divide between the prepared cake pans, about 26 ounces each.

3. Bake until the cakes are golden and firm, about 40 minutes (or 210°F). A cake tester inserted into the center will emerge with a few crumbs still attached, and your fingertip will leave a slight indentation in the puffy crust when pressed gently. Cool until no trace of warmth remains, about 2 hours.

4. Run a knife around the inside of the cake pans to loosen the cooled cakes. Place a wire rack over the cake pans and invert the cakes onto the racks. Peel off the parchment. Place the racks on top of the cakes,

continued

Strawberry Shortcake with Brave Tart's Classic Yellow Layer Cake

Makes one 8-inch layer cake

Yellow Cake

3½ cups bleached cake flour, such as Swans Down

1 cup unsalted butter, pliable but cool

2 cups granulated sugar

1 tablespoon baking powder

1 tablespoon potato flour, such as Bob's Red Mill

1 teaspoon Diamond Crystal kosher salt (half as much if iodized)

½ cup egg yolks, brought to 70°F

4½ teaspoons vanilla extract

1½ cups milk, brought to 70°F

Simple Syrup

⅔ cup granulated sugar

⅔ cup water

½ cup St-Germain elderflower liqueur (or whatever you like, really)

Strawberry Shortcake with
Brave Tart's Classic Yellow Layer Cake

Strawberry Shortcake Cream

1 tablespoon unflavored
powdered gelatin

3 tablespoons cold water

4 ounces cream cheese,
at room temperature

¾ cup granulated sugar

½ teaspoon kosher salt

½ cup Pastry Cream (page 303)

½ cup sour cream,
at room temperature

½ teaspoon vanilla extract

2 cups heavy cream

3 pints strawberries, hulled and
evenly sliced

¼ cup semisweet chocolate
shavings

and invert the cakes onto the racks. Let cool. The cooled cakes can be tightly wrapped in plastic and kept at room temperature for 2 days, or frozen for up to 1 month.

5. Make the syrup. In a heavy-bottomed saucepot set over medium-high heat, bring the sugar and water to a boil. Once the sugar has fully dissolved, let the syrup boil for 45 seconds, then remove from the heat and cool. Stir in the St-Germain.

6. Make the shortcake cream. In a small microwave-safe bowl, sprinkle the gelatin over the water and allow to sit for a few minutes until the gelatin swells (or blooms) from absorbing the water. Once bloomed, melt the gelatin in the microwave for about 30 seconds and set aside.

7. In the bowl of a stand mixer fitted with the paddle attachment or in a large bowl using a handheld mixer, beat the cream cheese, sugar, and salt on medium-high speed for 3 to 5 minutes, until smooth, stopping midway through to scrape down the bottom and sides of the bowl with a rubber spatula. Add the pastry cream and sour cream and mix on medium speed for 1 minute, until combined. Reduce the speed to low and stream in the vanilla and gelatin mixture. Remove the bowl from the mixer and, using a rubber spatula, scrape the mixture into a large bowl.

8. Clean the mixer bowl, return it to the stand and using the whisk attachment, whip the cream to medium peaks. Remove the bowl from the mixer, then add a rubber spatula's worth of whipped cream to the cream cheese mixture in the bowl. Gently fold in the cream in three portions, using a figure-8 motion, until the cream is fully incorporated. It's best to use the shortcake cream right away, since the gelatin will start to set the cream quickly and it will become difficult to work with.

9. Using a large serrated knife, trim the domed tops of the cakes so they're flat; save the scraps for snacking. Cut each cake horizontally into two even layers, creating four layers in total; set the top layers aside.

10. Brush the bottom layer of one cake evenly with the simple syrup. Spread about 1 cup of the shortcake cream evenly over the layer and top with a layer of strawberries, followed by another layer of cream. Place the second layer right on top, brush with syrup, and repeat this step until you have all four layers stacked. Once you place the fourth layer on top, liberally brush the layer with simple syrup, then cover the entire cake with the cream. Decorate as desired with fresh strawberries, chocolate shavings, toasted coconut, mixed berries, or whatever brilliance you can come up with. Let the cake set up in the refrigerator for a minimum of 2 hours before serving. Store any leftovers in an airtight container in the refrigerator for up to 4 days.

Here's the thing about upside-down cakes, y'all: there are no rules beyond caramel + fruit + cake batter = upside down cake. Experiment with the fruit you love that's in season and think beyond pineapple (even though I do love pineapple). I would go so far as recommending you invest in a mandoline so you can cut paper-thin slices of fruit for social media–worthy shingling, should that be something you're after. But, practically speaking, cutting fruit exactly and consistently will yield better results in baking because all the fruit will cook much more evenly. Some of my favorite alternatives to the classic pineapple are peaches, plums, bananas, citrus, apples, pears, and rhubarb. I won't tell you an exact amount of fruit to add because it depends on the actual fruit, the season, and your personal taste. The important part is to ensure the cake has a single, even layer of fruit.

1. Make the caramel sauce. In a heavy-bottomed saucepot, combine the brown sugar and butter and cook over medium-high heat until the sugar dissolves and the mixture is at a full rolling boil, about 1 minute. Remove from the heat, stir in the salt, and set aside.

2. Make the cake. Preheat the oven to 325°F. Liberally butter the sides and bottom of a 9-inch round cake pan with 2-inch-high sides. Pour the sauce into the pan and arrange the fruit(s) over the caramel sauce in an even layer.

3. In a medium bowl, whisk together the all-purpose flour, almond flour, baking powder, and salt. In another bowl, stir together the sour cream and buttermilk. In the bowl of a stand mixer fitted with the paddle attachment or in a large bowl using a handheld mixer, cream the butter with the granulated sugar and brown sugar on medium speed, until light and fluffy, about 4 minutes. Stop the mixer and scrape down the bottom and sides of the bowl with a rubber spatula halfway through. Beat in the eggs, one at a time, mixing well after each addition, followed by the vanilla. Alternately beat in the dry ingredients and the sour cream, beginning and ending with the dry ingredients. Mix just until the ingredients are incorporated.

4. Transfer the batter to the prepared cake pan, pouring it directly over the fruit. Bake on the center rack in your oven for about 1 hour, rotating the pan after 30 minutes, until golden brown and a cake tester comes out clean when inserted into the center.

5. Set the cake on a wire rack and let cool in the pan for 10 minutes. Place a serving plate with a raised edge over the pan, very carefully invert the cake onto the plate, and remove the pan. You can serve the cake immediately or let it cool completely and serve at room temperature. The cake can be stored well wrapped in foil or in an airtight container at room temperature for up to 4 days.

Upside-Down Cake

Makes one 9-inch cake

Caramel Sauce

1 cup firmly packed
dark brown sugar

½ cup unsalted butter

¾ teaspoon kosher salt

Sour Cream Cake

1 cup unsalted butter,
at room temperature, plus
more for greasing the pan

Sliced fruit of your choice
(see recipe introduction)

2 cups all-purpose flour

½ cup almond flour

¾ teaspoon baking powder

½ teaspoon kosher salt

½ cup sour cream,
at room temperature

¼ cup buttermilk,
at room temperature

1 cup granulated sugar

¾ cup firmly packed
light brown sugar

4 eggs, at room temperature

1 teaspoon vanilla extract

Dump Cake

Makes one 9 by 13-inch cake

1 (21-ounce) can cherry pie filling

1 (29-ounce) can sliced peaches in syrup

1 teaspoon kosher salt

1 teaspoon vanilla extract

1 box white cake mix

¾ cup unsalted butter, sliced thinly

Ya know, there's no reason for me to include this recipe other than that it's ridiculously delicious. Despite everything that's in it (a whole host of ingredients that I would not purchase under any other circumstances) . . . it's surprisingly good. I almost couldn't decide between including this dump cake or the "cuppa cuppa" cake that Truvy, Dolly Parton's character in *Steel Magnolias*, speaks so fondly of—both remind me of my childhood and my grandmothers and exemplify the American South. Dump Cake won out, just because I think it's the more delicious of the two.

1. Preheat the oven to 350°F. Pour the cherry pie filling and the peaches in their syrup directly into a 9 by 13-inch baking pan, along with the salt and vanilla. Stir to combine. Sprinkle the cake mix right over the top of the fruit and dot the cake mix with the butter.

2. Bake the cake for 50 to 60 minutes, rotating the pan after 25 minutes, until golden brown and bubbling.

3. Set the cake on a wire rack and cool for 20 minutes before cutting and serving. This cake keeps well wrapped in foil or plastic wrap and refrigerated for up to 5 days.

The first time I watched my mom make this cake, I ended up on the kitchen floor—crying, kicking, and screaming in FULL protest of anyone putting any vegetable in CAKE. I like to use this as an example of the ways I've matured through the years. This recipe is straightforward, simple, and honest-to-goodness reliably delicious.

Carrot Cake

Makes one 9-inch layer cake

Carrot Cake

1 pound carrots, peeled
and shredded

1½ cups vegetable oil

3 eggs, at room temperature

½ cup buttermilk,
at room temperature

1 teaspoon vanilla extract

2 cups granulated sugar

1 tablespoon grated fresh ginger

1 teaspoon kosher salt

3 cups all-purpose flour

2 teaspoons baking powder

1 teaspoon baking soda

1½ teaspoons ground cinnamon

1 teaspoon ground cardamom

Boozy Simple Syrup

⅔ cup granulated sugar

⅔ cup water

⅓ cup Cointreau or spiced rum

Cream Cheese Icing

1½ pounds cream cheese,
at room temperature

1½ cups unsalted butter,
at room temperature

3¾ cups powdered sugar, sifted

1 tablespoon finely grated
orange zest

1 tablespoon finely grated
fresh ginger

1. Make the cake. Preheat the oven to 350°F. Lightly coat two 9-inch round cake pans with cooking spray, then line the bottoms of the pans with parchment paper and lightly spray the paper.

2. In a large bowl, whisk together the carrots, oil, eggs, buttermilk, vanilla, sugar, ginger, and salt. In a medium bowl, whisk together the flour, baking powder, baking soda, cinnamon, and cardamom. Add the dry ingredients to the wet ingredients and mix by hand until smooth. Using a rubber spatula, divide the batter evenly between the prepared cake pans (about 3½ cups per pan) and bake on the center rack of the oven for about 30 minutes, rotating the pans after 15 minutes, until the tops are golden and a cake tester comes out clean when inserted into the center of each cake. Transfer the cakes to a wire rack and let cool in the pans for 10 minutes. Place a rack over each pan, invert the cakes onto the racks, and remove the pans. Peel off the parchment. Cool completely.

3. Make the syrup. In a heavy-bottomed saucepot set over medium-high heat, bring the sugar and water to a boil. Once the sugar has fully dissolved, let the syrup boil for 45 seconds, then remove from the heat. Let cool for 30 minutes, then stir in the Cointreau.

4. Make the icing. In the bowl of a stand mixer fitted with the paddle attachment or in a large bowl using a handheld mixer, beat the cream cheese and butter on medium-high speed until smooth. Decrease the speed to low and stream in the powdered sugar. Beat until just combined. Stop the mixer and scrape down the bottom and sides of the bowl with a rubber spatula. Increase the speed to medium-high and beat until smooth and light, 4 to 5 minutes. Stop the mixer and scrape down the sides of the bowl again to ensure that the frosting is as smooth as possible. Return the mixer to low speed and beat in the orange zest and ginger until just combined.

5. Using a large serrated knife, trim the domed tops of the cakes so they're flat; save the scraps for snacking. Cut each cake horizontally into two even layers, creating four layers in total. Place one layer on a cake plate or stand. Brush the top with about one-quarter of the syrup. Top with 1½ cups of the icing. Place a second layer on top. Repeat the process with the next two layers and top with the remaining cake layer; brush the top with simple syrup. Spread the top and sides of the cake with the rest of the icing.

6. Refrigerate the cake for at least 5 hours before serving to set. The cake will keep covered or in an airtight container in the refrigerator for up to 5 days. Bring to room temperature before serving.

Spiced Rum Bundt Cake

Makes one 10-cup Bundt cake

Rum Bundt Cake

1 cup unsalted butter, at room temperature, plus more for greasing the pan

4 cups all-purpose flour, plus more for flouring the pan

3 cups granulated sugar

2 (3.4-ounce) boxes instant vanilla pudding mix

1 tablespoon plus 1 teaspoon baking powder

1 cup vegetable oil

2 teaspoons kosher salt

1 cup whole milk, at room temperature

8 eggs, at room temperature

1 cup spiced rum

1½ teaspoons vanilla bean paste

Soaker Syrup

2 cups granulated sugar

½ cup water

1 cup unsalted butter

1 cup spiced rum

1 teaspoon vanilla extract

If you've ever stepped foot in New Orleans, you understand why it's referred to as the northernmost Caribbean city. The connections run deep, from the climate and the music to the celebratory spirit and the food. A few years ago, when I bought my house, one of my neighbors brought me a rum cake to welcome me to the neighborhood (she also assigned me the nickname "cornbread," which she still calls me years later). It's a gesture that has stuck with me, and now we trade baked goods on every holiday. Even the rest of the women on my block have joined in the fun. I make everyone pies, but I make German Chocolate Cake (page 272) for that one enthusiastic neighbor, and she delivers me this cake, without fail, with as much pride as I've ever seen anyone take in honoring their roots. Understandably so—this cake is unbelievably delicious.

1. Make the cake. Preheat the oven to 325°F. Liberally butter and lightly flour every crevice of a 10-cup Bundt pan.

2. In the bowl of a stand mixer fitted with the paddle attachment or in a large bowl using a handheld mixer, mix the butter, flour, sugar, pudding, baking powder, oil, and salt on medium speed until well combined. Stream in the milk, followed by the eggs, mixing well after each addition. Stop the mixer and scrape down the bottom and sides of the bowl with a rubber spatula to ensure a smooth batter. Stir in the rum and vanilla paste.

3. Pour the batter evenly into the prepared pan. Place in the center of the oven and bake for 85 to 95 minutes, rotating the pan after 40 minutes, until the cake is golden and a cake tester comes out clean when inserted into the center of the cake.

4. Meanwhile, make the syrup. In a heavy-bottomed saucepot, bring the sugar and water to a boil, stirring to dissolve the sugar. Add the butter and allow to melt. Remove from the heat and stir in the rum and vanilla. Keep warm for soaking. (You can make this syrup ahead of time and bring to a simmer over medium-high heat when your cake is about to come out of the oven.)

5. Remove the cake from the oven and immediately place a serving plate over the pan. Very carefully invert the cake onto the plate and remove the pan. Using a fork or a paring knife, poke holes in the cake and immediately (and very generously) spoon or brush the syrup onto the cake while still hot.

6. You can serve the cake immediately or let it cool and serve it at room temperature. This cake will keep in an airtight container at room temperature for up to 5 days.

What's Mine Is Yours

I think this cake is best with age. Don't get me wrong, it's super delicious hot and fresh, but I think it really hits its peak on days two and three. If you're feeling extra indulgent, butter a slice of cake on both sides and griddle until golden brown to enjoy for breakfast (or lunch . . . or dinner. . . . or just whenever 'cause you make your own rules).

This cake was inspired by Edna Lewis and Lisa Donovan. Part of the magic of this cake (and my favorite part) are the bites where the cake meets the frosting. When the frosting is still slightly warm, it seeps into the cake and creates almost gooey bites. If it were acceptable to eat only the middle of a cake, this might be the one I'd choose. Just note that the caramel icing needs to be applied with a sense of urgency because the cooler it gets, the more difficult it will be to work with. Once the cake is iced, it keeps at room temperature for up to 5 days . . . assuming it would ever last that long.

1. Make the cake. Preheat the oven to 350°F. Lightly coat two 9-inch round cake pans with cooking spray, then line the bottoms with parchment paper and lightly spray the paper.

2. In a medium bowl, whisk together the flour, baking soda, and salt. In the bowl of a stand mixer fitted with the paddle attachment or in a large bowl using a handheld mixer, cream the butter and sugar on medium speed until light and creamy. Decrease the speed to low and beat in the eggs, one at a time, mixing well after each addition. Stop the mixer and scrape down the bottom and sides of the bowl with a rubber spatula. Increase the speed to high and beat until light and fluffy, 4 to 5 minutes. Beat in the vanilla. Add the dry ingredients, in three portions, alternating with the buttermilk, beginning and ending with the dry ingredients. Mix until just incorporated.

3. Divide the batter evenly between the prepared cake pans (about 4½ cups per pan). Bake for 30 to 35 minutes, rotating the pans after 15 minutes, until the cakes are golden brown and a cake tester comes out clean when inserted into the center of each cake.

4. Set the cakes on a wire rack and let cool in the pans for about 10 minutes. Place a wire rack over each pan, invert the cakes onto the racks, and remove the pans. Peel off the parchment paper. Cool completely.

5. Before making the icing, prep the cake layers. Using a large serrated knife, trim the domed tops of the cakes so they're flat; save the scraps for snacks. Place one cake layer on a cake platter or cake stand.

6. Make the icing. Attach a candy thermometer to the rim of a large heavy-bottomed saucepot. Melt the butter over medium-high heat, then stir in the sugar, buttermilk, evaporated milk, and baking soda. Cook, stirring constantly, until the mixture foams up and then "deflates," about 5 minutes. Be mindful of where your hands and arms are, as the mixture will hiss, bubble, and steam and, well, that can make a painful burn. Cook, stirring, until the caramel mixture is very dark brown and

continued

Caramel Cake

Makes one 9-inch layer cake

White Buttermilk Cake
3¾ cups all-purpose flour

1 teaspoon baking soda

2 teaspoons kosher salt

1 cup unsalted butter, at room temperature

2½ cups granulated sugar

3 eggs, at room temperature

1½ teaspoons vanilla extract

2¾ cups buttermilk, at room temperature

Caramel Icing
1½ cups unsalted butter

2½ cups granulated sugar

1 cup buttermilk

½ cup evaporated milk

1 tablespoon baking soda

1½ teaspoons vanilla extract

½ teaspoon kosher salt

continued
Caramel Cake

reaches a temperature of 240°F, about 4 minutes. Carefully pour the mixture into the bowl of a stand mixer fitted with the paddle attachment or pour it into a large bowl and use a handheld mixer. Add the vanilla and salt and beat on low speed for 3 to 5 minutes, until the icing is thick but still pourable.

7. Once the icing is ready (again, working quickly because the icing will set up and thicken as it cools), spread about 1½ cups of the icing to the edge of the first layer of cake. Place the second cake directly and evenly on top and pour the remaining icing evenly over the cake, using a rubber or offset spatula to smooth out and spread it into any uniced spots.

8. Refrigerate the cake for at least 1½ to 2 hours before serving to allow the icing to fully cool and set. The cake can be stored in an airtight container at room temperature for up to 5 days.

Making Perfect Cake

I know we've talked a lot about the importance of ingredients being as close to the same temperature as possible in baking to create stable emulsifications. In that same vein, it is equally as important to make sure you're mixing your ingredients correctly and in the right order to create the perfect texture and crumb. If you add the dry ingredients (or even the wet ingredients) all at once, you're literally breaking down the structure of the batter and therefore all the work you've already done. This results in an overmixed, overdeveloped protein structure and, in a lot of cases, a broken emulsion. In the long run, that means you'll produce tough, chewy, and heavy baked goods.

When you take the time to alternate adding your ingredients, you're balancing the structure and emulsion the whole way through, allowing for optimum delicate, fluffy, and soft outcomes! Being patient and doing the "work" for the batter, rather than dumping everything in and letting the batter work it out through mixing and friction, is always the way to go.

Hummingbird Cake

Makes one 9-inch layer cake

Hummingbird Cake

3 cups all-purpose flour

2 cups granulated sugar

1 teaspoon baking soda

1 teaspoon ground cinnamon

¼ teaspoon ground organic rose petals

¼ teaspoon ground cardamom

3 eggs, at room temperature

¾ cup vegetable oil

¼ cup coconut oil, at room temperature

1½ teaspoons vanilla extract

½ teaspoon kosher salt

½ cup sour cream, at room temperature

8 ounces crushed pineapple with juice

2 cups mashed very ripe bananas (about 5)

1 cup chopped pecans or pecan pieces

Frosting

1½ pounds cream cheese, at room temperature

¾ cup unsalted butter, at room temperature

5¼ cups powdered sugar

1 teaspoon finely grated orange zest

½ teaspoon vanilla bean paste

This was one of those cakes that had a place in our home during most holidays when I was growing up. Like much of the baking my mom did, I thought the name "hummingbird" was something she completely made up using poetic license. Years into my professional career, I came to understand the cake I grew up eating was actually created in Jamaica and named after the island's national bird. It gained unprecedented popularity in the American South when the recipe was first published in a 1978 issue of *Southern Living*.

1. Make the cake. Preheat the oven to 325°F. Lightly coat two 9-inch round cake pans with 4-inch-high sides with cooking spray, then line the bottoms of the pans with parchment paper and lightly spray the paper. (If you don't have 4-inch-deep pans, 2-inch-deep will work.)

2. In a large bowl, combine the flour, sugar, baking soda, cinnamon, rose petals, and cardamom and mix well. In a medium bowl, lightly whisk the eggs with the vegetable oil, coconut oil, vanilla, and salt, then stir in the dry ingredients, mixing just until they are moistened. Stir in the sour cream. Using a large spatula, fold in the crushed pineapple and juice, bananas, and pecans. Divide the batter evenly between the prepared pans. Bake the cakes in the center of the oven for about 45 minutes, rotating the pans after 20 minutes, until the cakes are golden brown and a cake tester comes out clean when inserted into the center of each cake. Let the cakes cool in the pans on a wire rack for 15 to 20 minutes. Place a rack over each pan, invert the cakes onto the racks, and remove the pans. Peel off the parchment paper. Cool completely.

3. Make the frosting. In the bowl of a stand mixer fitted with the paddle attachment or in a large bowl using a handheld mixer, beat the cream cheese and butter on medium-high speed until smooth. Sift the powdered sugar into the bowl; beat until incorporated and smooth. Stop the mixer and scrape down the bottom and sides of the bowl with a rubber spatula to ensure that the frosting is as smooth as possible. Beat in the orange zest and vanilla paste.

4. Using a serrated knife, trim the domed tops of the cakes so they're flat; save the scraps for snacking. Cut each cake horizontally into two even layers, creating four layers in total. Set one layer on a cake stand or plate and spread with the frosting. Continue to stack and frost the layers, then spread a thin layer of frosting all over the cake.

5. Refrigerate for 15 minutes, until set. Spread the remaining frosting evenly all over the sides and top of the cake. The cake will keep at room temperature for about 4 days, if it ever actually sticks around that long.

What's Mine Is Yours

Rose petals are not traditional in a hummingbird cake, but back when I was working in San Francisco, I met Kathy FitzHenry, who owned Juliet Mae spices. She introduced me to the idea of adding rose to cinnamon to help highlight cinnamon's floral nuances. As someone who had never truly loved (or even appreciated) cinnamon, this blend literally changed my life!

Some people like to press pecans onto the sides of the cake. I think that looks really nice, especially when the top is just stark white.

I'm a fan of my mom's approach of using the microwave oven as a cake box for storing cake, but you can also put the cake on a stand or plate and invert a large bowl or pot over the cake to protect it. Once the cake is sliced, however, it will start to dry out pretty quickly, so place a piece of plastic wrap against the cut sides to help lengthen the life of the cake.

Let's Call It Love

Here's a random fact: Hummingbird Cake was the inspiration for the "What's Mine Is Yours" advice in this book. See, Carrie Brownstein is the guitarist for the American indie rock band Sleater-Kinney—my favorite band in the world—and that's the title of one of their songs that's particularly relevant to my creative process. In her book *Hunger Makes Me a Modern Girl*, Brown explains that on the album *The Woods*, there are moments that break apart, disintegrate, and allow the opportunity to rebuild. The idea of breaking open your comfort zone, undoing tradition, and rebuilding through experimentation and exploration to really define the root of a dish is how I've approached every creative exercise in my career. I love Sleater-Kinney.

Hummingbird Cake is one of my favorite recipes to tear apart and reassemble in new ways because I love the flavor combinations so much. And no matter how far I deviate from the original cake as far as texture, technique, and temperature, the moment I put the flavors together, it always triggers that emotional response for me and brings the entire adventure of experimentation and exploration full circle.

In the past, one of my favorite versions of hummingbird cake used this recipe (minus the pecans). I passed the batter through a fine sieve, then charged it with NO_2 (nitrogen dioxide) in an iSi canister (like making homemade canned whipped cream). I filled Dixie cups (unwaxed, if you can find them) with the aerated batter and microwaved the cups for about 30 seconds to create the little cake "sponges" that gained popularity in the 2000s. I served them topped with braised pineapple, pecan butter, and cream cheese ice cream. How's that for taking apart and rebuilding?

German Chocolate Cake

Makes one 9-inch layer cake

I'm not proud of the fact that coconut was an acquired taste for me. Only in my late twenties did I grow to love its flavor (the texture still kind of freaks me out). When confronted with German chocolate cake as a kid, I would eat around the frosting and just enjoy the chocolate cake. It is now one of my favorite cakes. I make mine with a chocolate-buttermilk cake, which is the recipe I use 98 percent of the time when chocolate cake is involved. It has a really light crumb, it's easy and really delicious—plus, it just gets better on day two.

Buttermilk-Chocolate Cake

1½ cups plus 1 tablespoon unsweetened Dutch-processed cocoa powder

1⅓ cups warm water

1½ cups cake flour

1⅓ cups all-purpose flour

1½ teaspoons baking powder

1½ teaspoons baking soda

1 teaspoon kosher salt

2⅔ cups firmly packed dark brown sugar

½ cup plus 2 tablespoons unsalted butter, at room temperature

2 eggs, at room temperature

2 egg yolks, at room temperature

⅔ cup buttermilk, at room temperature

1½ teaspoons vanilla extract

1. Make the cake. Preheat the oven to 350°F. Lightly coat two 9-inch cake pans with cooking spray, then line the bottoms of the pans with parchment paper and lightly spray the paper.

2. In a medium bowl, whisk together the cocoa and water to form a paste. In a separate bowl, sift together the cake flour, all-purpose flour, baking powder, baking soda, and salt. In the bowl of a stand mixer fitted with the paddle attachment or in a large bowl using a handheld mixer, mix the brown sugar and butter on medium speed until well combined and smooth. Reduce the speed to low and add the cocoa paste. Increase the speed to medium and beat to incorporate the cocoa paste evenly. Add the whole eggs and egg yolks, one at a time, mixing well after each addition. Stop the mixer and scrape down the bottom and sides of the bowl with a rubber spatula.

3. Return the mixer to low speed. Add the dry ingredients in three portions, alternating with the buttermilk and beginning and ending with the dry ingredients. Beat until combined, then beat in the vanilla. Using a rubber spatula, divide the batter evenly between the prepared cake pans. Place the cake pans on a baking sheet and bake in the center of the oven for 35 to 45 minutes, rotating the pans after 15 minutes, until a cake tester comes out clean when inserted into the center of each cake and they spring back when pressed with a fingertip. Transfer the cakes to wire racks to cool in the pans for 15 to 20 minutes. Place a wire rack over each pan, invert the cakes onto the racks, and remove the pans. Peel off the parchment paper. Cool completely. These cakes can be wrapped in plastic wrap and stored in the refrigerator for up to 3 days or frozen for up to 1 month.

4. Make the frosting. Preheat the oven to 325°F. Spread the pecans on a rimmed baking sheet in a single layer and bake for about 15 minutes, stirring every 5 minutes, until golden brown and aromatic. Remove from the oven and cool completely.

5. In a heavy-bottomed saucepot, whisk together the evaporated milk, sugar, butter, and egg yolks. Place over medium-high heat and cook, whisking constantly, until the mixture thickens and turns a caramelly brown color, about 12 minutes. Remove from the heat and stir in the pecans, coconut, vanilla paste, and salt. Transfer to a medium bowl and let cool completely. This frosting can be refrigerated in an airtight container for up to 2 days. Bring to room temperature before using.

6. Make the syrup. In a heavy-bottomed saucepot set over medium-high heat, bring the sugar and water to a boil. Once the sugar has fully dissolved, let the syrup boil for 45 seconds, then remove from the heat and stir in the liqueur. Set aside to cool. The syrup can be made a day or two ahead of time and stored in an airtight container at room temperature.

7. Using a large serrated knife, trim the domed tops of the cakes so they're flat; save the scraps for snacking. Cut each cake horizontally into two even layers, creating four layers in total. Place one layer on a cake plate or stand and, using a pastry brush, coat the top with the syrup. Spread 1 cup of the frosting over the top and to the edges of the layer. Place another cake layer on top, brush with syrup, and top with frosting. Repeat until all four layers are stacked. Brush the top layer with syrup and coat the entire top and side of the cake with the remaining frosting.

8. Let the cake stand for at least 1 hour for the frosting to set before slicing and serving. You can keep this cake in an airtight container at room temperature or in the refrigerator, if you prefer, for up to 3 days.

Coconut and Pecan Frosting

3¾ cups pecan pieces

2¼ cups evaporated milk

2¼ cups granulated sugar

1¼ cups plus 2 tablespoons unsalted butter

10 egg yolks, at room temperature

3¾ cups sweetened coconut flakes

1½ teaspoons vanilla bean paste

¾ teaspoon kosher salt

Simple Syrup

1 cup granulated sugar

½ cup water

½ cup Cathead Pecan Vodka or any sort of nut liqueur

This is the cake my mom made all the time when I was growing up because it's super easy. I'd slice little slivers of it all day long, often on the same schedule as my brother and sister, until it was gone. It's one of my favorite cakes, but because it's rich and dense, it's almost like a brownie. I really enjoy it warmed until the frosting and marshmallows become soft again and then topped with vanilla ice cream.

1. Make the cake. Preheat the oven to 350°F. Lightly coat with cooking spray or butter a 9 by 13-inch baking pan. In a large saucepot over medium-low heat, melt the butter. Whisk in the cocoa. Remove from the heat and stir in the sugar and eggs, mixing well. Add the flour, salt, pecans, chocolate chips, and vanilla and mix well.

2. Using a rubber spatula, scrape the batter into the prepared pan and bake in the center of the oven for 35 to 45 minutes, rotating the pan after 15 minutes, until a cake tester comes out clean when inserted into the center of the cake.

3. While the cake is baking, make the frosting. Sift the powdered sugar and cocoa together into the bowl of a stand mixer fitted with the paddle attachment or into a medium bowl and use a handheld mixer. Add the butter and beat on medium-high speed until no visible clumps remain. Stop the mixer occasionally and scrape down the bottom and sides of the bowl with a rubber spatula to ensure the mixture is as smooth as possible. Return the mixer to medium-high speed and stream in the milk. Mix until well incorporated.

4. Sprinkle the marshmallows on top of the warm cake and pour the frosting over the top while still warm. (You're just covering the warm cake with marshmallows so they both kind of melt into each other. It's nasty-good.) Serve warm or at room temperature. This cake keeps at room temperature for up to 4 days.

Mom's Mississippi Mud Cake

Makes one 9 by 13-inch cake

Double-Chocolate Cake

1 cup unsalted butter

½ cup unsweetened Dutch-processed cocoa powder, sifted

2 cups granulated sugar

4 eggs, at room temperature and lightly beaten

1½ cups all-purpose flour

Pinch of kosher salt

1½ cups pecans, chopped

1 cup chocolate chips (use whatever kind you like)

1 teaspoon vanilla extract

Frosting

2½ cups powdered sugar

⅓ cup unsweetened Dutch-processed cocoa powder

2 tablespoons unsalted butter, at room temperature

½ cup whole milk, at room temperature

About 3 cups mini marshmallows

Cakes

Blackout Cake

Makes one 10-inch layer cake

Devil's Food Cake

1½ cups plus 1 tablespoon unsweetened Dutch-processed cocoa powder

1½ cups cake flour

1⅓ cups all-purpose flour

1½ teaspoons baking powder

1½ teaspoons baking soda

½ teaspoon kosher salt

2¾ cups firmly packed dark brown sugar

½ cup plus 2 tablespoons unsalted butter, at room temperature

2 eggs, at room temperature

2 egg yolks, at room temperature

1 cup hot brewed coffee

1½ teaspoons vanilla extract

¼ cup hot water

1¼ cups buttermilk, at room temperature

Chocolate Ganache

1 pound 11 ounces dark chocolate (preferably Valrhona 70% cacao), chopped

3 cups heavy cream

Pinch of kosher salt

Simple Syrup

2 cups sugar

2 cups water

This cake was inspired by McKenzie's Bakery here in New Orleans. It was once one of the most popular bakeries in NOLA, and at its peak, it had about fifty locations around town! Sadly, after sixty-four years in business, the bakery closed in 2000. New Orleanians still romanticize McKenzie's at every opportunity, particularly around Mardi Gras, when no one makes a king cake that compares to theirs. Having a bakery here in NOLA, everyone asks for blackout cake, so I developed this one, based on the folklore and memories shared.

1. Make the cake. Preheat the oven to 350°F. Lightly coat two 10-inch round cake pans with cooking spray, then line the bottoms with parchment paper and lightly spray the paper. In a large bowl, sift the cocoa powder, cake flour, all-purpose flour, baking powder, baking soda, and salt.

2. In the bowl of a stand mixer fitted with the paddle attachment or in a large bowl using a handheld mixer, beat the brown sugar and butter on medium speed until well combined, with no pieces of butter visible. Beat in the whole eggs and egg yolks. Stop the mixer and scrape down the bottom and sides of the bowl with a rubber spatula. In a glass measuring cup, mix the coffee with the vanilla and water and set aside. With the mixer on low, add the dry ingredients in three portions, alternating with the buttermilk, beginning and ending with the dry ingredients. Beat in the coffee mixture. (It is important to add the buttermilk and coffee separately to avoid curdling.)

3. Divide the batter between the prepared cake pans, filling them three-quarters full (about 3½ cups per pan). Bake in the center of the oven for 32 to 40 minutes, rotating the pans after 20 minutes, until a cake tester comes out clean when inserted into the center of each cake and the cakes spring back when pressed with a fingertip. Let the cakes cool in the pans on a wire rack for 30 minutes. Place a wire rack over each pan, invert the cakes onto the racks, and remove the pans. Peel off the parchment and let cool completely.

4. Once the cakes are cool, preheat the oven to 325°F. Using a large serrated knife, trim the domed tops of the cakes so they're flat. Break the cake scraps into even pieces about the size of croutons and spread on a baking sheet. Toast for 15 to 20 minutes, until they are dry and crispy. Let cool then pulse a few times in a food processor to make fine crumbs (or put in a resealable bag and roll all over with a rolling pin to break up). Set aside.

continued

Blackout Cake

5. Meanwhile, make the ganache. Put the chocolate and salt in a heatproof bowl. Place a saucepot full of water over high heat and bring to a boil. Remove from the heat and set the bowl of chocolate over the hot water to melt; stir often to melt the chocolate evenly. In a second pot, bring the cream to a scald (you will see bubbles around the perimeter of the liquid and a wisp of steam from the surface); do not bring to a full boil. Remove from the heat. Pour one-third of the cream into the melted chocolate and whisk to combine. Carefully add the remaining cream in two portions, whisking after each addition, then whisk until the ganache is smooth, shiny, and incorporated. Cover and set aside at room temperature until the ganache cools; this can take several hours. Once cool, the ganache can be covered and refrigerated for up to 5 days (let it come back to room temperature, until it's easily stirred before you use it).

6. Make the syrup. In a heavy-bottomed saucepot set over medium-high heat, bring the sugar and water to a boil. Once the sugar has fully dissolved, let the syrup boil for 45 seconds, then remove from the heat and cool.

7. Carefully and evenly slice each cake horizontally into three equal layers, creating six layers in total. Place one of the layers on a cake stand or plate and, using a pastry brush, generously dab some of the syrup evenly onto the cake. Top the cake layer with about ½ cup of the ganache and use an offset spatula to spread the ganache evenly to the edge of the cake. Place the next layer directly on top of the ganache and repeat with the syrup and ganache; continue until you've stacked all six layers of the cake.

8. Brush the top layer with syrup. Using the remaining ganache, coat the top and side of the cake as evenly as possible, then coat the ganache with the cake crumbs. Pat the cake crumbs all over the whole damn cake, cover loosely with plastic wrap, and refrigerate for at least 2 hours to set up completely.

9. Bring the cake back to room temperature before serving. You can keep the cake at room temperature for up to 2 days, but I promise you it won't last that long!

What's Mine Is Yours

I think it's easier to assemble this cake when the cake layers are cold. I like to freeze the cake rounds and then assemble it. Then I let the cake sit out at room temperature overnight, and it's good to go the next day.

Red Velvet Cake

Makes one 9-inch layer cake

Beet Juice

4 red beets, washed and dried

4 teaspoons kosher salt

Beet Cake

6 ounces unsweetened chocolate, chopped

4 cups all-purpose flour

1 tablespoon baking soda

1 tablespoon kosher salt

6 eggs, at room temperature

2 cups vegetable oil

4½ cups granulated sugar

2 tablespoons vanilla extract

1 cup buttermilk, at room temperature

Cream Cheese Frosting

1½ cups unsalted butter, at room temperature

1¼ pounds cream cheese, at room temperature

1 tablespoon vanilla bean paste

7 cups powdered sugar, sifted

Simple Syrup

1 cup granulated sugar

¾ cup water

You know that dark red, towering, picture-perfect red velvet cake you are imagining right now? This is not it. This is an incredibly delicious, natural approach to red velvet cake, inspired by how my grandmothers and great-grandmothers would achieve the best cake possible without the means to buy expensive ingredients. This cake is tender, dark, and earthy in all the right ways, and, no it doesn't taste like beets.

1. Make the beet juice. Preheat the oven to 350°F. Sprinkle each beet with 1 teaspoon of the salt and wrap them separately in foil. Bake for 45 to 60 minutes, until the beets are tender enough to pierce with a fork. Decrease the oven temperature to 325°F. Cool for 20 minutes before unwrapping each beet and peeling off the skin. Roughly chop the beets and process using a juicer to yield 2 cups beet juice. Set aside to cool to room temperature. If you don't have a juicer, a blender works fine also; you just may need to add a touch of water to help break down the beets. If you use a blender, strain the pulp through a fine-mesh strainer. Alternatively, substitute store-bought 100% beet juice; the salt used for roasting the beets is minimal, so no need to add salt if using prepared beet juice.

2. Make the cake. Lightly coat three 9-inch round cake pans with cooking spray, then line the bottoms with parchment paper and lightly spray the paper.

3. In a small microwave-safe bowl, melt the chocolate in the microwave, stirring every 30 to 45 seconds, until smooth. Meanwhile, in a medium bowl, whisk together the flour, baking soda, and salt.

4. In the bowl of a stand mixer fitted with the whisk attachment or in a large bowl using a handheld mixer, whisk the eggs on high speed until light and fluffy, about 5 minutes. Reduce the speed to medium and stream in the oil, followed by the sugar and vanilla, whisking for about 1 minute to fully combine. Remove the bowl from the mixer and transfer the egg mixture to a large bowl. Using a rubber spatula, carefully fold in the dry ingredients in a few portions, mixing carefully so as not to deflate the batter. Stir in the melted chocolate, followed by the beet juice and buttermilk. Using the spatula, divide the batter evenly among the prepared cake pans. Bake for 40 to 45 minutes, rotating the pans after 20 minutes, until a cake tester comes out clean when inserted into the center of each cake.

5. Cool the cakes in the pans on a wire rack for 20 minutes. Place a wire rack over each pan, invert the cakes onto the racks, and remove the pans. Peel off the parchment paper. The cakes can be wrapped in plastic wrap and stored at room temperature or in the refrigerator for up to 1 day.

continued

continued
Red Velvet Cake

6. Make the frosting. In the bowl of a stand mixer fitted with the paddle attachment or in a large bowl using a handheld mixer, beat the butter and cream cheese on high speed for about 5 minutes, until well combined. Stop the mixer and scrape down the bottom and sides of the bowl with a rubber spatula. With the mixer on low speed, add the vanilla paste and mix to combine. With the mixer running, stream in the powdered sugar. When all the sugar has been added, increase the speed to medium-high and whip for 3 minutes, until smooth and fluffy. You can cover and refrigerate the frosting for up to 3 days. Bring to room temperature before using.

7. Make the syrup. In a heavy-bottomed saucepot set over medium-high heat, bring the sugar and water to a boil. Once the sugar has fully dissolved, let the syrup boil for 45 seconds, then remove from the heat and cool.

8. Using a large serrated knife, trim the domed tops of the cakes so they're flat; save the scraps for snacking. Cut each cake horizontally into two even layers, creating six layers in total. Place one layer on a cake plate. Brush with about one-sixth cup of the syrup, then spread with 1 cup of the frosting. Place a second layer on top. Repeat the process until all the layers have been stacked; brush the top with syrup. Spread the top and sides of the cake with the rest of the frosting.

9. Loosely cover the cake with plastic wrap and refrigerate for at least 5 hours before serving. The cake will keep, covered, in the refrigerator for up to 3 days. Bring to room temperature before serving.

What's Mine Is Yours

Roasting and juicing beets may not be your thing, and that is okay. It is common these days to find 100% pure beet juice in grocery stores. If you're unable to find it in your local grocery store, swing by your favorite juice drinks shop and get some freshly made.

If you prefer to butter your pans, do so liberally, then dust the pans with cocoa powder.

Lemon Doberge Cake

Makes one 9-inch layer cake

Buttermilk Genoise

8¾ cups cake flour

2½ tablespoons baking powder

2½ cups buttermilk,
at room temperature

2½ tablespoons sour cream,
at room temperature

1¾ cups plus 2 tablespoons
unsalted butter, at room
temperature

5 cups granulated sugar

1⅔ teaspoons kosher salt

2½ teaspoons finely grated
lemon zest

10 eggs, separated and at
room temperature

2½ teaspoons vanilla extract

Doberge cake is the birthday cake of choice in New Orleans—it's one of our most celebrated desserts. The cake was first created in Hungary by József Dobos, who sought to make a sturdy cake that didn't need refrigeration and could be shipped. He called his invention the dobos torte and made it by layering genoise with buttercream and covering it in a caramel glaze. Back in NOLA, during the Depression, a woman by the name of Beulah Ledner morphed the cake to suit our hot climate, swapping the buttercream for custard and renaming it Doberge Cake, so locals would find it more appealing. In 1949, Ledner sold the recipe to Joe Gambino, and Gambino's Bakery has been selling the cake ever since.

This makes one very tall cake, which takes a lot of cake batter. It requires a 7-quart stand mixer, but if you don't own one, you can make the cake batter in a very large bowl, using a hand mixer.

1. Make the genoise. Preheat the oven to 375°F. Lightly coat three 9-inch round cake pans with cooking spray, then line the bottoms with parchment paper and lightly spray the paper.

2. In a medium bowl, whisk together the flour and baking powder. In another bowl, whisk the buttermilk and sour cream. In the bowl of a 7-quart stand mixer fitted with the paddle attachment or in a very large bowl using a handheld mixer, beat the butter with the sugar and salt on medium speed until light, fluffy, and pale in color, 4 to 5 minutes. Stop the mixer and scrape down the bottom and sides of the bowl with a rubber spatula. Beat in the lemon zest, then beat in the egg yolks, one at a time, mixing well after each addition. Beat in the vanilla.

3. Sift one-third of the dry ingredients into the mixer, mixing on the lowest speed setting. When most of the first addition of dry ingredients has been incorporated, slowly add half the buttermilk mixture. Sift in another third of the dry ingredients, add the remaining buttermilk, and sift in the final batch of dry ingredients. Transfer the mixture to a large, clean bowl. Clean the mixer bowl thoroughly, making sure there are no traces of butter or buttermilk on the bowl. Switch to the whisk attachment.

4. In the clean bowl of the stand mixer, quickly whip the egg whites on medium speed until foamy. Increase the speed to high and whip the whites until stiff peaks form (the whites should hold their points when you pull the whisk out of the meringue), 4 to 5 minutes. Using a rubber spatula, gently fold the whipped egg whites into the cake batter, working carefully not to deflate the whites while incorporating.

continued

Lemon Doberge Cake

Lemon Custard

6 eggs, at room temperature

8 egg yolks, at room temperature

1 cup granulated sugar

½ cup finely grated lemon zest

1 cup fresh lemon juice

1 teaspoon kosher salt

½ cup unsalted butter,
at room temperature

German Buttercream

1¼ cups granulated sugar

2 cups whole milk

1 teaspoon vanilla bean paste

½ teaspoon kosher salt

3 tablespoons cornstarch

2 eggs, at room temperature

2 egg yolks, at room temperature

4 cups unsalted butter, at room
temperature, cut into pieces

Simple Syrup

3 cups granulated sugar

3 cups water

5. Divide the batter among the prepared cake pans and bake for 45 to 50 minutes, rotating the pans after 25 minutes, until the cakes are set and bounce back when gently pressed with a fingertip. Cool in the pans on wire racks for about 10 minutes. Place a wire rack over each pan, invert the cakes onto the racks, and remove the pans. Peel off the parchment and cool completely. The cakes can be made a day or two ahead if well wrapped in plastic wrap and stored at room temperature. I also find working with this cake while it is cold makes the job far easier, so feel free to keep the cake layers in the refrigerator for a couple of days.

6. Make the custard. Fill a large bowl with ice water and set it near the stove. In a large stainless-steel bowl set over a pot of simmering water, whisk the whole eggs and egg yolks with the sugar until super thick and foamy, about 5 minutes. Whisk in the lemon zest, lemon juice, and salt. Cook, whisking constantly, until the mixture thickens enough that when the whisk is gently removed, the trail from the whisk remains on the surface. Remove the bowl from the heat and quickly whisk in the butter, a few pieces at a time. Strain the custard through a fine-mesh sieve into a medium bowl and set the bowl in the ice bath. Continue whisking slowly while the custard cools. If not using immediately, store the custard in an airtight container in the refrigerator for up to 3 days.

7. Make the buttercream. In a heavy-bottomed saucepot, combine ½ cup plus 2 tablespoons of the sugar with the milk, vanilla paste, and salt. Place over high heat until it comes to a scald (you will see bubbles around the perimeter of the liquid and a wisp of steam rising from the surface); do not bring to a full boil.

8. Meanwhile, in a medium bowl, whisk together the cornstarch and the remaining ½ cup plus 2 tablespoons sugar. Whisk in the eggs and egg yolks until smooth. Start streaming a small amount of the hot dairy into the egg mixture, whisking constantly to prevent the eggs from cooking. Continue whisking in the milk mixture until three-quarters of it has been incorporated into the egg mixture. Pour the mixture in the bowl into the saucepot and place the pot over medium-high heat. Cook, again whisking constantly, until the mixture thickens and begins to bubble. Let it bubble for 1½ minutes, then remove from the heat and transfer to the bowl of a stand mixer fitted with the paddle attachment or transfer to a large bowl and use a handheld mixer. Mix on medium speed until completely cool, then beat in the butter, a few pieces at a time, until it is incorporated and the buttercream is creamy and smooth. The buttercream can be covered and refrigerated for up to 2 days; bring it to room temperature and beat it with the mixer to refresh it before using.

9. Make the syrup. In a heavy-bottomed saucepot set over medium-high heat, bring the sugar and water to a boil. Once the sugar has fully dissolved, let the syrup boil for 45 seconds, then remove from the heat and cool.

10. Using a large serrated knife, trim the domed tops of the cakes so they're flat; save the scraps for snacking. Cut each cake horizontally into three even layers, creating nine layers total. Place the first layer on a platter and brush with about ⅓ cup of the syrup. Spread ⅔ cup of the custard evenly over the cake, leaving about a ½-inch border around the perimeter. Top with another cake layer, brush with another ⅓ cup syrup, then spread evenly with another ⅔ cup of the custard, again leaving a ½-inch border. Repeat until you have stacked the last layer of cake. Brush the top layer with syrup. Refrigerate the cake for at least 45 minutes before frosting.

11. Apply a layer of buttercream to the sides of the cake with a large offset spatula. Smooth out the sides as evenly as possible and then spread a smooth, even layer of buttercream across the top.

12. Chill the cake for another hour to set before serving. This cake can be kept well wrapped in foil or plastic wrap and stored in the refrigerator for up to 5 days.

The chocolate version of Doberge is one of my favorite cakes, as a self-proclaimed chocolate enthusiast. Like the lemon version (page 284), this makes one very tall, stunning cake (and requires a 7-quart stand mixer or very large mixing bowl), often a part of any celebration in New Orleans. Once you master this recipe, and the lemon version, try combining the two by picking your favorite of the cakes and then alternating the chocolate and the lemon fillings between layers for the real New Orleans way of life.

1. Make the cake. Preheat the oven to 350°F. Lightly coat three 9-inch cake pans with cooking spray, then line the bottoms of the pans with parchment paper and lightly spray the paper.

2. In a medium bowl, sift together the flour, cocoa, and baking soda. In a large heatproof bowl, whisk together the eggs and sugar. Place the bowl over a pot of simmering water and whisk continuously until the mixture is warm enough to dissolve the sugar completely. Remove from the heat and transfer the eggs to the bowl of a stand mixer fitted with the whisk attachment or transfer to a very large bowl and use a handheld mixer. Whip on high speed until the mixture is thick and pale, 5 to 7 minutes. Add the vanilla paste and whip for 1 minute.

3. Remove the bowl from the mixer and, using a rubber spatula, gently fold in the sifted dry ingredients in three portions, being careful not to deflate the egg mixture in the process. When incorporated, stream in the butter, also folding it into the batter.

4. Divide the batter among the prepared cake pans and tap the pans gently on the counter to release any large air bubbles. Bake for about 20 minutes, rotating the pans after 8 minutes, until a cake tester comes out clean when inserted into the center of each cake. Let cool in the pans on a wire rack for 10 minutes. Place a wire rack over each pan, invert the cakes onto the racks, and remove the pans. Peel off the parchment. Let the cakes cool completely. The cakes can be wrapped in plastic wrap and kept at room temperature overnight or frozen for up to 1 month.

5. Make the pudding. In a heavy-bottomed saucepot set over medium-high heat, combine the cream, milk, and vanilla paste. In a medium bowl, whisk together the sugar, cocoa, cornstarch, and salt. Add the eggs and whisk until smooth. Once the dairy mixture comes up to a scald (you will see bubbles around the perimeter of the liquid and a wisp of steam rising from the surface), remove the pot from the heat. Start streaming a small amount of the hot dairy into the egg mixture, whisking constantly to prevent the eggs from cooking. Continue whisking in the milk mixture,

continued

Chocolate Doberge Cake

Makes one 9-inch layer cake

Chocolate Sponge Cake

2 cups cake flour

1 cup unsweetened Dutch-processed cocoa powder

¾ teaspoon baking soda

18 eggs, at room temperature

2¼ cups granulated sugar

1 tablespoon vanilla bean paste

¾ cup plus 3 tablespoons unsalted butter, melted and cooled

Cocoa Pudding

1½ cups heavy cream

1½ cups whole milk

½ teaspoon vanilla bean paste

½ cup granulated sugar

2 tablespoons unsweetened Dutch-processed cocoa powder, sifted

2 tablespoons plus 2 teaspoons cornstarch

2 teaspoons kosher salt

2 eggs, at room temperature

¼ cup unsalted butter, at room temperature

6 ounces dark chocolate (preferably Valrhona 70% cacao), chopped

Chocolate Doberge Cake

German Buttercream

1¼ cups granulated sugar

2 cups whole milk

1 teaspoon vanilla bean paste

½ teaspoon kosher salt

3 tablespoons cornstarch

2 eggs

2 egg yolks

4 cups unsalted butter,
cut into pieces and
at room temperature

Simple Syrup

2 cups granulated sugar

2 cups water

Chocolate Ganache Icing

1 pound dark chocolate
(preferably Valrhona
70% cacao), chopped

Pinch of kosher salt

2 cups heavy cream

until most of the liquid has been incorporated into the egg mixture. Pour the mixture in the bowl into the saucepot and place the pot over medium heat. Cook, again whisking constantly, until the mixture thickens and bubbles. When bubbling, remove the pot from the heat and immediately whisk in the butter and chocolate until melted and combined. Pour the pudding into a 9 by 13-inch baking pan and place a sheet of plastic wrap directly on the surface of the pudding, then poke a few holes in the plastic to allow the steam to escape. Let cool completely before building the cake. The pudding can be covered and refrigerated for up to 2 days.

6. Make the buttercream. In a heavy-bottomed saucepot, combine ½ cup plus 2 tablespoons of the sugar with the milk, vanilla paste, and salt. Place over high heat until it comes to a scald (you will see bubbles around the perimeter of the liquid and a wisp of steam from the surface); do not bring to a full boil.

7. Meanwhile, in a medium bowl, whisk together the cornstarch and the remaining ½ cup plus 2 tablespoons sugar. Whisk in the eggs and egg yolks until smooth. Start streaming a small amount of the hot dairy into the egg mixture, whisking constantly to prevent the eggs from cooking. Continue whisking in the milk mixture until three-quarters of it has been incorporated. Pour the mixture in the bowl into the saucepot and place the pot over medium-high heat. Cook, again whisking constantly, until the mixture thickens and begins to bubble. Let it bubble for 1½ minutes, then remove from the heat and transfer to the bowl of a stand mixer fitted with the paddle attachment or transfer to a large bowl and use a handheld mixer. Mix on medium speed until completely cool, then beat in the butter, a few pieces at a time, until it is incorporated and the buttercream is creamy and smooth. The buttercream can be covered and refrigerated for up to 2 days; bring it to room temperature and beat it with the mixer to refresh it before using.

8. Make the syrup. In a heavy-bottomed saucepot set over medium-high heat, bring the sugar and water to a boil. Once the sugar has fully dissolved, let the syrup boil for 45 seconds, then remove from the heat and cool.

9. Using a large serrated knife, trim the domed tops of the cakes so they're flat; save the scraps for snacking. Cut each cake horizontally into three even layers, creating nine layers total. Place the first layer on a platter and brush with about ⅓ cup of the simple syrup. Spread ⅔ cup of the pudding evenly over the cake, leaving about a ½-inch border around the perimeter. Top with another cake layer, brush with another ⅓ cup syrup, then spread evenly with ⅔ cup of the pudding, again leaving a ½-inch border. Repeat until you have stacked the last layer of cake. Brush the top layer with syrup. Refrigerate the cake for at least 45 minutes before frosting.

10. Apply a layer of buttercream to the sides of the cake with a large offset spatula. Smooth out the sides as evenly as possible and then spread a smooth, even layer of buttercream across the top. Chill the cake for another hour to set, while you make the icing.

11. Meanwhile, make the icing. Put the chocolate and salt in a heatproof bowl. Place a saucepot full of water over high heat and bring to a boil. Remove from the heat and set the bowl of chocolate over the hot water to melt; stir it often to melt the chocolate evenly. In a second pot, heat the cream to a scald (you will see bubbles around the perimeter of the liquid and a wisp of steam rising from the surface), then remove from the heat. Pour one-third of the cream into the melted chocolate and whisk to combine. Carefully add the remaining cream in two portions, whisking after each addition, until the ganache is smooth, shiny, and incorporated. Set aside until the ganache cools and is just thick enough to stick to the cake when poured over the top, 15 to 20 minutes.

12. Remove the cake from the refrigerator and pour the ganache evenly over the top. The cake can be served right away or stored in the refrigerator for up to 3 days.

What's Mine Is Yours

It bears repeating that when you're making a cake with a lot of wet ingredients, like the genoise here, you must have them all at room temperature so they create a stable emulsion. The end result will be light, airy, and tender.

German buttercream is less buttery than traditional Swiss or Italian buttercream because the base is more of a custard.

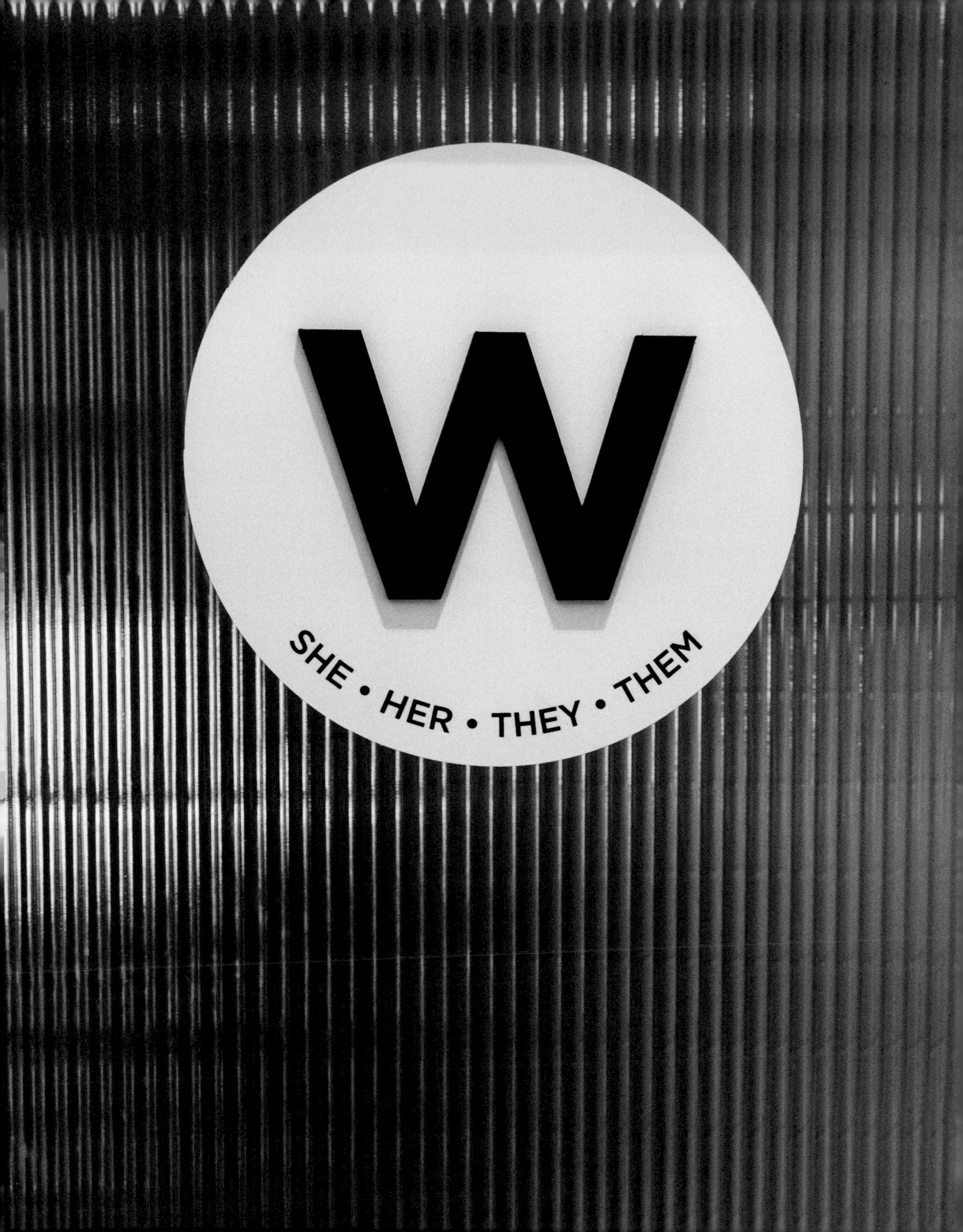
W
SHE • HER • THEY • THEM

Basics

Basic Poaching Liquid

Makes about 2 quarts

This is a basic poaching liquid that works well with apples, pears, apricots, and rhubarb. The important thing is to use your intuition to judge when the fruit is poached to your liking; this will depend on the freshness of the fruit itself. As a rule, once your fruit is soft and tender, it's done.

3 cups white or red wine (your choice)

3 cups water

3 cups granulated sugar

1 vanilla bean pod, split lengthwise and seeds scraped out

1 tablespoon fresh lemon juice

1. In a heavy-bottomed saucepot, combine the wine, water, sugar, vanilla pod, and vanilla seeds. Cook over high heat until the liquid boils and the sugar has fully dissolved. Remove from the heat and stir in the lemon juice.

Flavored Poaching Liquid

You can substitute various juices for the wine. I sometimes make poaching liquid with cranberry juice to give the poached fruit a really bright, beautiful color. You can always get creative with spices as well. Add star anise, cloves, cinnamon—whatever you'd like to celebrate the season you're in.

Poached Apples and Pears

To make the poached apples or pears for my turnovers (page 217), drop the peeled and chopped fruit right into the simmering poaching liquid and let cook until tender to the touch. Remove from the heat. Use a slotted spoon to transfer the fruit from the hot liquid to a bowl to cool; cool the poaching liquid separately. Remove the vanilla pod, and wash, dry, and save it for another use. Once cool, pour the poaching liquid over the fruit, cover, and store in the cooled liquid in the refrigerator for up to 3 days, until ready to use.

Poached Peaches, Apricots, or Rhubarb

To poach peaches, apricots, or rhubarb, place the fruit in a heatproof bowl. Pour the hot poaching liquid directly over the fruit and let cool in the liquid, until tender. Cover and store the poached fruit in the poaching liquid in the refrigerator for up to 1 week, until ready to use.

Caramel Sauce

Makes about 2 cups

Caramel sauce is one of those things everyone can and should know how to make. It's simple and, after you've made it a few times, not intimidating by any stretch of the imagination. It is also incredibly versatile and an amazing complement to almost any pastry or dessert (or even stirred into your morning coffee). I think it's a staple to always have in your fridge.

1¼ cups granulated sugar

⅓ cup water

⅓ cup heavy cream, slightly warmed

1½ tablespoons unsalted butter

1 teaspoon kosher salt

1. In a heavy-bottomed saucepot, stir the sugar and water to combine; do not stir again while the sugar is cooking. Cook over medium-high heat, until the sugar turns a deep caramel color, about 10 minutes (remember, color = flavor). Remove the pot from the heat and carefully whisk in the cream; be mindful that the sugar will hiss, steam, and bubble, so be aware of your hands and arms above the pot to prevent burns. Whisk in the butter until melted and incorporated, then season with the salt.

2. The caramel sauce can be stored in a jar or in an odorless plastic container in the refrigerator for up to 2 weeks. Reheat in the microwave in 30-second bursts, stirring between each burst.

Tahitian Vanilla Milk

Makes 1 quart

If you've been to Willa Jean, you might have tried my cookie plate. I serve three warm chocolate chip cookies alongside an egg beater of raw cookie dough and a glass of Tahitian Vanilla Milk. It's so easy that you have to try it the next time you make my cookies (page 92). It's the bomb.

1 tablespoon granulated sugar

½ Tahitian vanilla bean

1 quart whole milk

1. Put the sugar in a small bowl. Place the vanilla bean on a small baking sheet in a warm oven for 30 seconds or pop it in the microwave for 15 seconds, then use a sharp paring knife to split the bean lengthwise. Scrape the back of your knife down both sides of the vanilla pod to remove as many of the seeds as possible. Using your fingers, mix the vanilla seeds into the sugar, breaking up the clusters of seeds.

2. Put the milk in a large pitcher. Whisk in the sugar. Refrigerate for several hours for the flavors to infuse before serving.

What's Mine Is Yours

Caramel is one of the most versatile things we make in the pastry world. When you boil it down (pun intended), you're really just controlling the liquid content of sugar. That being said, think about experimenting with what that liquid actually is. Fresh juice, vinegar, wine, liquor, and even beer work well in caramel sauce in place of the cream. Just be sure to remove the pan from the flame before adding any of those things so as not to catch something, or yourself, on fire. The only real variables in experimenting are:

First, do you want to add the butter or leave it out? This is up to you. There is no wrong answer. Taste the caramel (when it's cool enough) and decide.

Second, how thick do you want the sauce? All of these liquids will create different outcomes for the caramel. The best test is to drop a small amount of the caramel on a room-temperature plate, let it sit for about 15 seconds, then hold the plate vertically and see how quickly (or not), the caramel sauce moves across it. If it's too thin, just keep reducing the caramel over medium heat until it is your desired consistency. Remember, the longer it cools, the thicker it gets.

Third, caramel takes on great flavors from fresh herbs. So, if you're thinking about making a seasonal fruit somethin'-or-other, feel free to throw in a few leaves or stalks of a well-paired, hearty herb, such as rosemary, thyme, or basil, to complement your dish. Just remember to strain the caramel sauce before serving.

Cajeta

Makes about 1 quart

Cajeta is a caramel sauce similar to dulce de leche (see page 139) but made with goat's milk. The result is a super-delicious, silky sauce with the most perfect bit of tang to balance the sweetness. You can purchase cajeta from your local Latin market or from the internet, where it's sometimes labeled as "goat's-milk caramel," or you could make your own with the following recipe. It's great to have around to drizzle on your ice cream or even to add to your coffee when you want a little café con leche moment.

1 quart goat's milk

½ teaspoon baking soda

1 cup granulated sugar

1 cinnamon stick

1 teaspoon vanilla bean paste

½ teaspoon kosher salt

1. In a small bowl, mix ½ cup of the goat's milk with the baking soda to dissolve. In a large heavy-bottomed saucepot, combine the remaining 3½ cups goat's milk with the sugar and cinnamon stick. Cook over medium-high heat, stirring often, until the mixture comes to a full simmer. Remove from the heat and whisk in the baking soda mixture; be careful, as the mixture will bubble, froth, and rise to about twice its volume (hey, that's what baking soda does), so be extra mindful of where your hands and arms are (steam burns are the worst).

2. Return the pot to the stove and bring it back to a simmer over medium-low heat, stirring often to keep the mixture from burning on the bottom of the pot, until it's thick and caramel colored, about 1 hour. When the caramel is thick enough that your spoon leaves a trail and you can see the bottom of the pot when you stir it, it is done.

3. Remove the caramel from the heat and stir in the vanilla paste and salt. Discard the cinnamon stick. Cool to room temperature. Transfer to a glass jar or an airtight, odorless plastic container and store in the refrigerator for up to 3 weeks.

Roasted Strawberries in Their Own Sauce

Makes 1 quart

These roasted strawberries go with everything: cheesecake, panna cotta, chess pie, cornbread bread pudding, angel food cake, rum cake, even ice cream sundaes—you name it. The sauce should be served chilled with cheesecake, but it is great served warm over other cakes.

6 cups strawberries (about 1½ pounds), washed, dried, hulled, and halved lengthwise

¼ cup firmly packed light brown sugar

1 teaspoon vanilla bean paste

1 cup unsalted butter, melted, plus ¼ cup, cut into cubes and chilled

¼ cup fresh orange juice

¼ cup Grand Marnier

1. Preheat the oven to 400°F. In a large bowl, toss the strawberries, brown sugar, and vanilla paste in the melted butter. Transfer the strawberries to a large rimmed baking sheet or a casserole pan, cut-side down, and bake for 10 to 12 minutes, until they feel soft. Let cool for about 15 minutes.

2. Remove the berries from the baking sheet and pour the juices left on the pan into a skillet set over medium heat. Add the orange juice and Grand Marnier to the skillet and bring to a simmer. Turn off the heat and whisk in the cold butter. Add the strawberries and stir to combine.

3. The strawberries and sauce can be stored in an airtight container in the refrigerator for up to 4 days. Reheat in a skillet over low heat.

Sweet Whipped Cream

Makes about 3 cups

Having grown up in a Cool Whip household, discovering real whipped cream was a revelation—a pivotal moment, even—in my life. It's so simple and goes with everything. This recipe can literally be served with any recipe in this book. I recommend finding and using the best cream available, preferably from a local dairy producer.

2 cups cold heavy cream
½ teaspoon vanilla extract
2 teaspoons powdered sugar, sifted

1. Chill the bowl and whisk attachment for your stand mixer or a bowl and the beaters for a handheld mixer. Fit the bowl and whisk attachment on the mixer. Add the cream, vanilla, and powdered sugar and whip on medium-high speed until soft peaks form.

2. Whipped cream can be stored, tightly covered, in the refrigerator for a day (or overnight).

Pastry Cream

Makes 3 cups

Pastry cream has become so commonplace in my world that it's on the same level of condiment as Duke's mayonnaise—that is, it's always in my fridge. I add it to the bottoms of pies, spread it over laminated doughs, whip it with cheese for spreads, and even make it the base of my icings instead of just sugar. I'll even just eat it hot out of the mixing bowl or treat it like a dip for fresh fruit, with strawberries being my favorite. There's really no wrong way.

1 egg
3 egg yolks, at room temperature
¼ cup plus 1 tablespoon cornstarch
½ teaspoon kosher salt
¼ cup plus 1 tablespoon granulated sugar
2 cups whole milk
¼ cup unsalted butter, cut into pieces
1 teaspoon vanilla extract

1. Line a large rimmed baking sheet with plastic wrap, leaving an overhang of approximately 1 inch on all sides. Set aside.

2. In a large bowl, whisk together the whole egg, egg yolks, cornstarch, salt, and 2 tablespoons of the sugar; set aside. In a medium saucepot, bring the milk and the remaining 3 tablespoons sugar to a scald (you will see bubbles around the perimeter of the liquid and a wisp of steam rising from the surface) over medium-high heat. Start streaming a small amount of the hot milk mixture into the egg mixture, whisking constantly to prevent the eggs from cooking. Continue whisking in the milk until most of the liquid has been incorporated into the egg mixture. Pour the mixture in the bowl into the saucepot and place over medium-high heat. Cook, again whisking constantly, until the mixture comes to a boil, about 1½ minutes. Remove the pot from

continued

continued
Pastry Cream

the heat and whisk in the butter, one piece at a time, followed by the vanilla. Pour the custard onto the prepared baking sheet.

3. Place a sheet of plastic wrap directly on the surface of the custard and poke a few holes in the plastic to let the steam escape. Set aside to cool. Once cool, transfer the pastry cream to an airtight container and refrigerate for up to 3 days.

Cream Cheese Filling

Makes 2¼ cups

Use in the Fruit Danish (page 78) if you're not in a pastry cream–filling mood or to fill hand pies (see pages 210–216).

12 ounces cream cheese, at room temperature

3 tablespoons ricotta cheese

2 tablespoons granulated sugar

1½ teaspoons fresh lemon juice

¾ teaspoon finely grated lemon zest

¾ teaspoon vanilla bean paste

¾ teaspoon kosher salt

1 tablespoon sour cream

1. In the bowl of a stand mixer fitted with the paddle attachment or in a large bowl using a handheld mixer, cream the cream cheese, ricotta, and sugar. Once smooth, mix in the lemon juice, lemon zest, vanilla paste, and salt. Once well incorporated, mix in the sour cream.

2. The filling will keep in an airtight container in the refrigerator for up to 4 days.

What's Mine Is Yours

When storing pastry cream or any of these doughs or fillings, make certain your containers are dry and odor-free. Any remnants of savory smells like garlic, onions, or bacon will automatically seep into and flavor what's stored in the container.

Creole Cream Cheese

Makes 1½ quarts

When I moved back to New Orleans after culinary school and landed the pastry chef position at Restaurant August, I was completely unqualified for the job. My real exposure to what folks were baking in New Orleans and the surrounding areas was more limited than I care to admit. I rode along with the chef de cuisine and a sous to my first farmers' market on a Wednesday, right after I started in the kitchen. It was late spring, and I predictably bought all the Louisiana strawberries I could handle. One of the guys bought a cheesecake from a local dairy, Mauthe's (now Progress Dairy), and we sat on the curb and dug into that Creole cream cheese cheesecake with the next best thing to silverware: strawberries. It is one of my fondest work and food memories, and now, some sixteen years later, the simplicity of that delicious moment is one I think about when I consider how I want people to experience the work I do.

What made the cheesecake special was the Creole cream cheese, which is Louisiana's answer to ricotta or burrata cheese. It's made with skim milk, buttermilk, and rennet and has a dry texture, though it's slightly sweeter and more tart than ricotta or burrata. Traditionally, it's eaten with cream, sugar, and fruit spooned over the top (just like the Italians eat their ricotta!) or even as a substitute for yogurt.

Creole cream cheese nearly became extinct in recent history, and there was a huge local movement to help save it from disappearing. More recently, there's been an uptick in popularity, and it's now a flavor in almost all ice cream shops in NOLA. I personally like to smear it on a biscuit and top that with fruit preserves as a breakfast go-to (or, let's be honest, a middle-of-the-day snack). At Willa Jean, we use it in various applications: as an ice cream on our red velvet dessert and also as the (not-so) secret ingredient in our banana bread. We periodically offer cheesecakes and Creole cream cheese custards at our front counter as well. To make your own Creole cream cheese, you will need rennet tablets, which are available at many health foods stores (a common brand is called Junket) and online.

2 quarts skim milk
¼ cup buttermilk
1 rennet tablet

1. In a large heavy-bottomed saucepot over medium heat with a kitchen thermometer attached to the rim, warm the milk and buttermilk to 85°F. Add one-quarter of the rennet tablet and transfer the mixture to a plastic container or bowl. Cover with plastic wrap and then poke a few holes in the plastic to allow the steam to escape. Let stand at room temperature in a cool spot in your house for 48 hours.

2. Use a slotted spoon to transfer the solids to a double layer of cheesecloth set over a bowl and discard the liquid. Wrap the solids in the cheesecloth and hang it over the bowl (to catch the whey) in the refrigerator for 24 hours.

3. Discard the whey. Pack the cheese into an airtight plastic container and store in the refrigerator for up to 1 week.

Whipped Cranberry Cream Cheese

Makes 2 cups

As a kid (and, let's be real, as an adult, too), I cut slivers of cream cheese and ate it plain. When I was working for Susan Spicer at Spice Inc., one of the bakers would slice a fresh-from-the-oven loaf of bread every morning and slather it with a thick slab of cream cheese. Obviously, I instantly took to the snack, and there are few things I love more. This recipe can be whipped up for any bread, quick bread, toast, muffin, or even for pancakes. I call for cranberries because they pair so beautifully with pumpkin (see page 42), but feel free to make this spread with whatever fresh berry is in season. I love making it with fresh mayhaws (if you're near the bayou), huckleberries, and cherries.

> 8 ounces cream cheese, at room temperature
>
> ½ cup unsalted butter, at room temperature
>
> ¼ cup granulated sugar
>
> Pinch of kosher salt
>
> ½ cup fresh or thawed frozen cranberries

1. In the bowl of a stand mixer fitted with the paddle attachment or in a large bowl using a handheld mixer, beat the cream cheese on high speed until light and fluffy, about 3 minutes. Add the butter and beat until incorporated, then add the sugar and salt. Whip the mixture on high speed for about 3 minutes before decreasing the speed to medium and adding the cranberries. Mix for about 2 minutes, allowing the cranberries to become slightly crushed and distributed throughout the cream cheese.

2. Transfer to an airtight container and store in the refrigerator for up to 5 days. Bring to room temperature to serve.

Single-Crust Pie Dough

Makes enough dough for one 9-inch piecrust

This is my go-to pie dough, which I use for just about all of my pies at Willa Jean. I have a few rules when it comes to making pie dough. First off, I like to keep everything in the freezer, from the flour, salt, and butter to the bowl and beater I use to mix the dough. This helps create the flakiest piecrust. Second, I use a little bit of white vinegar (it prevents the formation of gluten) to create a tender dough. And finally, I almost always parbake (aka blind-bake) my piecrust. Usually the amount of moisture in the pie filling determines which pies need to be parbaked, but I bend the rules, based on being in New Orleans, where it's 100 percent humidity 99 percent of the time. The closer I can get to crusty, flaky goodness, the better off I am. So, when in doubt, I always blind-bake. It's my rule of thumb, and it's not going to hurt a damned thing.

1¼ cups all-purpose flour, plus more for dusting

¼ teaspoon kosher salt

½ cup frozen unsalted butter, grated on the large holes of a box grater and frozen

½ teaspoon distilled white vinegar

¼ cup ice water

1. In the bowl of a stand mixer fitted with the paddle attachment or in a large bowl using a handheld mixer, combine the flour and salt. Add the butter and beat on medium speed just until the mixture resembles coarse meal, about 45 seconds. In a small bowl, combine the vinegar and water. With the mixer on low speed, mix in the vinegar-water mixture, 1 tablespoon at a time, until the dough just comes together. Turn the dough out onto a lightly floured work surface and pat it into a disk. Wrap in plastic wrap and refrigerate for at least 4 hours or up to 2 days or freeze for up to 1 month. If frozen, thaw in the refrigerator overnight before using.

2. Liberally dust a work surface and your rolling pin with flour. Working quickly to keep the pie dough from warming up too much, roll out the dough, rotating it a quarter turn every few rolls, until it's about ¼ inch thick. Roll the dough around the rolling pin and carefully unroll it into a deep 9-inch glass pie plate. Pat the dough into the pie plate. Fold the overhanging dough under itself and press the dough to make it even. To crimp the dough, use the index finger of one hand to press the dough between the index finger and thumb of another, allowing the crimp to extend past the edge of the pie pan a bit—this will prevent the rim of the dough from collapsing during baking. Place the pie shell in the freezer for at least 1 hour.

3. Parbake the crust. Preheat the oven to 425°F. Scrunch up a sheet of parchment paper so it's all wrinkled, then flatten it out and use it to line the pie shell. Fill with dried beans or pie weights.

4. Bake for 15 minutes, rotating the pie plate after 8 minutes, until the crust is light golden at the edges. Remove the parchment and beans or pie weights and let cool on a wire rack.

5. To fully bake the crust, after you've removed the parchment and pie weights, return the crust to the oven and bake for an additional 7 minutes, until lightly golden.

What's Mine Is Yours

This piecrust is just as easily made by hand. Place the cold flour and salt in a large cold bowl. Add the butter and cut it in with your hands, rubbing the butter into the mixture until it resembles coarse meal. This takes about 90 seconds. Make a well in the middle of the mixture and add the vinegar and ice water. At this point, I like to switch over to a spatula to start moving the dry ingredients into the liquid, folding the ingredients over until everything is just incorporated and a dough has formed. Turn the dough out onto a lightly floured work surface and continue as directed in the recipe.

Double-Crust Pie Dough

Makes enough dough for one 9-inch double-crust pie

While assembling a double-crust pie, just as for a single-crust pie, the crucial step is to keep the dough as cold as possible. Once you've rolled out both portions of dough, I recommend placing the top crust in the freezer while you're assembling the bottom crust and the filling. Double-crust pies are never blind baked, and work best with delicious fruit fillings.

2½ cups all-purpose flour, plus more for dusting

½ teaspoon kosher salt

1 cup frozen unsalted butter, grated on the large holes of a box grater and frozen again

1 teaspoon distilled white vinegar

½ cup ice water

1. In the bowl of a stand mixer fitted with the paddle attachment or in a large bowl using a handheld mixer, combine the flour and salt. Add the butter and beat on medium speed just until the mixture resembles coarse meal, about 45 seconds. In a small bowl, combine the vinegar and water. With the mixer on low speed, mix in the vinegar-water mixture, 1 tablespoon at a time, until the dough just comes together. Turn the dough out onto a lightly floured work surface, divide it in half, and pat it into two disks. Wrap in plastic wrap and refrigerate for at least 4 hours or up to 2 days or freeze for up to

1 month. If frozen, thaw in the refrigerator overnight before using. (Alternatively, make the pie dough by hand; see What's Mine Is Yours, page 308.)

2. Liberally dust a work surface and your rolling pin with flour. Remove one disk of dough from the fridge. Working quickly to keep the pie dough from warming up too much, roll out the disk of dough, rotating it a quarter turn every few rolls, until it's about ¼ inch thick. Roll the dough around the rolling pin and carefully unroll it into a deep 9-inch glass pie plate. Pat the dough into the pie plate. Trim the overhanging dough to about 1 inch, then fold the overhang under itself, pressing to make it even. Transfer the pie shell to the freezer to rest and chill while you roll out the dough for the top crust and prep your pie filling.

3. Roll out the second disk of pie dough in the same way you did the first disk. Carefully transfer the dough to a parchment paper–lined baking sheet and refrigerate for at least 15 minutes before using.

What's Mine Is Yours

I put the top crust in the fridge because I need it to rest but still be pliable enough to shape and work with once the filling is ready. Once the filling goes into that bottom crust, get that pie into the oven as quickly as possible.

Tart Dough

Makes one 10-inch tart shell

There's a big difference between pie dough and tart dough, in both flavor and texture. While with pie dough you work hard to create a delicate and tender texture, tart dough is more about creating a firm, crisp, and much more flavorful crust. Flavor can also come from adding ingredients like nut flours, cornmeal, citrus zests, or whatever spices tickle your fancy. I'm pretty sure there is also some rule about tarts being much shallower than their pie cousins, but I don't much care about those kinds of rules.

½ cup unsalted butter, at room temperature

3 tablespoons granulated sugar

1 cup all-purpose flour, plus more for dusting

½ teaspoon kosher salt

1 egg yolk, at room temperature

¼ teaspoon vanilla bean paste

1. In the bowl of a stand mixer fitted with the paddle attachment or in a large bowl using a handheld mixer, cream the butter and sugar on medium-high speed until pale, light, and fluffy, about 3 minutes. Stop the mixer and scrape down the bottom and sides of the bowl with a rubber spatula. With the mixer on low speed, add the flour and salt in two portions, mixing until just incorporated or until the mixture looks a bit like wet sand. Add the egg yolk and vanilla paste and mix just until the dough comes together, about 20 seconds.

2. Turn the dough out onto a floured surface. Turn the dough over onto itself several times, then form it into a disk and wrap in plastic wrap. Refrigerate for at least 2 hours and up to 3 days or freeze for up to 1 month. If frozen, thaw overnight in the refrigerator before using.

3. Remove the dough from the refrigerator and let it sit just long enough for you to work with it easily (find that amazing fine line between too cold and brittle versus too soft and pliable and therefore sticky). You'll want to flour your work surface and rolling pin much more liberally than you do for pie dough, since this dough gets sticky the warmer it gets. Roll the dough into an even 12-inch round, about ¼ inch thick, rolling from the center of the dough to the edge but not off the edge (this will create uneven thickness around the edges). Rotate the dough clockwise about 1½ inches every two rolls to help keep the dough round. If you're working quickly enough and with the dough cool enough, the dough may crack a little toward the edges. No need to panic—this will all work itself out. You're doing great.

4. Use the rolling pin to transfer the dough to a 10-inch tart pan. Just as with pie dough, press the dough into the bottom, corners, and sides of the pan. Trim any overhanging dough so it's flush with the top of the tart pan. Use any dough scraps to fill in any thin spots or cracks, pressing the excess into place. Place the tart shell in the refrigerator to rest for at least 1 hour or up to overnight before using.

Graham Cracker Crust

Makes one 9-inch piecrust

This is the stuff my childhood memories are filled with. I love graham crackers, and graham cracker crust may be my most favorite way to pie. I much prefer to make my own than to purchase the premade shells in the store. This way I have total control over the thickness, sweetness, and height of the crust, based on the pie pan I use. Feel free to add a signature move to yours; add a spice that complements the filling or even zest some citrus into the mix for added flavor.

> 2 cups graham cracker crumbs
> (about 16 whole crackers)
> 3 tablespoons granulated sugar
> 3 tablespoons firmly packed light brown sugar
> ¼ teaspoon kosher salt
> ½ cup unsalted butter, melted

1. Preheat the oven to 375°F. In a medium bowl, stir the graham cracker crumbs, granulated sugar, brown sugar, salt, and butter until combined.

2. Press the graham cracker mixture into the bottom, corners, and up the sides of a deep 9-inch pie pan. Bake for 7 to 10 minutes, until fragrant, dry, and toasty.

3. Let cool completely on a wire rack before filling.

Saltine Piecrust

Makes one 9-inch piecrust

Even though this crust is only called for with Aunt Jean's Lemon Chiffon Pie (page 195), you can use it any time you'd use a graham cracker crust or any other crushed cookie crust.

> 2 sleeves Saltine crackers
> 2 tablespoons granulated sugar
> ¾ cup unsalted butter, at room temperature

1. Preheat the oven to 350°F. Crush the crackers, using either a food processor or crushing them in the sleeve using a rolling pin. Transfer the crackers to a medium bowl and add the sugar. Add the butter, then knead by hand until the mixture holds together when pressed with your fingers (just like a graham cracker crust).

2. Press the Saltine mixture into the bottom and up the sides to the rim of a deep 9-inch pie pan and chill for 15 minutes. Bake for 10 minutes, or until lightly browned.

3. Let cool completely on a wire rack before filling.

Danish Dough

Makes one "book"

This is the foundational recipe I use for cinnamon rolls, sticky buns, morning buns, and fruit Danish. Once you get the hang of the technique and the timing, you can use this dough for just about any deliciousness you can think of. It works really well to form and freeze, too. Just pull out the items from your freezer and let them sit at room temperature until thawed and proofed (see specific items for those instructions).

Dough

1¾ teaspoons instant yeast (I use SAF brand)

4½ cups bread flour (it's really best if you can weigh this; it should be 1 pound 4½ ounces)

2 tablespoons instant milk powder

¾ cup water, at room temperature

2 eggs, at room temperature

¼ cup plus 1 tablespoon unsalted butter, at room temperature

3 tablespoons granulated sugar

2 teaspoons kosher salt

Laminate

1 pound 4 ounces unsalted butter, at room temperature

All-purpose flour, for dusting

1. Make the dough. Line a 9 by 13-inch baking pan with plastic wrap, leaving enough overhanging plastic wrap to wrap up the dough. In a large bowl, whisk the yeast into the bread flour and set aside. In a small bowl or measuring cup, dissolve the milk powder in the water.

2. In the bowl of a stand mixer fitted with the whisk attachment or in a large bowl using a handheld mixer, whisk the eggs until they are homogenous. Add the dissolved milk powder, flour mixture, butter, sugar, and salt. Using the dough hook, mix on low speed for 8 minutes, stopping and scraping down the bowl halfway through to ensure that all the ingredients are thoroughly incorporated.

3. When the dough is finished, turn it out onto a lightly floured surface. Shape the dough into a large ball, forming a smooth surface. Transfer the ball to the prepared pan and wrap completely using the overhanging plastic. Press the dough so it reaches all corners of the pan; the surface should be as level as possible. Let the dough rest in the pan in the refrigerator for at least 3 hours or up to overnight. It can also be well wrapped and frozen for up to 1 month. If frozen, thaw in the refrigerator for 30 minutes before laminating.

4. Line a 9 by 13-inch baking pan with plastic wrap, leaving enough overhang to wrap up the butter. Spread the softened butter evenly into the pan, so it's a 9 by 13-inch sheet. Cover the butter in the pan with the plastic wrap and refrigerate for a minimum of 1 hour. About 30 minutes before you start the lamination process, let the butter sit at room temperature to become pliable. If you notice it is not very pliable, beat the butter with a rolling pin until it has softened slightly.

5. Laminate the dough. Dust a work surface with flour. Unwrap the dough and dust it with flour until the dough is no longer sticky. With a lightly floured rolling pin, applying even pressure, roll out the dough lengthwise until it is doubled in length; you should have a 12 by 20-inch rectangle. Unwrap the butter, then carefully place it diagonally in the middle of the dough. Fold the four edges of the dough up over the butter so the points meet, encasing the butter. Roll out the dough until it is 10 by 28 inches. Fold the dough over itself in thirds, like a letter. Turn the dough 90 degrees and repeat this process once more, rolling out the dough to 10 by 28 inches and folding it over itself in thirds. Wrap the dough in plastic wrap and refrigerate for 20 minutes.

6. Take the dough out of the refrigerator. With the creased side facing you, roll out until the dough is approximately 9 by 32 inches. Trifold the dough, wrap it in plastic, and refrigerate for another 30 minutes.

You can keep the dough in the refrigerator, wrapped well in plastic wrap, for up to 3 days. If you want to keep it longer, you'll need to move the dough to the freezer, since it will start to oxidize and change color. Keep it well wrapped and freeze for up to 1 month. When you're ready to use it, thaw the dough overnight in the refrigerator or for 1 hour at room temperature, still wrapped (you don't want to expose the dough to the air for any length of time, since it will create a "skin" that will ultimately prevent the dough from rising to its fullest potential).

7. To use, lightly flour a work surface and your rolling pin. Dusting with flour as you work, roll out the dough until it is ⅓ inch thick and roughly 14 by 30 inches (unless you are making the Fruit Danish on page 78, which needs to be rolled out to ¾ inch thick), and proceed with the pastry recipe.

What's Mine Is Yours

When I say the butter should be "pliable," I mean just soft enough to bend but not soft to the touch or melty in any part. You literally want it as cold as it can be and still workable.

Acknowledgments

Willa Jean family, past and present, thank you for showing up so generously and graciously day after day. And for the support you've all shown me and one another. No collection of people could inspire me more. Thank you for not being afraid to feed people, work hard, dream big, and celebrate our failures as much as our successes, and for lighting up my days with the desire to do good and be great. You are all such a blessing.

Kate Heddings, you are the best copilot in the world. I am so proud to have worked with you on this book, and so grateful for the friendship that blossomed along the way. I am thankful every day that the world spun back around and put us together to make this happen. Thank you for your time, your energy, your meticulous eye, your love of food, your passion for pastry, and our mutual admiration of crab. I'd do it all again if it meant another opportunity to be in each other's corners.

Thank you, David Black, for thinking I had a voice to share, and giving me the microphone to do it. I would have never taken on this project without you and your support.

Thanks for taking such a risk on me, and continuing to champion and support this project, Lorena Jones. And thanks for putting the phenomenal Emma Campion in my corner.

Lizzie Faulkner, there are no actual words to express how thankful I am for you and your constant desire to do and be great, to learn, organize, and keep everything moving forward. No doubt you have the most challenging job in the world trying to keep me focused, on task, and on time. You are the true reason this book exists, and the definition of grace. Thank you.

Thank you, Oriana Koren, for giving your perspective and vision to these recipes. I am incredibly inspired by your work in life as well as behind the camera. Carolina Isabel Salazar, thank you for bringing your light, steadiness, tunes, and phenomenal eye to this project. Koshara Johnson, thank you for propping us up with the tools needed to create this vision.

Michelle Gatton and Tiffany Schleigh, this would've never ever happened without y'all. In short, y'all nailed it, take the cake, elevated it, whisked me away with your talents, and you can't be beat. I'm jazzed to have had the pleasure of working with you both.

Yolanda Torres, and Daniella, too, thank you for holding Willa Jean as your own and so generously pouring your heart and soul into everything you do. I am grateful to work beside you daily, and the life lessons we've learned together through highs and lows. Your support fuels me, and everyone around you, to push harder and be better. You are a gift, my friends.

Thanks to my mom, Shari Wooten, for the osmosis that seems to have occurred while you spent weekends always baking at home. I am sorry I cried when you made carrot cake, and I can now admit that I was wrong. Thank you for teaching me so young the value of eating a homegrown tomato straight off the vine, for the gift of canning and preserving the seasons, and the comforting gift of baking for others. Thanks for dealing with my teenage years and for tolerating my stubbornness while supporting this dream I dreamed.

To my dad, Sam Fields, thank you for taking the time to teach me that making homemade ice cream is absolutely worth it and for teaching me that the best way to eat chocolate cake is in a bowl of cold milk. Thanks for always being ready and willing to try a new food or restaurant. The support you've shown through your own curiosities about my world and my career inspires me.

To my sister, Kimberly, and my brother, Brodie, thanks for switching chores with me often so I could cook when I found some random recipe in a cookbook I wanted to try when we were kids. Thanks, Kim, for messing up those mashed potatoes so terribly that one time that everyone was in favor of me cooking . . . and giving me a good story to tell for life. The trust you have in me to cook for you makes me proud. Brodie, you've constantly encouraged me to be exactly who I am and how I am our entire lifetime, and I am beholden. Thanks to you and Janet for also gifting

the world with my two biggest sources of inspiration, Westin and Henry—the best nephews in the world.

Martine Boyer you're the best, period. Lisa Donovan, Michelle Battista, Cheetie, Brandy, Ann Marshall, Vitus Spehar, Katherine, Sarah Trapp, Gia, Amy Reynolds, Kat, Simone, and all you others, my love for y'all knows no bounds.

Patricia Morton, my life, and the world, is better because of you. Thank you for helping on this book. Thank you for sharing kitchen space with me for all these years, and, more important, for making the space and supporting and encouraging me to grow and heal along the way.

Sweet, sweet Mallory Page, you're an inspiration every day. Thanks for lending your work, ideas, support, and friendship along the way. You are power.

Huge thanks to Keith Kreeger for so generously sharing your work and your heart with us on this project. I could not be more excited to present these recipes and stories on your wares.

And, even though you're never going to read this, the greatest of thanks to R. S. Kinney for coming into my life and overflowing it with unconditional love and admiration. You've made me the best version of myself.

To all of my amazing friends, fellow chefs, farmers, and stewards of the American South, my life is so full of love and kindness because of you. Thank you for all that you do. The world is such a beautiful place with all of you in it.

About the Authors

Kelly Fields was born into a Charleston family with a strong Lowcountry Southern baking tradition. She has worked as a pastry chef for more than twenty years, starting with Susan Spicer and then the restaurant August, after which she opened her own Willa Jean bakery in New Orleans. *Eater* New Orleans awarded her Chef of the Year and *Garden & Gun* magazine named her one of the most influential people in the South. In 2017, she co-founded the Yes Ma'am foundation to inspire, encourage, and mentor the next generation of women in the restaurant and hospitality industry. Two years later, she won the James Beard Foundation's Outstanding Pastry Chef Award. And, like every good Southerner, she has a good dog (Kinney) by her side.

Kate Heddings was the food editor at *Food & Wine* for more than seventeen years, managing the test kitchen and overseeing the magazine's branded cookbooks. Before *Food & Wine*, she was a book editor at William Morrow and a recipe developer and tester for *Martha Stewart Living*. Kate is a graduate of Boston University and received her grande diplome from the International Culinary Center (formerly The French Culinary Institute). She is currently a contributing editor at *Food & Wine* and has written for *The Washington Post* and *Thrillist*.

Index

Published in the United States by Lorena Jones Books,
an imprint of Random House, a division of Penguin
Random House LLC, New York.
www.crownpublishing.com
www.tenspeed.com

Lorena Jones Books and the Lorena Jones Books colophon
are trademarks of Penguin Random House, LLC.

Library of Congress Cataloging-in-Publication Data
    Names: Fields, Kelly, 1978– author. | Heddings, Kate, author.
    Title: The good book of southern baking : a revival of
        biscuits, cakes, and cornbread / Kelly Fields with
        Kate Heddings.
    Description: California : Lorena Jones Books, 2020. |
        Includes index.
    Identifiers: LCCN 2020003835 (print) | LCCN
        2020003836 (ebook) | ISBN 9781984856227
        (hardcover) | ISBN 9781984856234 (ebook)
    Subjects: LCSH: Cooking, American—Southern style. |
        Baking. | LCGFT: Cookbooks.
    Classification: LCC TX715.2.S68 F45 2020 (print) |
        LCC TX715.2.S68 (ebook) | DDC 641.5975—dc23
    LC record available at https://lccn.loc.gov/2020003835
    LC ebook record available at https://lccn.loc.gov
        /2020003836

Grateful acknowledgment is made to W. W. Norton &
Company, Inc. for permission to reprint "Classic Yellow
Layer Cake" from *Bravetart: Iconic American Desserts*
by Stella Parks, copyright © 2017 by Stella Parks.
Used by permission of W. W. Norton & Company, Inc.

Hardcover ISBN: 978-1-9848-5622-7
Ebook ISBN: 978-1-9848-5623-4

Prop styling by Kashara Johnson
Food styling by Michelle Gatton

Printed in China

10 9 8 7 6 5 4 3 2 1

First Edition